Contents

Contents	ii–iii
Introduction	iv–v

Metacognition and self-regulation	2
1.1 Working as a scientist	2
1.2 Plan, monitor, evaluate	4

Working and Thinking Scientifically Unit Opener — 6

1.1	Asking scientific questions	8
1.2	Working safely	10
1.3	Planning investigations	12
1.4	Recording data	14
1.5	Presenting data	16
1.6	Analysing data	18
1.7	Evaluating data	20

Biology 1 Unit Opener — 22

Chapter 1: Cells — 24

1.1	Observing cells	26
1.2	Plant and animal cells	28
1.3	Specialised cells	30
1.4	Movement of substances	32
1.5	Unicellular organisms	34

Chapter 1 Summary: Cells — 36

Chapter 2: Structure and function of body systems — 38

2.1	Levels of organisation	40
2.2	Gas exchange	42
2.3	Breathing	44
2.4	Skeleton	46
2.5	Movement: joints	48
2.6	Movement: muscles	50

Chapter 2 Summary: Structure and function of body systems — 52

Chapter 3: Reproduction — 54

3.1	Adolescence	56
3.2	Reproductive systems	58
3.3	Fertilisation and implantation	60
3.4	Development of a foetus	62
3.5	The menstrual cycle	64
3.6	Flowers and pollination	66
3.7	Fertilisation and germination	68
3.8	Seed dispersal	70

Chapter 3 Summary: Reproduction — 72

Chemistry 1 Unit Opener — 74

Chapter 1: Particles and their behaviour — 76
- 1.1 The particle model — 78
- 1.2 States of matter — 80
- 1.3 Density — 82
- 1.4 Melting and freezing — 84
- 1.5 Boiling — 86
- 1.6 More changes of state — 88
- 1.7 Diffusion — 90

Chapter 1 Summary: Particles and their behaviour — 92

Chapter 2: Elements, atoms, and compounds — 94
- 2.1 Elements — 96
- 2.2 Atoms — 98
- 2.3 Compounds — 100
- 2.4 Chemical formulae — 102

Chapter 2 Summary: Elements, atoms, and compounds — 104

Chapter 3: Reactions — 106
- 3.1 Chemical reactions — 108
- 3.2 Word equations — 110
- 3.3 Oxidation reactions — 112
- 3.4 Decomposition reactions — 114
- 3.5 Using ratios — 116
- 3.6 Conservation of mass — 118
- 3.7 Exothermic and endothermic — 120

Chapter 3 Summary: Reactions — 122

Chapter 4: Acids and alkalis — 124
- 4.1 Acids and alkalis — 126
- 4.2 Indicators and pH — 128
- 4.3 Neutralisation — 130
- 4.4 Making salts — 132

Chapter 4 Summary: Acids and alkalis — 134

Physics 1 Unit Opener — 136

Chapter 1: Forces — 138
- 1.1 Introduction to forces — 140
- 1.2 Squashing and stretching — 142
- 1.3 Drag forces and friction — 144
- 1.4 Forces at a distance — 146
- 1.5 Balanced and unbalanced — 148

Chapter 1 Closer: Forces — 150

Chapter 2: Sound — 152
- 2.1 Waves — 154
- 2.2 Sound — 156
- 2.3 Loudness and pitch — 158
- 2.4 Detecting sound — 160
- 2.5 Echoes and ultrasound — 162

Chapter 2 Closer: Sound — 164

Chapter 3: Light — 166
- 3.1 Light — 168
- 3.2 Reflection — 170
- 3.3 Refraction — 172
- 3.4 The eye and the camera — 174
- 3.5 Colour — 176

Chapter 3 Closer: Light — 178

Chapter 4: Space — 180
- 4.1 The night sky — 182
- 4.2 The Solar System — 184
- 4.3 The Earth — 186
- 4.4 The Moon — 188

Chapter 4 Closer: Space — 190

Glossary — 192
Index — 200
Periodic Table — 204

Introduction

Learning objectives
Each spread has a set of learning objectives. These tell you what you will be able to do by the end of the lesson.

Reactivate your knowledge
Here you will find some short questions that will help to remind you what you already know about a topic.

Maths skills
Scientists use maths to help them solve problems and carry out their investigations. These boxes contain activities to help you practise the maths you need for science. They also contain useful hints and tips.

Link
Links show you where you can learn more about something mentioned in the topic.

Summary Questions
1 Each spread has a set of Summary Questions. Questions with one dot symbol ask you to recall information.

2 Questions with two dot symbols are a bit more challenging.

3 Questions with three dots are more challenging. You will need to think carefully and apply your knowledge.

Welcome to your *Activate* Student Book

This introduction shows you all the different features *Activate* has to support you on your journey through Key Stage 3 Science.

Being a scientist is great fun. As you work through this Student Book, you'll learn how to work as a scientist, and get answers to questions that science can answer.

This book is packed full of activities to help build your confidence and skills in science.

Q These boxes contain short questions. They will help you check that you have understood the text.

Working scientifically
Scientists work in a particular way to carry out fair and scientific investigations. These boxes contain activities and hints to help you build these skills and understand the process so that you can work scientifically.

Key words
The key words in each spread are highlighted in bold and summarised in the key-word box. They can also be found in the Glossary.

Literacy skills
As a scientist, you need to be able to communicate and share your ideas. These boxes contain tasks and tips to help build your reading, writing, listening, and speaking skills.

Opener

Each unit begins with an opener spread. This introduces you to the awe and wonder of science and helps you to understand your place in the scientific world.

It asks some important questions that you will find the answers to in the unit, and shows you the key topics you will study.

Chapter map

This shows all the chapters in this unit and what each one contains.

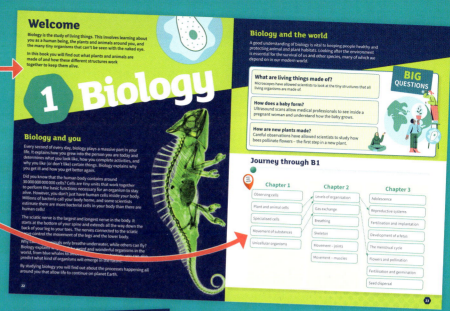

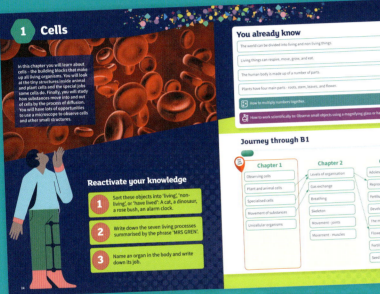

Each chapter has an opener spread to reactivate what you already know, and to show you what's coming up in the chapter. It also shows you the Working Scientifically and Maths skills that you will learn. The chapter map shows how far through the unit you have progressed.

Summary

This summarises the key ideas you have learnt so far and shows you your progress through the unit.

Metacognition and self-reflection

You can use these techniques to reflect on your own strengths and challenges when working through the chapter.

End-of-chapter questions

You can use these exam-style questions to test how well you know the topics in the chapter.

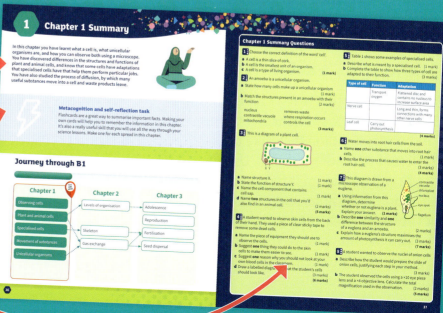

v

Working as a scientist

Often secondary-school science lessons are very different from what you may be used to in primary school. Secondary-school students need to work more independently – this could be doing an experiment in small groups, or working on your own to understand a new topic. It is important that you have a range of strategies to use when learning new scientific content.

Mastering secondary science

At secondary school you often need to approach learning in a much more independent way, so it is important to make sure you know what resources you have available to help you. This includes reviewing the notes in your book, using online resources like Kerboodle, and knowing when to ask a partner or your teacher for help. Knowing who or what can help you will mean you can tackle any task with confidence.

Sometimes when you start to learn a new topic it can feel like you will never remember it all. However, by practising your skills, learning from your mistakes, and seeking help when needed you will soon master any new topic. You can use the flowchart shown in Figure 1 to help you master secondary school science.

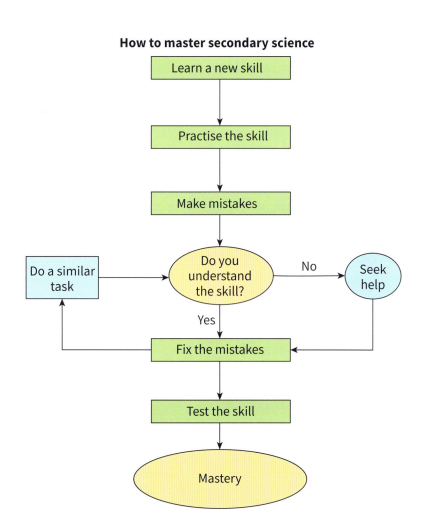

▲ **Figure 1** A flowchart to help you master secondary-school science.

Working as a scientist

Reading scientific texts is a big part of secondary-school science. Reading and understanding texts like this is different to reading a book. Usually there will be a lot of information given in short paragraphs and there will be lots of examples, diagrams, and data for you to understand. You can use the SURE strategy to help you read and understand scientific texts.

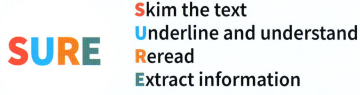

Finish with a one-sentence summary.

When extracting information from a text it is important to keep to key facts. This may mean that you just write a list of bullet points that cover the key ideas, including any equations or diagrams. Or you may feel the need to write notes with more detail. You can also use the Cornell notes method shown in Figure 2 when taking notes. To help you understand what using the Cornell notes method would look like in a lesson, you can see Figure 3.

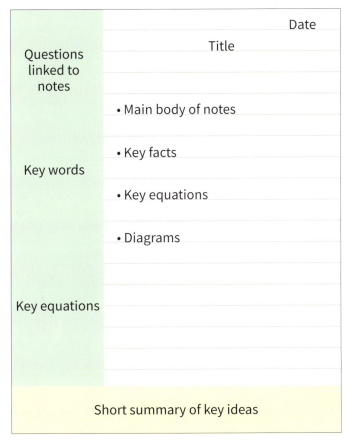

▲ **Figure 2** The Cornell notes method. This is a strategy to help you when taking notes.

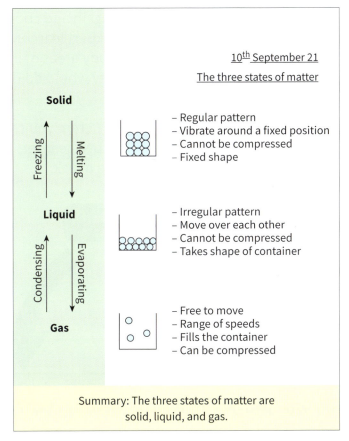

▲ **Figure 3** An example of using the Cornell notes method in a lesson on the three states of matter.

Discuss

Think and discuss with a partner what resources you can use if:

- you are stuck with a question in a lesson
- you are stuck with a question when doing homework
- you are unsure about what to do during a practical investigation
- you are unsure if your answer is correct.

Plan, Monitor, Evaluate

Expert learners approach new and unfamiliar tasks in a structured way. Often, they will start by picking apart the question or task, thinking carefully about what subject knowledge they are going to need or whether they have seen something similar before.

During a task an expert learner will keep checking to make sure they are on track by regularly looking back at the question. Sometimes they may even decide to start the task again and choose a different approach. After they have finished, an expert learner will reflect on how they have done by thinking about any areas of improvement and putting a plan together for what they would do differently next time.

The Plan, Monitor, Evaluate cycle is a structure you can follow to help you approach a new task like an expert learner. This cycle should be used every time you complete a task.

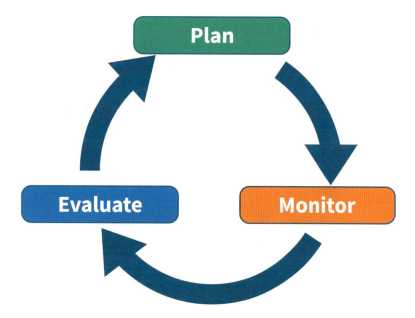

Discuss

Think and discuss with a partner your answers to these questions:

- When does the planning phase take place?
- How can you monitor your progress during the monitoring phase?
- Why is the evaluation phase important?

Plan

The planning phase takes place **before** you start the task. This is where you plan your approach to the task by thinking about what you already know and what pieces of information relate to the task:

Here some examples of the types of questions you could be asking yourself before you start a new task.

- How many marks does this question have?
- What scientific knowledge do I need to recall to answer the question?
- Have I answered a similar question before? What did success look like then?
- What have I learnt from the examples my teacher has shown me?

Evaluate

When you have completed a task, it is important to **reflect** on how you have done. An expert learner learns from their mistakes and uses teacher feedback to move their own learning forward.

Here are some examples of the types of questions you should be asking yourself after a task:
- What went well?
- Did I miss any marks? If so, for what?
- Is there any other strategy that I could have used to complete this task?
- What areas do I need to improve upon for next time?

Monitor

Once you have started the task it is important to monitor your own progress. Sometimes by **pausing and reviewing** the task you may choose to change your approach. You may even decide that you need to go back and re-read some scientific content to help you complete the task:

Here are some examples of the types of questions you should be asking yourself during a task.
- How do I feel now that I am answering the question? Confident or unsure?
- Am I meeting the requirements of the task or question?
- Do I need to stop and change anything I have done?
- Have I followed the examples that my teacher showed me?

Welcome

When you carry out scientific experiments or try to solve problems, it is important to think and work in a scientific way. This chapter will help you to develop your Working Scientifically skills, taking ideas and turning them them into scientific questions that can be tested. You will use scientific equipment to collect and record measurements and observations, then examine your data to see if it can answer your scientific questions. You will also learn how to work safely and begin to evaluate your work to spot errors and suggest improvements.

Working Scientifically

Working Scientifically and you

You were born a scientist. Humans are naturally curious and wonder, 'How, why, what?' about the world we live in. Ever since you were little you posed questions to try to understand the world around you. As your knowledge grew, you were able to ask more difficult questions, and begin to understand the answers you got. This is how our understanding of science develops.

By learning to work scientifically you will be able to ask scientific questions based on observations you make. You will also start to make sense of the answers you find by carrying out practical investigations and doing experiments.

Scientific research is happening all the time, all over the world. In 2020, scientists from many different countries worked together to develop vaccines, drugs, and testing kits in the fight against Covid-19. But research doesn't just happen in a laboratory, or in hospitals. Science and research take place at the tops of mountains, at the bottom of oceans, and even on Mars!

Working Scientifically and the world

It is important to understand how science works so that we can make decisions about things that affect us. We are bombarded every day by new information. Scientific knowledge can help us to understand the information, and to figure out whether it is reliable and believable. Scientists have a key role in exposing 'fake news', and helping the population to be well-informed using accurate information.

How do scientists find out how things happen?
Scientists make observations of the world. This leads to questions about how or why something happens. They then work scientifically to find the answer.

How do you carry out an investigation?
To answer a scientific question, you need to choose equipment and follow a method carefully to collect results.

How do scientists use data to answer their questions?
Scientists carefully examine the results of an investigation to see if there are any patterns or trends. These help us to answer scientific questions.

Working Scientifically through Book 1

Asking scientific questions	Working safely	Planning investigations	Recording data	Presenting data	Analysing data	Evaluating data
There are some questions that we can use science to answer and some that we can't.	During an investigation, safety is very important. How can you make sure you are working safely?	How can we investigate our scientific question to find the answer?	What is the best way to record our observations and the results of the investigation?	There are many different ways to present the results – how do you choose?	What does the data tell us about our investigation?	Have the investigation and data helped to answer our scientific question?

1.1 Asking scientific questions

Learning objectives
After this topic, you will be able to:
- develop an idea into a question that can be investigated
- identify independent, dependent, and control variables
- make a scientific prediction.

Reactivate your knowledge
1. What name is given to observations and measurements made during an investigation?
2. What is a fair test?
3. Name some sources of data.

Is the temperature of the world rising? Why are the polar ice caps melting (see Figure 1)? We can ask lots of different questions about the world around us. Some are questions that science can answer.

What is a scientific question?

Scientists make **observations** of the world around them, and then ask questions such as 'Why is the sky blue?' or 'Can we bring an extinct animal back to life?'. These are examples of scientific questions because they can be answered through scientific **investigations**.

Scientific investigations are experiments where you collect **data** (observations or measurements) to answer your question.

▲ **Figure 1** What is causing the polar ice caps to melt?

Suggesting ideas

Tom and Katie are watching a tennis match. Tom observes that new tennis balls are brought out from a refrigerator during the match. Observations like this can give you ideas that you can scientifically investigate.

Developing ideas into questions

In Figure 2, Katie and Tom discuss why the new balls are kept in a fridge.

Key words
observation, investigation, data, variable, independent variable, dependent variable, control variable, prediction

▲ **Figure 2** Why are the new balls kept in a fridge?

Reactivate your knowledge answers
1 Data (or results) 2 A test that keeps everything the same except for the variable (thing) being tested 3 For example, books, internet, other people

Working and thinking scientifically

What is a variable?

In science, anything that can change during an investigation is called a **variable**. There are three types of variable:

- **Independent variable:** this is the variable you change in an investigation.
- **Dependent variable:** this variable changes when you change the independent variable.
- **Control variables:** these are the variables you need to keep the same in an investigation.

Katie and Tom decide they want to investigate if the temperature affects the height a ball bounces. In their experiment, temperature is the independent variable. How high the ball bounces is the dependent variable.

> **A** A scientist investigates how the brightness of a torch affects how far you can see at night. Identify the independent variable.

Control variables

The temperature of the ball is not the only thing that might affect the height of the bounce. Katie and Tom think about other variables that might affect how high tennis balls bounce. Here is their list:

- the height you drop the ball from
- the surface that you drop it onto
- the size of the ball

Katie and Tom need to keep these variables the same during their investigation so that they do not affect the bounce height. These are their control variables.

> **B** Suggest one other control variable in Katie and Tom's investigation.

Making a prediction

Scientists often have an idea about what they might expect to happen in an investigation. This is called their **prediction**. Predictions don't always turn out to be true, though!

Katie predicts that '*the higher the temperature of the ball, the higher it will bounce*'. She can then test these ideas out when she completes her experiment.

Name those variables!

Imagine that Katie and Tom decided to investigate whether the **size** of a ball affects how high it bounces.
a State the dependent and independent variables.
b List all the variables that Katie and Tom would need to control.

Summary Questions

1 Copy and complete the following sentences.

The _____ variable is the variable you change.
A _____ variable should be kept the same during an investigation.
The _____ variable is the variable which changes when the independent variable is changed. (3 marks)

2 A student is looking at an ice cube melting.
a Suggest a scientific question that could be investigated. (1 mark)
b Explain why this is a question that science can answer. (2 marks)

3 A student investigates how the length of a leaf affects how long it takes to fall from a tree to the ground.
a Identify the independent variable. (1 mark)
b Identify the dependent variable. (1 mark)
c Name **three** control variables for this investigation. (3 marks)

9

1.2 Working safely

Learning objectives

After this topic, you will be able to:
- recognise commonly used hazard symbols
- identify possible hazards in practical work
- understand the purpose of a risk assessment.

Reactivate your knowledge

1. List two ways of keeping yourself safe when using a kettle.
2. Why do most countries have signs to show when there is a sharp bend in the road?
3. What is a scientific investigation?

▲ **Figure 1** Hazard signs are used in many places to help people work safely.

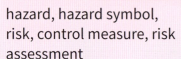

Key words

hazard, hazard symbol, risk, control measure, risk assessment

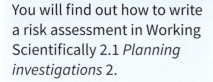

Link

You will find out how to write a risk assessment in Working Scientifically 2.1 *Planning investigations* 2.

Have you ever noticed the symbols on the back of lorries or products in the cupboards or posters on the walls in public places, such as those in Figure 1?

These are **hazard symbols**. They warn people of dangers and tell them how to work safely.

What is a hazard?

A **hazard** is anything that can harm us or people around us. This could involve chemicals, working on a ladder, using electrical appliances, or working with animals.

Safety is one of the first things scientists must think about before carrying out an experiment. They must think about their own safety and the safety of others.

Katie and Tom's experiment involves bouncing tennis balls. In Figure 2 Katie and Tom discuss the hazards they should think about during their investigation.

The ball might bounce into someone's face.

The control measure for this would be to wear safety goggles to protect their eyes.

▲ **Figure 2** Potential hazards of bouncing balls.

A State one way Katie and Tom can make sure they carry out the experiment safely.

Reactivate your knowledge answers

1 For example, don't touch hot surfaces, avoid scalding in steam 2 For example, warn drivers of the bend, warn drivers to slow down/reduce speed 3 An experiment where you collect data to answer a scientific question.

Working and thinking scientifically

Hazard symbols

Hazard symbols are placed on the outside of containers, on walls, signs, and vehicles. They let us know the danger so we can be safe. Figure 3 shows some common hazard symbols.

Before 2017, different countries used to use different hazard symbols. However, in 2017 all countries agreed to use the same symbols to label dangerous substances and situations. These symbols are called the Globally Harmonized System (GHS).

> **B** Suggest why hazard symbols need to be the same all over the world.

What is a risk?

A **risk** is the chance that a hazard will cause harm. Scientists need to think how likely it is that someone will be exposed to the hazard, or how serious the effects of the hazard could be.

You can put a **control measure** in place to reduce the risk of a hazard causing harm. A control measure could involve choosing a different method, using safety equipment, or a less hazardous substance.

Is it safe?

A plan for an experiment should include the steps you will take to stay safe. In many scientific investigations you will need to wear goggles; when using a Bunsen burner, you should also tie long hair back out of the way.

If you are following someone else's plan, it will often include a **risk assessment**. This explains what you must do – or not do – to avoid injuring yourself or other people.

> **C** Explain why you should tie long hair back when using a Bunsen burner.

Oxidising   Flammable   Corrosive

Compressed gas   Toxic   Health hazard

Irritant   Explosive   Environmental hazard

▲ **Figure 3** These are the international hazard symbols and their meanings.

Summary Questions

1 Match each symbol to the hazard:

   Flammable

   Corrosive

   Environmental hazard

   Irritant

(3 marks)

2 An experiment involves using a flammable chemical. The students using the chemical are wearing goggles. State **one** other control measure that should be in place to protect the students. (1 mark)

3 A student measured 20 cm^3 of dilute acid using a glass measuring cylinder.

a Identify the possible hazards for this part of their method. (2 marks)

b Suggest control measures for each of these hazards. (4 marks)

1.3 Planning investigations

Learning objectives
After this topic, you will be able to:
- write a plan for a scientific investigation
- use simple measuring equipment
- take accurate measurements.

Reactivate your knowledge
1. Name some pieces of science equipment used to take measurements.
2. What is meant by an independent variable?
3. What is meant by a control variable?

▲ **Figure 1** You have to follow a clear plan when carrying out scientific investigations.

Have you ever cooked from a recipe? Did it turn out the way you wanted? The plan for a science investigation or experiment is a bit like a recipe. It lists what equipment and materials you are going to use, and says what you are going to do with them.

Look at the students doing a chemistry experiment in Figure 1.

How do you plan a scientific investigation?

▲ **Figure 2** Katie is talking about changing the independent variable in their investigation. Tom is suggesting how to measure the dependent variable.

In Figure 2 Katie and Tom want to know whether the temperature of a ball affects how high it bounces. They now need to write a **plan** for their scientific investigation to find the answer to their question. A scientific plan includes the following information:

- the scientific question that you are trying to answer
- the independent and dependent variables
- a list of variables you will control, and how you will do this
- a prediction
- a list of the equipment you will need; this can include a diagram
- a step-by-step **method** of how you will collect data or observations
- any safety precautions which you should take

Key words
plan, method, accurate data, true value, range, interval

Reactivate your knowledge answers
1 For example, ruler, stopwatch, balance 2 The variable you change 3 A variable which does not change during an investigation

Working and thinking scientifically

How do you choose the right equipment?

Your equipment should be able to produce measurements or observations to help you answer your scientific question. For example, you could use a microscope to see very small objects, or a ruler to measure length. You need to choose equipment to measure both the independent and dependent variables.

Equipment	Quantity measured
ruler or tape measure	length
thermometer	temperature
stopwatch	time
balance	mass
measuring cylinder	volume

▲ Table 1 Common scientific equipment.

A What equipment should Katie and Tom use to measure the temperature of the tennis balls?

B What equipment should Katie and Tom use to measure how high the ball bounces?

You must be able to use each piece of equipment correctly to stay safe and collect **accurate data**. Accurate data is close to the **true value** of what you are trying to measure. For example, in Figure 3 Tom needs to look directly at the ruler to get an accurate measurement of the bounce height.

▲ Figure 3 Look straight at a scale to make an accurate measurement.

How many measurements?

To answer a scientific question, you often need a number of observations to see a pattern or trend. This means you will need to take several measurements of both the independent and dependent variables. If possible, you should take each measurement three times.
Katie and Tom need to choose which temperatures to test for their plan. They need to decide:

- the biggest and smallest temperatures – this is called the **range**
- how many different temperatures, usually five or more
- the **interval** (gap) between their temperature measurements.

Summary Questions

1 Copy and complete the following sentences.
The plan for an investigation includes a list of the _____ that you will use. You should name the independent and _____ variables, and also any variables you need to _____. You then include a step-by-step _____ which shows how you will carry out your investigation. (4 marks)

2 A student decides to investigate how the volume of water in a beaker affects the mass of sugar which can dissolve in it.

a State which piece of equipment could be used to measure the volume of water. (1 mark)

b State which piece of equipment could be used to measure the mass of sugar and describe how to use it. (3 marks)

3 A student investigates whether the type of surface affects the bounce height of a ball. She uses four different surfaces, and tests each one two times.

a Explain why she should read the scale on the ruler by looking straight at it when measuring the bounce height. (2 marks)

b Suggest why it is a good idea for the student to repeat her results. (2 marks)

c State and explain whether she needs to write any safety precautions for this experiment. (2 marks)

13

1.4 Recording data

Learning objectives
After this topic, you will be able to:
- design a results table
- present data in a correctly designed results table
- calculate a mean from repeat measurements.

Reactivate your knowledge
1. What is a dependent variable?
2. What piece of safety equipment is used to protect your eyes?
3. Name the piece of equipment used to measure mass.

School team	Played	Won	Drawn
Albester	12	6	5
Barnshot	11	7	2
Clovehill	10	7	1
Donston	10	7	1
Erdham	11	6	2

▲ **Table 1** Football league table showing a selection of data.

Have you ever looked for numerical information, such as the records from school sports day, or how fast a certain type of car can accelerate?

Table 1 shows data from a school football league. When organising lots of data together, scientists use results tables to make the data easier to understand and interpret.

What does a simple results table look like?

Results tables are always drawn in the same way in science. Table 2 shows their features.

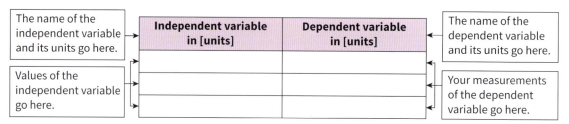

▲ **Table 2** How to draw a simple results table.

A results table helps you to organise your data. Not all data are numbers. Sometimes you need to use words, and record observations in a table using scientific language. For example, you could record a colour change in a chemical reaction.

> **A** Where should you record the units of a quantity in a results table?

How do you record repeat measurements?

Katie and Tom decided to collect data on how high a ball bounces, at five different ball temperatures. They also decided to repeat each result three times to check their results were correct. Their results table is shown in Table 3.

Key words
mean, anomaly

Reactivate your knowledge answers
1 A variable which is affected by changing the independent variable 2 Goggles 3 Balance

14

Working and thinking scientifically

Temperature of ball in °C	Height of bounce in cm			
	1st measurement	2nd measurement	3rd measurement	Mean
0				
10				
20				
30				
40				

- Values of the independent variable go from smallest to largest.
- Repeat measurements go here.
- The mean bounce height will be written here.

▲ **Table 3** Katie and Tom's results table.

How do you calculate a mean?

The **mean** is a type of average. To calculate the mean, you add up all the results and divide by the number of results.

$$\text{Mean average} = \frac{\text{result 1 + result 2 + result 3 + ...}}{\text{number of results}}$$

For example, Katie and Tom collected the following results at 0 °C:

Result 1: 25 cm   Result 2: 35 cm   Result 3: 30 cm

$$\text{Mean} = \frac{25 + 35 + 30}{3} = \frac{90}{3} = 30 \text{ cm}$$

How do you check for anomalous results?

As they collect their data, Katie and Tom fill in their results table in Table 4.

Temperature of ball in °C	Height of bounce in cm			
	1st measurement	2nd measurement	3rd measurement	Mean
0	25	35	30	30
10	45	35	40	40
20	50	55	(15)	
30	60	60	60	60
40	65	75	70	70

This is an anomaly, as it is much lower than the other results at 20 °C.

▲ **Table 4** Results table for bouncing a ball with different temperatures.

You should check your data for an anomalous result. This means a result that is very different to the others. You should repeat the measurement to replace an anomalous result. In Table 4, the third measurement for the 20 °C ball temperature, 15 cm, is an **anomaly**. Katie and Tom repeat this result before calculating their mean – the ball bounces to 60 cm.

B Calculate the new mean bounce height for the ball at 20 °C.

Summary Questions

1 Copy and complete the following sentences.

Scientists collect data from experiments into a _____ table. The first column contains the _____ variable. The second column contains the _____ variable. _____ are written next to the variable name. (4 marks)

2 A student collects three repeat measurements when investigating how temperature affects how long it takes sugar to dissolve. Their results are shown in Table 5:

Temperature in °C	Dissolving time in s		
	1st	2nd	3rd
50	40	16	48
80	17	14	14

▲ **Table 5** The student's results.

a Identify the anomaly in the student's results. (1 mark)
b Calculate the mean dissolving time at 80 °C. (2 marks)

3 A group of students investigate how the volume of an ice cube affects how long it takes to melt. They collect data on five different volumes, and take each measurement three times.

a Design a results table to hold the students' data. (3 marks)
b Explain **one** way to deal with an anomaly in a set of repeated measurements. (1 mark)

15

1.5 Presenting data

Learning objectives
After this topic, you will be able to:
- classify data as continuous, discrete, or categorical
- present data as a chart or graph.

Reactivate your knowledge
1. Name some different types of graph.
2. What is an anomaly?
3. How do you calculate a mean?

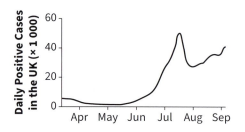

▲ **Figure 1** During the Covid pandemic, the government used line graphs to show how the number of positive cases varied over time.

How do you share large numbers of measurements or observations with others? Scientists use graphs to make it easier to see patterns or trends within data. Figure 1 shows an example.

What are the three types of scientific data?

When you carry out an investigation, the data you collect might be in the form of words or numbers. Data can be:

- **continuous** – the data can have any value within a range, such as length or temperature
- **discrete** – the data can have only whole-number values, such as shoe size or the number of woodlice collected
- **categorical** – the value is a word, such as 'blue' or 'fizzing'.

You will use three main types of graph or chart in science. These are:

- **bar chart** – used to plot discrete and categorical data
- **line graph** – used when both the independent and dependent variables are continuous
- **pie chart** – used to plot discrete and categorical data.

How do you draw a bar chart?

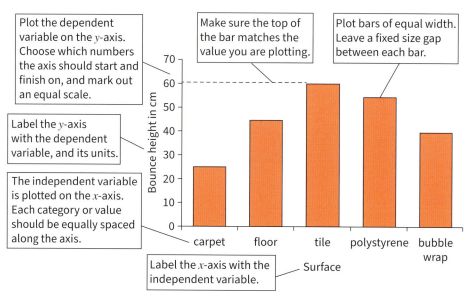

▲ **Figure 2** Bar chart of bounce height of a tennis ball on different surfaces.

Reactivate your knowledge answers
1. Bar chart, line graph, pie chart 2. A result which is very different (when repeating results) 3. Add up measurements, divide by number of values

Working and thinking scientifically

A group of students bounced a tennis ball on different surfaces. Their results are shown in the bar chart in Figure 2.

A Using the graph in Figure 2, find the bounce height on a tiled surface.

How do you draw a line graph?

Figure 3 shows how Katie and Tom plotted a graph from their experimental data. They chose a line graph as their experiment produced continuous data.

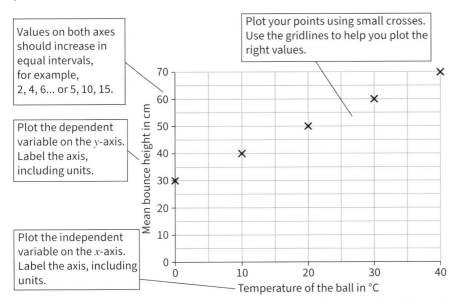

▲ **Figure 3** Line graph of Katie and Tom's results showing the effect of temperature on the mean ball bounce height.

How do you draw a pie chart?

Pie charts like the one in Figure 4 use segments of a circle to represent the data. To plot a pie chart, you will need to use a protractor to measure the angle of each segment.

- Draw a line from the centre of the circle to the edge.
- Use a protractor to measure the angle of each segment as you draw them.
- Remember to label each segment.
- Shade each segment a different colour.

▲ **Figure 4** Pie chart of Katie and Tom's survey results showing the types of floor covering used in hallways.

B Using Figure 4, identify which is the most common floor covering.

Key words

continuous, discrete, categorical, bar chart, line graph, pie chart

Summary Questions

1 Name the following chart types: (3 marks)

A

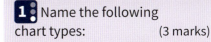

B

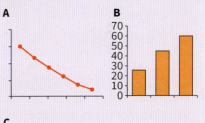

C

2 Plot a bar chart of the following data:

School transport type	Number of students
Walk	20
Cycle	12
Bus	6
Car	8

(4 marks)

3 A group of students studied how the mass of a seed affected how long it took to fall a distance of 1 m.
 a State which type of graph the students should choose to display their data. (1 mark)
 b Explain your answer. (2 marks)

17

1.6 Analysing data

Learning objectives
After this topic, you will be able to:
- identify patterns or trends in data using a graph or chart
- interpret data to draw conclusions.

Reactivate your knowledge
1. What are the three main types of graph or chart used in science?
2. What type of graph is used to plot continuous data?
3. What is a prediction?

Key words
analyse, pattern, trend, line of best fit, conclusion

How can we monitor how human activity affects our planet? Collecting data and then plotting graphs helps scientists and others to clearly see any patterns or trends over time.

How do you identify a pattern or trend?

When you **analyse** your data, plotting a line graph or chart helps you to spot a **pattern** or **trend**. It shows how the dependent variable is affected by the independent variable. For example, the bar chart in Figure 1 shows that the Amazon rainforest is getting smaller over time.

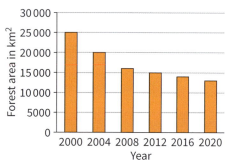

▲ **Figure 1** Chart showing how the size of the Amazon rainforest has changed over time.

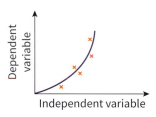

▲ **Figure 2** If the independent variable increases then the dependent variable increases.

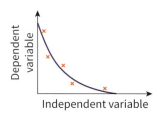

▲ **Figure 3** If the independent variable increases then the dependent variable decreases.

To make the trend easier to see on a graph, you should add a **line of best fit**. This is a straight line or smooth curve that goes through, or very close to, as many points as possible. There should be equal numbers of points above and below the line. If there are any anomalies, you should ignore these when you draw your line of best fit.

What does a line of best fit show?

The line of best fit tells you about the trend in the data.

- If the line slopes *upwards*, like in Figure 2, it means that as the independent variable *increases*, the dependent variable *increases* too.
- If the line slopes *downwards*, like in Figure 3, it means that as the independent variable *increases*, the dependent variable *decreases*.
- If the line is horizontal, like in Figure 4, it means that as the independent variable *increases*, the dependent variable *does not change*.

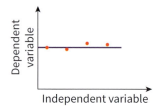

▲ **Figure 4** If the independent variable increases the dependent variable does not change.

Reactivate your knowledge answers
1 Bar chart, pie chart, line graph 2 Line graph 3 A statement where you say what you think will happen

Working and thinking scientifically

Look at the graph in **Figure 5**. Katie and Tom added a line of best fit to their graph showing how temperature affects how high a ball bounces.

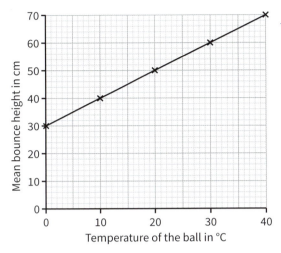

Figure 5 Changes in the temperature of the ball affect the bounce height.

The line is sloping upwards. This means that as the independent variable (temperature) increases, the dependent variable (bounce height) increases as well. So the trend can be written as: *As the temperature increases, the bounce height also increases*.

A State the trend shown in Figure 1.

How do you write a conclusion?

Once you have analysed your graph you can write a **conclusion**. This is where you write down what you have found out. Start by describing the pattern in your data or the relationship you can see between the two variables from your graph or chart. Katie writes:

When the ball is warmer, the ball bounces higher.

Saying what your results show is only part of analysing results. You also need to use scientific knowledge to explain the pattern or trend.

Tom begins to explain the relationship between temperature and the height of the bounce:

The ball bounces higher when it is warmer because the ball is softer.

However, to come up with a good explanation he needs to understand why balls bounce. You may want to do some research to help you explain why something has happened.

Finally, you can compare your results with your prediction.

B Katie predicted that if the ball was hotter, it would bounce higher. State whether or not Katie's prediction was correct.

Summary Questions

1 Copy and complete the following sentences.
To analyse your data you plot a graph and work out the relationship between the _____. Then you write a _____ that includes what you have found out, and explains why. Finally, you compare your results with your _____.
(4 marks)

2 A student plots a graph of water temperature and the time that it takes sugar to dissolve.

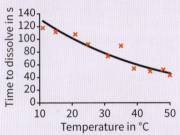

a Explain why they plotted a line of best fit.
(1 mark)

b Use the graph to describe what happens when water temperature increases.
(2 marks)

3 Look at the graph.

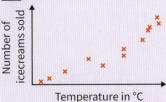

a Describe what the graph shows. (1 mark)

b Suggest an explanation for the trend. (1 mark)

19

1.7 Evaluating data

Learning objectives
After this topic, you will be able to:
- describe the stages in evaluating data
- suggest ways to improve a practical investigation.

Reactivate your knowledge
1. How do you show a pattern on a line graph?
2. What should a conclusion contain?
3. What name is given to a measurement which is very different to other repeat results?

▲ **Figure 1** Evaluating your performance after a race helps you to identify areas to improve.

Top-level athletes (like those in Figure 1) constantly look for ways to improve their performance. They identify areas where they can make changes to perform at a higher level in future events.

What is an evaluation?

There are three parts to a scientific investigation:
- Identify the strengths and weaknesses in your results.
- Decide how confident you are in your conclusion.
- Suggest and explain improvements to your method, so you can collect data of better quality if you did it again.

Katie and Tom have collected data and analysed it. Now they need to **evaluate** their data and their method.

How do you identify strengths and weaknesses in data?

1. Identify anomalies

Katie and Tom had only one anomaly in their experiment – the third measurement at 20 °C (see page 15). If there were lots of anomalies then they would have less **confidence** in their conclusion.

2. Look at the spread of data

The **spread** is the difference between the highest and the lowest readings in a set of repeat measurements. In Katie and Tom's results the spread of the data for 0 °C is 10 cm (35 cm–25 cm). A small spread in the data will give you more confidence in your conclusion. Your method is **repeatable** if your repeat results are very similar.

3. Check for errors

There is an experimental error in any measurement you make. This is why there is often a small spread in experimental data. However, there are two types of error that can cause much bigger changes in scientific measurements:

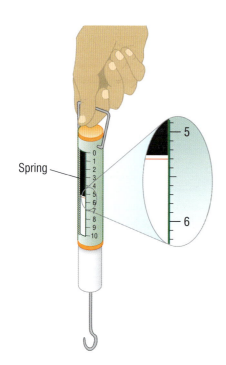

▲ **Figure 2** This newtonmeter shows a systematic error, as it has a reading when there is no load on the meter.

Reactivate your knowledge answers
1 Line of best fit 2 Description of the trend, explanation of trend, comparison to prediction 3 Anomaly

Working and thinking scientifically

- **random error** – this is where an unexpected change affects your results. An example is the temperature of the room suddenly changing because someone opens a door.
- **systematic error** – this is where something consistently affects all of your results. Systematic errors are often caused by faulty measuring equipment, such as in Figure 2.

> **A** A balance shows a reading of 0.2 g when unloaded. State whether this is an example of a random error or a systematic error.

You should think about errors, anomalies, and spread to help you to decide how confident you are in your conclusion.

How can you improve an investigation?

It is always possible to improve the quality of your measurements in an investigation. Improvements would make you more confident that your conclusion is correct.

1. Range of results

Remember, the **range** is the smallest and largest values of the independent variable. The wider the range, the more certain you can be that your conclusion is always true. Tom and Katie used a range of 0 °C to 40 °C. To be more certain of their conclusion, they could test hotter balls.

Remember – within the range, you should always investigate at least five values of the independent variable.

> **B** Suggest another temperature of ball Katie and Tom could test to improve their experiment.

2. Repeat readings

If you have not taken repeat readings you cannot be certain if any of the results were a 'fluke'. You should always take at least three repeat readings for each value of the independent variable.

3. Using different equipment

If you had several anomalies, or a large spread of data, you might want to consider using different equipment to collect your measurements. For example, Katie and Tom could have used a video camera to record the highest bounce point; it is difficult to take an accurate measurement of a moving object.

Key words

evaluation, confidence, spread, repeatable, random error, systematic error, range

Summary Questions

1 Match the term to its definition. (3 marks)

Range	An error which consistently affects a set of results
Spread	An error caused by an unexpected event
Random error	The difference in readings within a set of repeat results
Systematic error	The smallest and largest values of the independent variable

2 Draw a flowchart to show the stages you should follow when writing an evaluation.
(4 marks)

3 A group of students collect the following data about how the mass of a paper aeroplane affects how far it can fly.

Mass of aeroplane in g	Distance travelled in m	
	Measurement 1	Measurement 2
20	1.8	2.0
40	1.4	3.8
60	1.2	1.0

a Identify the anomaly in this results table. (1 mark)

b The students conclude: 'The bigger the mass of a paper aeroplane, the less distance it can fly'. Evaluate the students' results. (4 marks)

21

Welcome

Biology is the study of living things. This involves learning about you as a human being, the plants and animals around you, and the many tiny organisms that can't be seen with the naked eye.

In this book you will find out what plants and animals are made of and how these different structures work together to keep them alive.

1 Biology

Biology and you

Every second of every day, biology plays a massive part in your life. It explains how you grew into the person you are today and determines what you look like, how you complete activities, and why you like (or don't like) certain things. Biology explains why you get ill and how you get better again.

Did you know that the human body contains around 30 000 000 000 000 cells? Cells are tiny units that work together to perform the basic functions necessary for an organism to stay alive. However, you don't just have human cells inside your body. Millions of bacteria call your body home, and some scientists estimate there are more bacterial cells in your body than there are human cells!

The sciatic nerve is the largest and longest nerve in the body. It starts at the bottom of your spine and extends all the way down the back of your leg to your toes. The nerves connected to the sciatic nerve control the movement of the legs and the lower body.

Why can some animals only breathe underwater, while others can fly? Biology explains why all of the weird and wonderful organisms in the world, from blue whales to amoebas, exist. Using biology, you can also predict what kind of organisms will emerge in the future.

By studying biology you will find out about the processes happening all around you that allow life to continue on planet Earth.

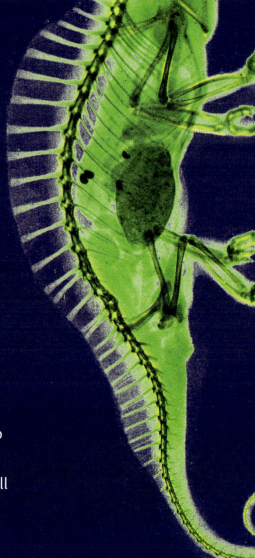

Biology and the world

A good understanding of biology is vital to keeping people healthy and protecting animal and plant habitats. Looking after the environment is essential for the survival of us and other species, many of which we depend on in our modern world.

BIG QUESTIONS

What are living things made of?
Microscopes have allowed scientists to look at the tiny structures that all living organisms are made of.

How does a baby form?
Ultrasound scans allow medical professionals to see inside a pregnant woman and understand how the baby grows.

How are new plants made?
Careful observations have allowed scientists to study how bees pollinate flowers – the first step in a new plant.

Journey through B1

Chapter 1
- Observing cells
- Plant and animal cells
- Specialised cells
- Movement of substances
- Unicellular organisms

Chapter 2
- Levels of organisation
- Gas exchange
- Breathing
- Skeleton
- Movement – joints
- Movement – muscles

Chapter 3
- Adolescence
- Reproductive systems
- Fertilisation and implantation
- Development of a foetus
- The menstrual cycle
- Flowers and pollination
- Fertilisation and germination
- Seed dispersal

23

1 Cells

In this chapter you will learn about cells – the building blocks that make up all living organisms. You will look at the tiny structures inside animal and plant cells and the special jobs some cells do. Finally, you will study how substances move into and out of cells by the process of diffusion. You will have lots of opportunities to use a microscope to observe cells and other small structures.

Reactivate your knowledge

1 Sort these objects into 'living', 'non-living', or 'have lived': A cat, a dinosaur, a rose bush, an alarm clock.

2 Write down the seven living processes summarised by the phrase 'MRS GREN'.

3 Name an organ in the body and write down its job.

You already know

- The world can be divided into living and non-living things.
- Living things can respire, move, grow, and eat.
- The human body is made up of a number of parts.
- Plants have four main parts - roots, stem, leaves, and flower.

 How to multiply numbers together.

 How to work scientifically to: Observe small objects using a magnifying glass or hand lens.

Journey through B1

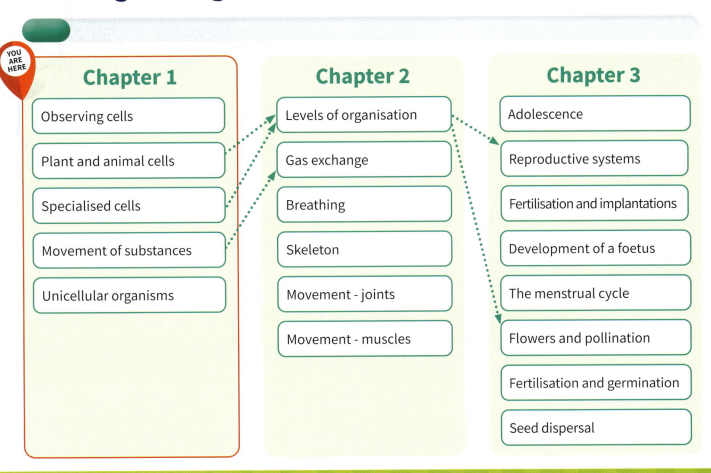

Chapter 1 (YOU ARE HERE)
- Observing cells
- Plant and animal cells
- Specialised cells
- Movement of substances
- Unicellular organisms

Chapter 2
- Levels of organisation
- Gas exchange
- Breathing
- Skeleton
- Movement - joints
- Movement - muscles

Chapter 3
- Adolescence
- Reproductive systems
- Fertilisation and implantations
- Development of a foetus
- The menstrual cycle
- Flowers and pollination
- Fertilisation and germination
- Seed dispersal

25

1.1 Observing cells

Learning objectives
After this topic, you will be able to:
- define what a cell is
- describe how to use a microscope to observe very small objects
- calculate the total magnification used to observe an object.

Reactivate your knowledge
1. What equipment can you use to look at small objects in detail?
2. What are the main structures in a plant?
3. Name some organs found in the human body.

▲ **Figure 1** This is the drawing that Hooke made of cork cells.

Key words
organism, cell, microscope, observation

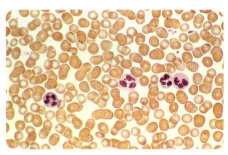

▲ **Figure 2** There are different types of cells in your blood.

Look around you. Can you see any dust? Most household dust is actually made of dead cells. These come from anything living in your house. To see the cells, you need to look through a microscope.

What are living organisms made of?

All living things, often called **organisms**, are made of **cells**. Cells are the building blocks of life and are the smallest units found in an organism. Organisms like bacteria are made up of only a single cell. Larger organisms, like you, are made up of millions of cells that are joined together.

A How many cells do you think make up a cat? Hundreds, thousands, or millions?

Seeing cells

Cells were first seen around 350 years ago when Robert Hooke, a scientist, looked down a **microscope** at a thin slice of cork. He saw tiny room-like structures, shown in Figure 1, which he called 'cells'. Cork is a type of tree bark, so what Hooke saw were plant cells.

B State what a microscope is used for.

Making an observation

To see a very small object in detail, you need to use a microscope. A microscope magnifies images using lenses. Looking carefully and in detail at an object is called making an **observation**. To make an observation with a microscope, the object you wish to observe needs to be very thin so that light can travel through it. Sometimes, you might need to add coloured dye to make the object easier to see, like the different types of blood cell shown in Figure 2.

Reactivate your knowledge answers
1 Hand lens/magnifying glass/microscope 2 Roots/stem/leaf/flower 3 Examples include: heart/lungs/stomach/eyes

B1 Chapter 1: Cells

Parts of a microscope

You can see the different parts of a microscope in Figure 3. Follow the steps below to observe an object using a microscope:

1. Move the stage to its lowest position.
2. Place the object you want to observe on the stage.
3. Select the objective lens with the lowest magnification.
4. Look through the eyepiece and turn the coarse-focus knob slowly until you see your object.
5. Turn the fine-focus knob until your object comes into focus.
6. Repeat Steps 1 to 5 using an objective lens with a higher magnification to see the object in greater detail.

C Name the part of a microscope that holds slides.

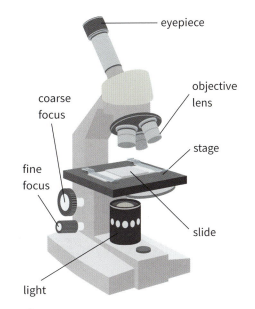

▲ **Figure 3** The parts of a microscope.

Magnification

The eyepiece lens and objective lens in a microscope have different magnifications. Together, they magnify the object.

For example, if you have an eyepiece lens of ×10 and an objective lens of ×4, the object would be magnified 40 times. This means the object looks 40 times bigger than it actually is. You can calculate magnification using the formula below:

Total magnification = eyepiece lens magnification × objective lens magnification
= 10 × 4
= 40

Magnification

You are going to observe an onion cell using a microscope. The eyepiece lens has a ×10 magnification and the objective lens has a ×40 magnification.

Calculate the total magnification using the formula:

Total magnification = eyepiece lens magnification × objective lens magnification

Summary Questions

1 Copy and complete the following sentences:

All living organisms are made up of _____ , which are the _____ units in an organism. To _____ cells in detail you need to use a _____ . This _____ the object. (5 marks)

2 Describe the function of these parts of the microscope.

a lens (1 mark)
b stage (1 mark)
c focusing knob (1 mark)

3 A drop of dye is added to a white flower petal before it is observed under a microscope.

a State why the dye was added. (1 mark)
b Choose which magnification (×40/×100/×400) should be used first to observe the petal, giving a reason for your answer. (3 marks)

27

1.2 Plant and animal cells

Learning objectives
After this topic, you will be able to:
- describe the function of each part of a cell
- compare the parts of plant and animal cells
- use a microscope to view plant and animal cells.

Reactivate your knowledge
1. Which parts of a microscope magnify an image?
2. What are the smallest units in an organism?
3. How do plants make food?

Key words
nucleus, cell membrane, cytoplasm, mitochondria, respiration, cell wall, vacuole, chloroplast, photosynthesis

When you look at cells through a microscope, you will see smaller parts inside them. These parts (components) all have important functions. Animal cells and plant cells contain some of the same components. However, some parts are different.

What's inside an animal cell?

Some animal cells are shown in Figure 1. They have an irregular shape and contain four components: a **nucleus**, a **cell membrane**, **cytoplasm**, and many **mitochondria** (singular: mitochondrion).

A Name the four parts that make up an animal cell.

Figure 2 shows the components of an animal cell. Each component has a different function:

cell membrane – This is a barrier around the cell. It controls what can come in and out of the cell.

cytoplasm – This is a 'jelly-like' substance where the chemical reactions in a cell take place.

nucleus – This controls the cell and contains genetic material. Genetic information is needed to make new cells.

mitochondria – This is where respiration takes place. **Respiration** is a special type of chemical reaction that transfers energy for the organism.

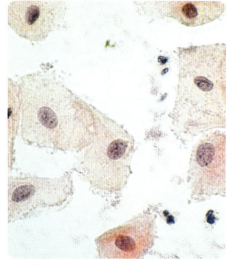
▲ **Figure 1** These are human cheek cells viewed under a microscope. Can you spot the nucleus inside each one?

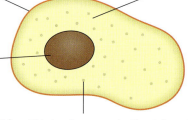
▲ **Figure 2** An animal cell.

Link
You can learn more about respiration in B2 2.5 *Aerobic respiration*.

B Name the two parts of a cell where chemical reactions take place.

Reactivate your knowledge answers
1 Eyepiece and objective lenses 2 Cells 3 By photosynthesis

B1 **Chapter 1:** Cells

What's inside a plant cell?

Plant cells, like the one in Figure 3, have a more regular structure than animal cells. This allows them to fit together like bricks. They contain seven components. Like animal cells, they contain a nucleus, a cell membrane, cytoplasm, and many mitochondria. However, they also contain three extra components: a **cell wall**, a **vacuole**, and **chloroplasts**.

▲ **Figure 3** These are leaf cells viewed under a microscope. Can you spot the chloroplasts?

C Name the cell components that are only found in plant cells.

Figure 4 shows the components of a plant cell. Each component has its own function:

chloroplasts – This is where photosynthesis happens. Chloroplasts contain a green substance called chlorophyll, which traps energy transferred from the Sun.

vacuole – This contains a watery liquid called cell sap. It keeps the cell firm.

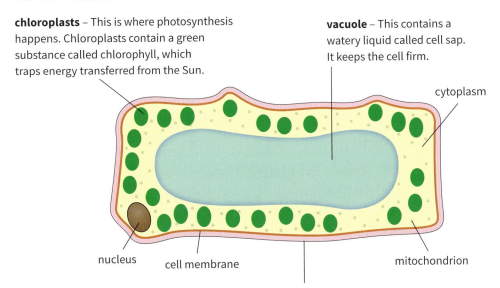

cytoplasm

nucleus cell membrane mitochondrion

cell wall – This strengthens the cell and provides support. It is made of a tough fibre called cellulose, which makes the wall rigid.

▲ **Figure 4** A plant cell.

Prefixes

'Chlorophyll' and 'chloroplast' both start with the prefix 'chloro', which means 'green'. Prefixes can give you a clue about what the word means. Other prefixes in biology include 'bio', 'photo', and 'micro'.

Summary Questions

1 Match each component of a cell to its function.

**vacuole   nucleus   cell wall
cytoplasm   chloroplasts
cell membrane   mitochondria**

a controls the cell's activities
b controls what comes in and out of a cell
c where chemical reactions take place
d where respiration takes place
e where photosynthesis takes place
f contains cell sap
g rigid structure that supports the cell   (6 marks)

2 Animal cells contain a number of components.

a Sketch an animal cell. (1 mark)
b Label **three** cell components on your sketch.   (3 marks)

3 Most plant cells contain chloroplasts.

a Identify the plant cells that do *not* contain chloroplasts:
**cells from a leaf
cells from a root
cells from a stem**   (1 mark)
b Explain your answer. (2 marks)

29

1.3 Specialised cells

Learning objectives
After this topic, you will be able to:
- describe the function of specialised cells
- describe the features of specialised animal cells
- describe the features of specialised plant cells.

Reactivate your knowledge
1. Where is the genetic material stored in cells?
2. Which chemical reaction happens inside the mitochondria?

Key words
specialised cell, adaptations, nerve cell, red blood cell, sperm cell, egg cell, leaf cell, root hair cell

Link
You can learn about how plants and animals are adapted to survive in B2 3.6 *Adapting to change*.

As you are reading this, your body is doing many different things. Each function carried out in the body is performed by different cells, and each type of cell has slightly different features.

How do animal cells differ?
Most cells in your body contain a nucleus, cell membrane, cytoplasm, and mitochondria. However, many cells have different shapes and structures so that they are suited to carrying out a particular job. These cells are called **specialised cells**.

If you look carefully at a specialised cell, its shape and special features, known as **adaptations**, can provide clues about what it does.

Nerve cell
Nerve cells, like the one in Figure 1, carry electrical impulses around your body.

They are long and thin and have connections at each end where they can join to other nerve cells. This allows them to transmit messages around the body.

> **A** Give two adaptations of a nerve cell.

▲ **Figure 1** A nerve cell. Its scientific name is a neurone.

Red blood cell
Red blood cells, shown in Figure 2, transport oxygen around the body. They contain haemoglobin, a red pigment that joins to oxygen. Unlike most animal cells they have no nucleus. They also have a disc-like shape that increases their surface area and helps them to carry oxygen.

> **B** Name the cell component missing in a red blood cell.

▲ **Figure 2** A red blood cell.

Reactivate your knowledge answers
1 Nucleus 2 Respiration

B1 Chapter 1: Cells

Sperm and egg cell

Sperm cells carry male genetic material. They have a streamlined head and a long tail that allow the cell to move through liquids. They contain lots of mitochondria to transfer energy because the tail requires a lot of energy to 'swim'. When the sperm cell meets an **egg cell**, the head of the sperm burrows into the egg. A sperm cell and an egg cell are shown in Figure 3.

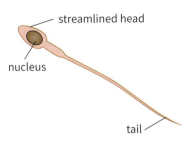

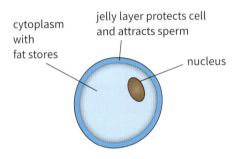

▲ **Figure 3** An egg cell and a sperm cell.

How do plant cells differ?

Not all plant cells are the same. Cells from different parts of a plant are specialised to perform their job.

Leaf cells

Figure 4 shows a **leaf cell**. Leaf cells found near the top of a leaf carry out photosynthesis. The cells are long and thin and packed with chloroplasts. This gives them a large surface area perfect for absorbing energy transferred from the Sun.

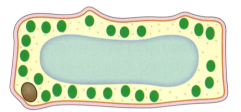

▲ **Figure 4** A cell from the top of a leaf. Its scientific name is a palisade cell.

C Give two adaptations of a leaf cell.

Root hair cells

Root hair cells absorb water and nutrients from the soil. The root hairs create a large surface area for absorbing water and nutrients. As there is no light underground, root hair cells have no chloroplasts and do not carry out photosynthesis. You can see the components of a root hair cell in Figure 5.

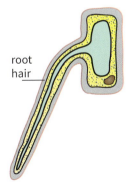

▲ **Figure 5** A root hair cell.

D Give two adaptations of a root hair cell.

Summary Questions

1 Copy and complete the following sentences.

_____ cells have special _____ that allow them to carry out their function. Red blood cells carry _____ around the body. Leaf cells are packed full of _____ to carry out _____.
(5 marks)

2 State the function of the following specialised cells:

Nerve cell (1 mark)
Root hair cell (1 mark)

3 Sperm cells are an example of a specialised animal cell.
  a Describe the function of a sperm cell. (1 mark)
  b Explain how sperm cells are adapted to perform their function. (3 marks)

31

1.4 Movement of substances

Learning objectives
After this topic, you will be able to:
- name some substances that move into cells and out of cells
- describe the process of diffusion
- describe examples of diffusion.

Reactivate your knowledge
1. What is a specialised cell?
2. Which type of plant cell absorbs water from the soil?
3. What piece of equipment is used to observe cells?

If someone starts cooking, the chances are that you will smell the food before you see it. The movement of the smell is a scientific process. The same process moves substances into and out of cells.

Key words
diffusion, concentration, vacuole

Which substances move into cells?
All the cells inside your body need glucose (a substance gained from food) and oxygen for respiration. During respiration, energy is transferred. Glucose and oxygen are carried around your body in your blood and are then passed onto the cells that need them.

Which substances move out of cells?
Some chemical reactions inside cells make waste products. For example, carbon dioxide is produced during respiration and passes out of cells into the blood. The blood then transports the carbon dioxide to the lungs, where it is breathed out.

> **A** Name a gas that moves into a body cell and a gas that moves out of a body cell.

Stink-bomb alert!
Imagine you work for a company that makes stink bombs.

A toy shop is interested in selling your stink bombs but wants to know how they work. Using what you know about diffusion, write a reply to the toy shop that explains simply how stink bombs work.

What is diffusion?
Substances move into and out of cells by **diffusion**. Diffusion is the movement of particles from a place where they are at a high **concentration** to a place where they are at a low concentration. The concentration of a substance means the number of particles of a substance present in a volume, or space.

Someone burns toast. Particles that make up the smell of burnt toast move from a place of high concentration (the kitchen) to one of low concentration (the rest of the house). At first, you may only be able to smell the burnt toast in the kitchen later. You may be able to smell the burnt toast in the living room. Diffusion continues until the concentration of particles is the same everywhere, as shown in Figure 1.

Link
You can learn more about diffusion in C1 1.6 *Diffusion*.

Reactivate your knowledge answers
1 Cell with special features that enable it to perform a function   2 Root hair cell   3 Microscope

B1 Chapter 1: Cells

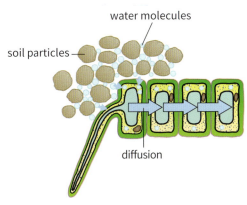

▲ **Figure 1** This diagram shows how you smell burnt toast in another room.

▲ **Figure 2** Water diffuses into the plant through the root hair cells. It then travels from the root hair cells to other cells in the plant by diffusion.

Diffusion in plant cells

Oxygen diffuses into a leaf and then into a plant's cells through tiny holes on the bottom of the leaf. The plant then uses the oxygen for respiration. The carbon dioxide produced diffuses back out of the leaf through the same holes.

Plants need a constant supply of water for photosynthesis. Water diffuses into the plant through the root hair cells, as shown in Figure 2. The water molecules move from the soil (high water concentration) into the root hair cell (low water concentration).

Why do plants wilt?

If plants are not watered regularly, they will wilt and eventually die. Inside the cells, water fills up the **vacuole**. This pushes outwards on the cell wall and makes the cell rigid. This helps the plant to stand upright. If the plant does not have enough water, the vacuole shrinks and the cells become floppy. This causes the plant to wilt, as shown in Figure 3.

cell from a leaf with enough water | healthy plant | wilted plant | cell from a leaf with no water

▲ **Figure 3** If a plant does not have enough water it will wilt.

B Name the process that causes water to move out of the vacuole.

Summary Questions

1 Copy and complete the following sentences.

Substances move from an area where they are at a _____ concentration to an area where they are at a _____ concentration. This process is called _____. (3 marks)

2 Various substances move into and out of cells.

a Name one substance, used for respiration, that moves into body cells. (1 mark)

b Name one substance, used for photosynthesis, that moves into plant cells. (1 mark)

3 Explain why oxygen moves into your body cells from the blood. (3 marks)

1.5 Unicellular organisms

Learning objectives
After this topic, you will be able to:
- define what a unicellular organism is
- describe the features of an amoeba
- describe the features of a euglena.

Reactivate your knowledge
1. Which process moves substances into a cell?
2. What components are found in an animal cell?
3. Which chemical reaction takes place inside chloroplasts?

Not all living organisms are as complicated as you are. The first organisms that existed on Earth were made up of just a single cell. Even today, many organisms exist as only one cell.

What is a unicellular organism?

A **unicellular** organism is an organism that is made up of just one cell. Unicellular organisms are not plants or animals, as these are made up of many cells.

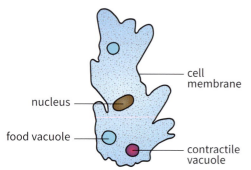

▲ **Figure 1** Parts of an amoeba.

Amoebas

An **amoeba** is a unicellular organism that has no fixed shape. Amoebas, shown in Figure 1, look a bit like a blob of jelly. They can be found in fresh water, salt water, wet soil, and even inside animals.

Just like an animal cell, an amoeba consists of a cell membrane filled with cytoplasm. They also contain a nucleus which controls growth and reproduction.

Amoebas move by changing the shape of their body. They do this by moving part of their body in the direction they want to travel. The rest of the cell then slowly follows.

> **A** Name two components found in both animal cells and amoebas.

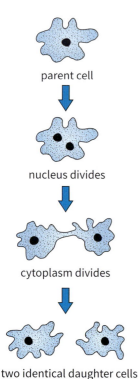

▲ **Figure 2** Amoebas divide by binary fission.

What do they eat?

Amoebas eat algae, bacteria, and plant cells by surrounding tiny particles of food and forming a food vacuole. This is known as engulfing. The food vacuole then digests the food.

Excess water and waste is removed by the contractile vacuole. Without this, the amoeba could swell up and burst.

Reactivate your knowledge answers
1 Diffusion 2 Nucleus, cell membrane, cytoplasm, mitochondria 3 Photosynthesis

How do they reproduce?

To reproduce, an amoeba splits itself into two identical cells. This is known as **binary fission**, shown in Figure 2.

Euglena

A **euglena**, shown in Figure 3, is a microscopic unicellular organism found in fresh water.

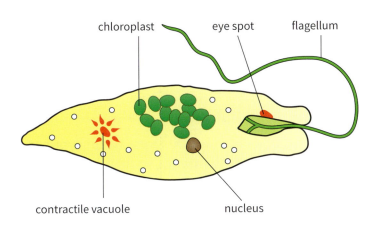

▲ **Figure 3** Parts of a euglena.

Like amoebas, euglenas have a cell membrane, cytoplasm, contractile vacuole, and a nucleus.

Unlike amoebas, they also contain chloroplasts that give them a green colour. The chloroplasts absorb energy transferred from the Sun so that the euglena can make food by photosynthesis.

Euglenas also have an eye spot to detect light as well as a **flagellum**. This tail-like structure spins like a propeller, causing the euglena to 'swim' towards the light to photosynthesise. This allows the euglena to maximise the amount of food it makes.

> **B** Give one way in which a euglena is different to an amoeba.

What do they eat?

When a euglena doesn't have enough light to make its own food, it finds other things to eat, usually other microorganisms like bacteria and algae. Just like amoebas, they eat by surrounding and engulfing their food.

How do they reproduce?

Like amoebas, euglenas reproduce by binary fission.

Link

You can learn more about photosynthesis in B2 2.1 *Photosynthesis*.

Key words

unicellular, amoeba, binary fission, euglena, flagellum

Summary Questions

1 Copy and complete the following sentences.

Amoebas and euglenas are examples of _____ organisms. This means that they are only made up of _____ cell. Both organisms reproduce by _____ _____. Amoebas have to _____ food to survive but euglenas can carry out _____ to produce their own food.
(6 marks)

2 Amoebas contain two types of vacuole:
 a Describe the function of the food vacuole. (1 mark)
 b Describe the function of the contractile vacuole. (1 mark)

3 A student suggested that a euglena could be classified as a plant cell.
 a Describe **one** piece of evidence to support the student's suggestion. (2 marks)
 b Give **one** structural reason why a euglena would not be classed as a plant cell. (1 mark)

1 Chapter 1 Summary

In this chapter you have learnt what a cell is, what unicellular organisms are, and how you can observe both using a microscope. You have discovered differences in the structures and functions of plant and animal cells, and know that some cells have adaptations that specialised cells have that help them perform particular jobs. You have also studied the process of diffusion, by which many useful substances move into a cell and waste products leave.

Metacognition and self-reflection task

Flashcards are a great way to summarise important facts. Making your own cards will help you to remember the information in this chapter. It's also a really useful skill that you will use all the way through your science lessons. Make one for each spread in this chapter.

Journey through B1

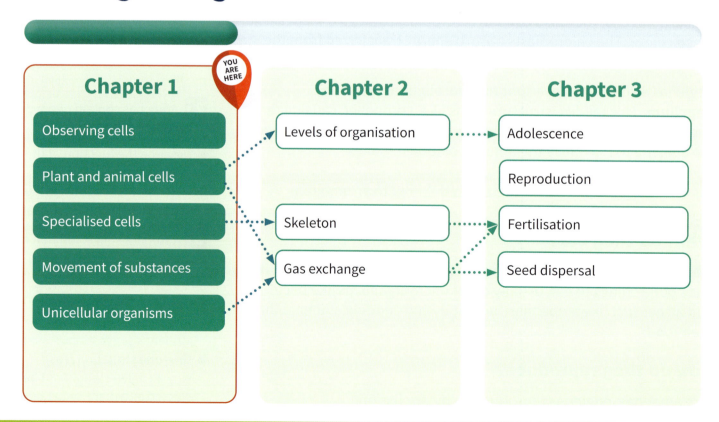

Chapter 1 Summary Questions

1 Choose the correct definition of the word 'cell'.
  a A cell is a thin slice of cork.
  b A cell is the smallest unit of an organism.
  c A cell is a type of living organism. **(1 mark)**

2 An amoeba is a unicellular organism.
  a State how many cells make up a unicellular organism **(1 mark)**
  b Match the structures present in an amoeba with their function **(2 marks)**

  nucleus   removes waste
  contractile vacuole   where respiration occurs
  mitochondria   controls the cell
  (3 marks)

3 This is a diagram of a plant cell.

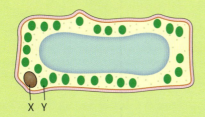

  a Name structure X. **(1 mark)**
  b State the function of structure Y. **(1 mark)**
  c Name the cell component that contains cell sap. **(1 mark)**
  d Name **two** structures in the cell that you'd also find in an animal cell. **(2 marks)**
  (5 marks)

4 A student wanted to observe skin cells from the back of their hand. They used a piece of clear sticky tape to remove some dead cells.
  a Name the piece of equipment they should use to observe the cells. **(1 mark)**
  b Suggest **one** thing they could do to the skin cells to make them easier to see. **(1 mark)**
  c Suggest **one** reason why you should not look at your own blood cells in the classroom. **(1 mark)**
  d Draw a labelled diagram of what the student's cells should look like. **(3 marks)**
  (6 marks)

5 Table 1 shows some examples of specialised cells.
  a Describe what is meant by a specialised cell. **(1 mark)**
  b Complete the table to show how three types of cell are adapted to their function. **(3 marks)**

Type of cell	Function	Adaptation
	Transport oxygen	Flattened disc and contains no nucleus to increase surface area
Nerve cell		Long and thin, forms connections with many other nerve cells
Leaf cell	Carry out photosynthesis	

  (4 marks)

6 Water moves into root hair cells from the soil.
  a Name **one** other substance that moves into root hair cells. **(1 mark)**
  b Describe the process that causes water to enter the root hair cell. **(3 marks)**
  (4 marks)

7 This diagram is drawn from a microscope observation of a euglena.

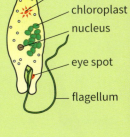

  a Using information from this diagram, determine whether or not euglena is a plant. Explain your answer. **(2 marks)**
  b Describe **one** similarity and **one** difference between the structure of a euglena and an amoeba. **(2 marks)**
  c Explain how a euglena's structure maximises the amount of photosynthesis it can carry out. **(3 marks)**
  (7 marks)

8 A student wanted to observe the nuclei of onion cells
  a Describe how the student would prepare the slide of onion cells, justifying each step in your method. **(3 marks)**
  b The student observed the cells using a ×10 eye piece lens and a ×4 objective lens. Calculate the total magnification used in the observation. **(2 marks)**
  (5 marks)

2 Structure and function of body systems

In this chapter you will look at the levels of organisation that exist in a multicellular organism.

You will focus on two organ systems in detail – the respiratory and skeletal systems. You'll find out how your lungs help you to breathe and how your skeleton does more than you might think.

Reactivate your knowledge

1. Draw a simple plant or animal cell and label its cell components.

2. Write down a definition of diffusion.

3. Name a bone and describe its function in the body.

You already know

Cells are the smallest functional unit in an organism.

The shape and structure of a specialised cell enables it to perform a particular function.

Glucose and oxygen diffuse into cells from the blood.

Skeletons are made of bones.

 How to interpret a simple pie chart.

 How to work scientifically to: Measure lengths using a ruler.

Journey through B1

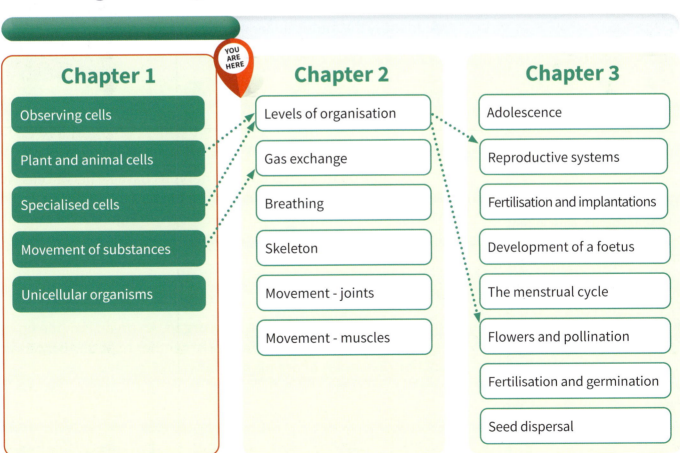

Chapter 1
- Observing cells
- Plant and animal cells
- Specialised cells
- Movement of substances
- Unicellular organisms

Chapter 2 (YOU ARE HERE)
- Levels of organisation
- Gas exchange
- Breathing
- Skeleton
- Movement - joints
- Movement - muscles

Chapter 3
- Adolescence
- Reproductive systems
- Fertilisation and implantations
- Development of a foetus
- The menstrual cycle
- Flowers and pollination
- Fertilisation and germination
- Seed dispersal

39

2.1 Levels of organisation

Learning objectives
After this topic, you will be able to:
- define the terms tissue, organ, and organ system
- describe the hierarchy of organisation in a multicellular organism.

Reactivate your knowledge
1. What is a unicellular organism?
2. What does the nucleus do?
3. Name some specialised animal cells.

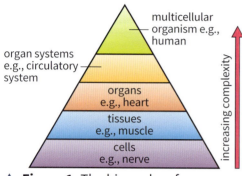

▲ Figure 1 The hierarchy of organisation in a multicellular organism.

Do the trees outside look like a euglena? No, not really! As well as being much larger, they are much more complicated. Large, complicated organisms, like trees, consist of many cells working together. A tree is an example of a multicellular organism.

What are multicellular organisms?

Multicellular organisms are made up of many cells. They have five layers of organisation, often called a hierarchy, as shown in Figure 1. Cells are the building blocks of life and make up the first level of organisation. Nerve, muscle, and red blood cells are examples of animal cells. Root hair and leaf cells are examples of plant cells.

> **A** Identify the multicellular organism from the list: bacteria, amoeba, fish.

What is a tissue?

The second level of organisation is a **tissue**. A tissue is a group of similar cells that work together to perform a certain function.

One example of an animal tissue is nervous tissue – nerve cells work together to transmit messages around the body. Another example of an animal tissue is muscle tissue, shown in Figure 2. An example of a plant tissue is the xylem – these are tubes that carry water around the plant.

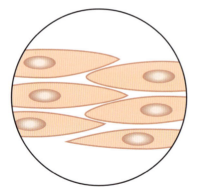

▲ Figure 2 Muscle tissue is a type of animal tissue. Muscle cells contract together to make the body move.

Key words
multicellular organism, tissue, organ, organ system, circulatory system, gas exchange system, digestive system, reproductive system

What is an organ?

The third level of organisation is an **organ**. An organ is made up of a group of different tissues that work together to perform a certain function. Examples of organs are shown in Figure 3.

Reactivate your knowledge answers
1 Organism made up of one cell 2 Controls the cell and contains genetic material 3 Nerve cell, muscle cell, red blood cell

B1 Chapter 2: Structure and function of body systems

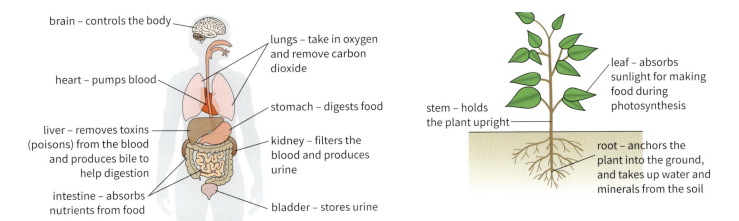

▲ **Figure 3** These are the main organs in plants and animals.

B Name two organs involved in the digestion of food.

What is an organ system?

The fourth level of organisation is an **organ system**. An organ system is a group of different organs that work together to perform a certain function. Some examples of animal organ systems include:
- **circulatory system** – transports substances around the body in the blood
- **gas exchange system** – takes in oxygen and removes carbon dioxide
- **digestive system** – breaks down and then absorbs food molecules.

Plants are mainly made up of organs and tissues but do contain some organ systems. Flowers contain the male and female sex organs that together form an organ system. The role of this organ system is to produce new organisms. Organ systems that make new organisms are called **reproductive systems**.

C Name an organ system found in both plants and animals.

The fifth level of organisation is a multicellular organism. A multicellular organism is made up of several organ systems working together to perform all the processes that are needed to keep the organism alive.

Summary Questions

1 Match the level of organisation to its function.

cell	group of organs working together
tissue	group of tissues working together
organ	group of similar cells working together
organ system	group of organ systems working together
organism	building blocks of life

(5 marks)

2 Organise the following terms into a hierarchy. Start with the bottom level.

*nervous tissue   chimpanzee
brain   nervous system
nerve cell*

(4 marks)

3 The circulatory system is an example of an organ system.

a Describe the function of the circulatory system. (1 mark)
b Name an organ found in this system. (1 mark)
c Describe the function of this organ. (1 mark)

41

2.2 Gas exchange

Learning objectives
After this topic, you will be able to:
- define the process of gas exchange
- describe how parts of the gas exchange system are adapted to their function
- compare inhaled and exhaled air.

Reactivate your knowledge
1. What is an organ system?
2. What do your lungs do?
3. Where in the cell does respiration occur?

If you are travelling on a bus, the windows may sometimes steam up. This is because the air in the bus contains lots of water vapour.

What happens when we breathe?

When you breathe, you take in oxygen and give out carbon dioxide. The transfer of gases between an organism and its environment is called **gas exchange**.

Gas exchange takes place inside your **lungs**. Lungs are made of elastic tissue that expands when you breathe in – this allows you to take in lots of oxygen. However, your lungs are delicate, so they are protected by your ribs. These are hard and strong bones that make up your **ribcage**. Your ribs and lungs can be seen in Figure 1.

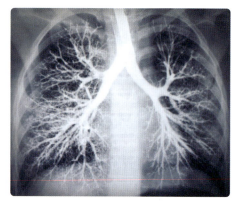

▲ **Figure 1** You can see your lungs and ribs on a chest X-ray.

A Name the organ where gas exchange occurs in humans.

Link
You can learn more about how you breathe in B2 2.3 *Breathing*.

Figure 2 shows the main components of your gas exchange system (respiratory system). Follow the arrows with your finger to see how air travels through your mouth and nose and ends up in the blood around your lungs. The blood then carries the oxygen to all the cells in your body.

Key words
gas exchange, lungs, ribcage, trachea, alveolus, inhale, exhale, condense

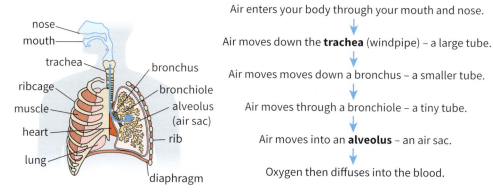

▲ **Figure 2** Air has to travel from your mouth and nose to your lungs for you to get oxygen into your bloodstream.

Reactivate your knowledge answers
1 Groups of organs working together 2 Take in oxygen and remove carbon dioxide 3 Mitochondria

B1 Chapter 2: Structure and function of body systems

There are millions of alveoli (singular: alveolus) in your lungs. They create a large surface area and have thin walls that are only one cell thick. These features help gas exchange occur quickly and easily.

Why do we breathe in and out?

When you breathe in you **inhale** to take in oxygen. The oxygen is used in respiration to transfer energy. Respiration produces carbon dioxide, which needs to be removed from the body. When you breathe out you **exhale** to remove carbon dioxide.

The amount of oxygen required by your body determines how fast you need to breathe. You need larger amounts of oxygen when you exercise. This is because your cells respire more to transfer more energy to your body cells.

> **B** Suggest what happens to your breathing rate when you start running.

The pie charts in Figure 3 show how much of each gas is present in both inhaled and exhaled air.

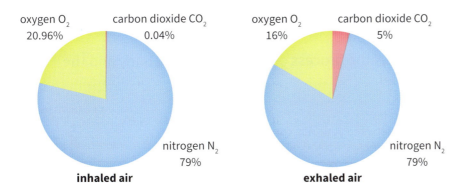

▲ **Figure 3** These pie charts show the approximate amounts of each gas in inhaled and exhaled air.

> **C** Use the pie chart to identify the gas, present in air, which is not used by the body.

Why do bus windows steam up on cold days?

If you breathe onto a cold window, it steams up. This is because the air you breathe out contains water vapour. Water is a waste product of respiration. When warm, exhaled water vapour hits the glass it **condenses**, turning it back into a liquid. This is what you see on the bus windows.

Which chart?

The compositions of inhaled and exhaled air are shown in a pie chart in Figure 3.

Why is this the best chart to use?

Link

You can find out more about condensing in C1 1.4 *Boiling and condensing*.

Summary Questions

1 Copy and complete the following table to show the differences between inhaled and exhaled air. Use the words *less, more, same, hotter,* and *colder*. Words can be used once, more than once, or not at all.

	Inhaled	Exhaled
oxygen		
carbon dioxide		
temperature		
water vapour		

(4 marks)

2 Describe how the ribcage is adapted to perform its function.
(2 marks)

3 Explain **two** ways alveoli are adapted for gas exchange.
(4 marks)

43

2.3 Breathing

Learning objectives

After this topic, you will be able to:
- describe the changes that occur when a person inhales and exhales
- describe how a bell jar can be used to model breathing
- describe a method used to estimate lung volume.

Reactivate your knowledge

1. Why do you inhale?
2. What happens in the alveoli?
3. What is diffusion?

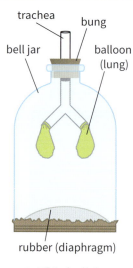

▲ **Figure 1** This bell-jar model can be used to represent breathing.

Even when you are sitting still, your ribcage is moving. This allows your lungs to fill with oxygen and is essential for you to stay alive.

How do you breathe?

When you breathe, muscles in your chest tighten or contract. A bell-jar model, in Figure 1, can show you what is happening inside your lungs when you breathe in and out. The jar represents your chest, the balloons represent your lungs, and the rubber sheet represents a muscle called the **diaphragm**.

What happens when you inhale?

Figure 2 shows the process of inhalation in the body and the bell-jar model.

When you inhale:
- The muscles between your ribs contract – this pulls your ribcage up and out.
- The diaphragm contracts, so it moves down.
- The volume inside your chest increases.
- The pressure inside your chest decreases – this draws air into your lungs.

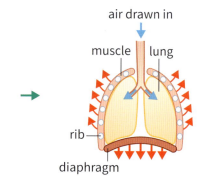

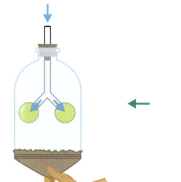

To show inhaling in the bell-jar model:
- The rubber sheet is pulled down.
- The volume inside the jar increases.
- The pressure inside the jar decreases – air rushes into the tube.
- The balloons inflate.

▲ **Figure 2** Inhaling in the lungs and in the bell-jar model.

Link

You can find out more about gas pressure in C1 1.7 *Gas pressure*.

Key words

diaphragm, lung volume, asthma

Reactivate your knowledge answers

1. To take in oxygen
2. Oxygen diffuses into the blood
3. Movement of substances from a high concentration to a low concentration area

B1 Chapter 2: Structure and function of body systems

> **A** List the two changes that increase the volume inside your chest when you breathe in.

What happens when you exhale?

Figure 3 shows the process of exhalation in the body and the bell-jar model.

When you exhale:
- The muscles between your ribs relax, pulling your ribcage down and in.
- The diaphragm relaxes, so it moves up.
- The volume inside your chest decreases.
- The pressure inside your chest increases – this pushes air out of your lungs.

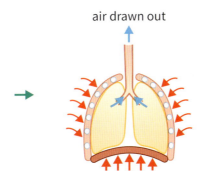

To show exhaling in the bell-jar model:
- The rubber sheet is pushed up.
- The volume inside the jar decreases.
- The pressure inside the jar increases – this makes air rush out of the tube.
- The balloons deflate.

▲ **Figure 3** Exhaling in the lungs and in the bell-jar model.

> **B** List the two changes that decrease the volume inside your chest when you breathe out.

How can we measure lung volume?

You can measure your **lung volume** using a plastic bottle, as shown in Figure 4. As you breathe out into the plastic tube, air from your lungs takes the place of the water in the bottle. If you breathe out fully, the volume of water pushed out of the bottle is equal to how much air your lungs can hold.

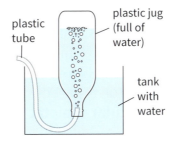

▲ **Figure 4** You can measure your lung volume by breathing into a bottle.

Lung volume can be increased with regular exercise. A large lung volume means that more oxygen can enter your body. Smoking, diseases such as **asthma**, and old age can reduce lung volume.

Lung volume 🧪

How big are your lungs? Calculate your own lung volume by breathing as hard as you can into a 3-litre bottle of water, set up like the one shown in Figure 4. Suggest why your doctor would not use this as an accurate measurement of your lung volume.

Summary Questions

1 Copy and complete Table 1 using the following words: *up and out, down and in, down, up, decreases, increases.* (3 marks)

Action	Inhaling	Exhaling
ribs move		
diaphragm moves		
chest volume		

▲ **Table 1**

2 Describe how you could measure the approximate lung volume of an athlete. (3 marks)

3 The bell jar model works in the same way as the lungs.
  a Describe how a bell-jar model can be used to represent inhalation. (4 marks)
  b Suggest **one** problem with the model. (1 mark)

45

2.4 Skeleton

Learning objectives

After this topic, you will be able to:
- label the main bones in the human skeleton
- describe the structure of a bone
- describe the functions of the skeletal system.

Reactivate your knowledge

1. Which structure protects the lungs?
2. What do muscles do?
3. What do red blood cells do?

Why are you not a blob of jelly? Most parts of your body have hard structures inside them. These are your bones. They stop you being shapeless, allow you to move, and have other important roles.

What are bones?

Although **bones** in a museum are old and dry, the bones in your body are different. Bone is a living tissue with a blood supply, and it is growing and changing all the time. Just like other parts of your body, it can repair itself when damaged, like the broken bone in Figure 1. Calcium and other minerals make the bone strong but slightly flexible. Exercise and a balanced diet are important to keep your bones healthy.

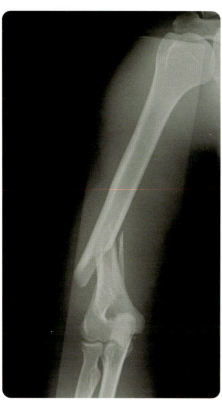

▲ **Figure 1** Doctors use X-rays to check if a bone is broken.

What is a skeleton?

Together, all the bones in your body make up your **skeleton**. They are joined together to form a framework. The average adult human skeleton consists of 206 bones, some of which are labelled in Figure 2. Your skeleton is part of your **muscular skeletal system**.

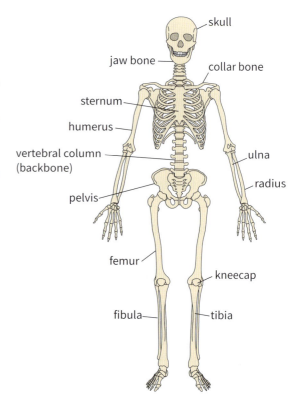

▲ **Figure 2** The main bones of the human body.

A Identify the two bones found in the lower leg.

Reactivate your knowledge answers
1 Ribcage 2 Contract to cause movement 3 Carry oxygen

B1 Chapter 2: Structure and function of body systems

Why do we have a skeleton?

The skeleton has four main functions:
- to support the body
- to protect vital organs
- to help the body move
- to make blood cells.

Support

The skeleton provides support for your body and holds your internal organs in place. Without bones the body would be floppy, like a jellyfish. The bones create a framework for your muscles and organs to connect to. Your vertebral column (backbone) holds the body upright.

Protect

Bones are hard and strong so they can protect vital organs from being damaged. For example:

- Your skull protects your brain.
- Your ribcage protects your heart and lungs.
- Your backbone protects your spinal cord.

Move

Muscles are attached to bones. If a muscle pulls on a bone, it will cause the bone to move. The skeleton moves at joints, such as your knee. The movement of bones at joints allows the body to move.

> **B** Name the tissue that causes your skeleton to move.

Making blood cells

Some bones inside your body, such as the long ones in your arms and legs, are not solid. In the middle of these bones is a soft tissue called **bone marrow**, shown in Figure 3. The bone marrow produces red and white blood cells. Red blood cells are needed to carry oxygen around the body, whilst white blood cells are used to protect against infection.

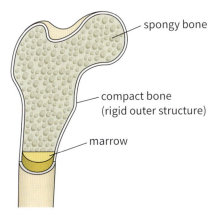

▲ **Figure 3** Structure of a bone.

> **C** Identify the outer layer of bone which makes bones strong.

Link

You can learn more about how your body moves in B1 2.5 *Movement: joints*.

Key words

bone, skeleton, muscular skeletal system, bone marrow

Summary Questions

1 Copy and complete the following sentences.

Your skeleton is made up of _____ . The skeleton has four important functions – to _____ the body, to _____ organs, to help the body move, and to make _____ . Red and white blood cells are produced in bone _____ which is found in the centre of some bones.
(5 marks)

2 Describe the structure of a bone. (2 marks)

3 Answer the following questions.

a Describe the function of the skull. (1 mark)
b One function of the radius is to produce blood cells.

Explain **one** other function of the radius. (2 marks)

47

2.5 Movement: joints

Learning objectives

After this topic, you will be able to:
- describe the role of joints in movement
- describe the structure of a joint
- describe how to measure the force exerted by different muscles.

Reactivate your knowledge

1. What are the functions of the skeleton?
2. Where does movement occur in the skeleton?
3. Name the cell component which transfers energy to cells.

Health and safety

Many people go to the gym and lift dumbbells to improve the strength of their muscles. What are the risks of trying to lift the heaviest dumbbells?

Without *muscles* and joints, we would all look like statues. Muscles move *bones*, and joints allow the skeleton to bend. The combination of muscle and joint movement is called *biomechanics*.

What are joints?

Joints occur where two or more bones join together. Most joints are flexible, but some bones in your skeleton are joined rigidly together and cannot move.

How do joints allow you to move?

Your joints need to be strong enough to hold your bones together, but flexible enough to let them move. Different types of joint allow movement in different directions. A pivot joint is shown in Figure 1.

Link

You can find out more about forces in P1 1.1 *Introduction to forces*.

Other types of joint include:
- hinge joints – for movement backwards and forwards. The knee and elbow are examples of hinge joints.
- ball-and-socket joints – for movement in all directions. The hip and the shoulder are examples of ball-and-socket joints.
- fixed joints – do not allow any movement. The skull is an example of a fixed joint.

A Name four types of joint found in the body.

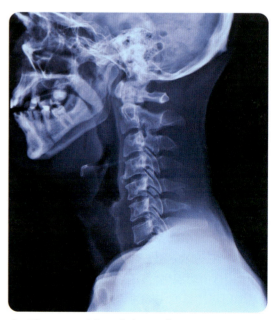

▲ **Figure 1** Pivot joints allow movement around a point. Your neck is a pivot joint. It allows you to rotate your head from side to side.

Key words

muscle, bone, biomechanics, ligament, cartilage, newtons

Reactivate your knowledge answers
1 Protection, support, movement, make blood cells 2 At joints 3 Mitochondria

B1 Chapter 2: Structure and function of body systems

What does a joint look like?

Most joints consist of two bones held together by **ligaments**. Two different types of joint are shown in Figure 2.

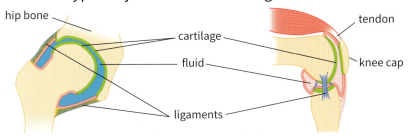

▲ **Figure 2** Structure of a hip joint and a knee joint.

If your bones moved against each other, they would rub, causing lots of pain. Eventually, the bone would wear away. To stop this happening, the ends of bones in a joint are covered with **cartilage**, a strong, smooth tissue. It is kept slippery by fluid in the joint. This allows the bones to move without rubbing together.

> **B** Name the tissue which holds bones together.

How can you measure muscle strength?

Different muscles in the body have different strengths. For example, arm muscles are much stronger than the muscles in your face that let you smile.

The strength of a muscle can be measured by how much force it exerts. You can measure the strength of your muscles using a newton scale. The harder you can push on the scale, the greater the force exerted. Force is measured in **newtons** (N).

> **C** Give the unit of force.

You can use a newton scale to measure the strength of many different muscles. For example:

- To measure the strength of your triceps – push down as hard as you can on the scale.
- To measure the strength of your biceps – put the scale under the table and push up as hard as you can as, shown in Figure 3 (ask another student to sit on the table to ensure it doesn't move).
- To measure the strength of your forearms – hold the scale in the air between your hands, and squeeze your hands together as hard as you can without using your thumbs.

In each technique you or your partner should read the force you exerted, in newtons, from the scale.

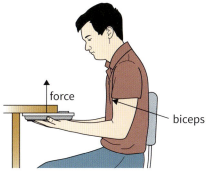

▲ **Figure 3** How to measure the strength of your biceps.

Summary Questions

1 Copy and complete the following sentences.

Joints occur where two or more _____ join together. Different types of joint allow _____ in different directions. For example, ball-and-socket joints in the _____ allow movement in all directions. _____ covers the ends of the bones in joints to stop them _____ together. Muscle strength is measured in _____ . (6 marks)

2 Describe how the structures in a joint prevent bones rubbing together. (3 marks)

3 The ankle joint allows forwards and backwards movement.

a Identify the type of joint present in the ankle. (1 mark)

b Compare the movement of the ankle joint with the skull and the shoulder joints. (4 marks)

49

2.6 Movement: muscles

Learning objectives
After this topic, you will be able to:
- describe the function of the major muscle groups
- describe how muscles cause movement in the body
- describe how antagonistic muscles control movement at a joint.

Reactivate your knowledge
1. Name some joints in the body.
2. Which structure holds bones together?
3. How do muscles move bones?

Key words
tendon, antagonistic muscles

Can you feel the muscle in the front of your arm working as you bend it? The muscle is pulling on one of the bones in your forearm, causing it to move upwards.

Muscles in the body

Muscles are found all over your body. They are a type of tissue – lots of muscle cells work together to cause movement.

There are many types of muscle in your body. For example, your heart is a muscle made of cardiac muscle tissue. This muscle pumps blood around the body.

Other muscles are found in your gut and help squeeze the food along. Figure 1 shows the major muscle groups in your body that are used for movement.

> **A** Give three functions of muscles.
>
> **B** Name three groups of muscles in the body used for movement.

How do muscles work?

To make you move, your muscles work by getting shorter – they contract. Muscles are attached to bones by **tendons**. When a muscle contracts, it pulls on a bone. If the bone is part of a joint, the bone will move.

> **C** Suggest what happens to the length of a muscle when it relaxes after contracting.

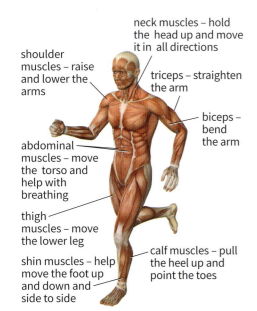

▲ **Figure 1** Major muscle groups used for movement.

- shoulder muscles – raise and lower the arms
- neck muscles – hold the head up and move it in all directions
- triceps – straighten the arm
- biceps – bend the arm
- abdominal muscles – move the torso and help with breathing
- thigh muscles – move the lower leg
- shin muscles – help move the foot up and down and side to side
- calf muscles – pull the heel up and point the toes

Reactivate your knowledge answers
1 Knee/elbow/hip/shoulder 2 Ligament 3 Pull on bones

B1 **Chapter 2: Structure and function of body systems**

How do pairs of muscles work together?

Muscles can only pull. They cannot push. This means that two muscles have to work together at a joint. If you only had one muscle in your arm, you may be able to bend your arm, but you would not be able to straighten it again.

At each joint a pair of muscles work together to cause movement. These are known as **antagonistic muscles**. When one muscle contracts, the other muscle relaxes.

The biceps and triceps are an example of a pair of antagonistic muscles. These are used to bend and straighten the arm at the elbow joint.

To bend the arm, look at Figure 2:
- the biceps muscle contracts
- the triceps muscle relaxes.

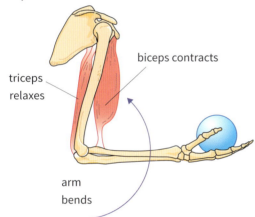

▲ **Figure 2** The biceps muscle contracts to bend the arm.

To straighten the arm, look at Figure 3:
- the biceps muscle relaxes
- the triceps muscle contracts.

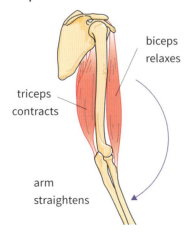

▲ **Figure 3** The triceps muscle contracts to straighten the arm.

Model limb

Design a model to show how antagonistic muscles allow your leg to move. Present your model to a partner, explaining how it represents antagonistic muscles.

Summary Questions

1 Copy and complete the following sentences.

Muscles are attached to bones by _____ . When a muscle _____ it shortens and _____ on a bone. If the bone is part of a _____ this will cause the bone to move. Pairs of muscles work together to control movement at a joint. They are called _____ muscles. (5 marks)

2 Describe the difference between a tendon and a ligament. (2 marks)

3 Look at Figure 4, which shows the main muscles of the human leg.

a Predict what happens when muscle **B** contracts. (1 mark)
b Predict what happens when muscle **C** contracts. (1 mark)
c Explain why antagonistic muscles **C** and **D** are required for movement at the ankle. (3 marks)

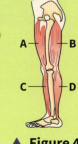

▲ **Figure 4**

51

2 Chapter 2 Summary

In this chapter you have learnt how multicellular organisms are organised into levels, starting with a cell at the lowest level and a fully-functioning multicellular organism at the top.

You then studied the main structures in the respiratory system, and how the process of breathing moves air into and out of the lungs. This allows oxygen to be taken into the body and carbon dioxide to be removed.

Metacognition and self-reflection task

Mind maps are a useful way of identifying how different parts of science are linked together. Take a topic, then on a large piece of paper write down the key concepts for that topic. Join the concepts together with lines to show how the concepts are connected, adding notes to describe the link. Make one mind map on levels of organisation, one on gas exchange, and one on the skeleton.

Journey through B1

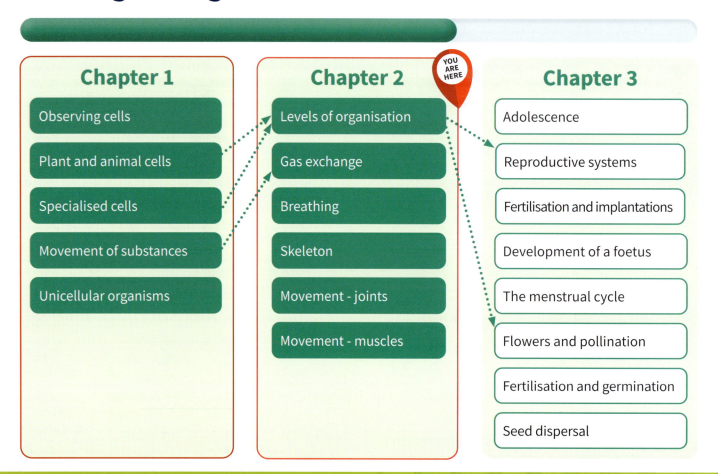

52

Chapter 2 Summary Questions

1. Your skeleton allows you to move.
   a Name the point in the skeleton where two bones meet. (1 mark)
   b Name the tissue that bones pull on to cause movement. (1 mark)
   c Give **one** other function of the skeleton. (1 mark)
   (3 marks)

2. Figure 1 shows how the body is organised into levels.

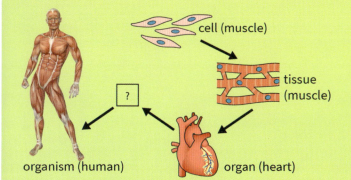

Figure 1

   a Name the type of cell shown in Figure 1. (1 mark)
   b State the function of this cell. (1 mark)
   c State what is meant by a tissue. (1 mark)
   d Name the level of organisation that is missing from Figure 1. (1 mark)
   (4 marks)

3. A student wanted to measure the strength of their biceps.
   a Name a piece of equipment they could use. (1 mark)
   b State the unit of force that they should use. (1 mark)
   c Explain why the student should repeat each measurement that they take. (1 mark)
   d Describe the experimental procedure the student should follow to measure the strength of their biceps. (3 marks)
   (6 marks)

4. Cells are the building blocks of life.
   a Name a cell component only found in plant cells. (1 mark)
   b Describe **two** features of an animal cell. (4 marks)
   (5 marks)

5. Gas exchange takes place in the respiratory system.
   a Name the bones that protect the lungs. (1 mark)
   b Name the process that causes oxygen to move into the blood in the alveoli. (1 mark)
   c State what the diaphragm is made of. (1 mark)
   d Describe what happens inside the chest cavity when you exhale. (3 marks)
   (6 marks)

6. Water diffuses into plants through the root hair cells.
   a Describe the process of diffusion. (2 marks)
   b Name a cell component through which the diffusion of water occurs. (1 mark)
   c Describe **one** adaptation of a root hair cell. (2 marks)
   (5 marks)

7. Explain **two** ways in which exhaled air is different to inhaled air. **(4 marks)**

8. Joints are essential to movement of the body.
   a Name the tissue that joins two bones together. (1 mark)
   b Name the tissue that joins a muscle to a bone. (1 mark)
   c Describe how the joint is adapted to stop the bones rubbing together. (3 marks)
   d Predict what would happen if the cartilage in this joint was damaged. (2 marks)
   e Explain how the elbow joint moves. (4 marks)
   (11 marks)

3 Reproduction

This chapter is about the biology of sexual reproduction between a male and a female. A person's sex can be different to their gender. Gender is the term used more broadly about a range of identities. They may or may not be the same as the biological definitions of male and female, which are based on reproductive functions.

You will look at both the physical and emotional changes that take place in male and female bodies during adolescence. You will study the structure and function of the male and female reproductive systems in detail. You'll also study reproduction in plants, including the structure of flowers, pollination, fertilisation, and germination.

Reactivate your knowledge

1 Produce a flow diagram showing the main stages in the human lifecycle.

2 Make a list of the changes that happen as males and females grow up.

3 Draw a diagram of a flower and label the main parts.

You already know

The shape and structure of a specialised cell enables it to perform a particular function.

The reproductive system produces new organisms.

Flowers are made of a number of parts.

Seed dispersal is the spreading out of seeds from the parent plant.

 What a percentage means out of 100.

 How to work scientifically to: Take a measurement and record it in a results table.

Journey through B1

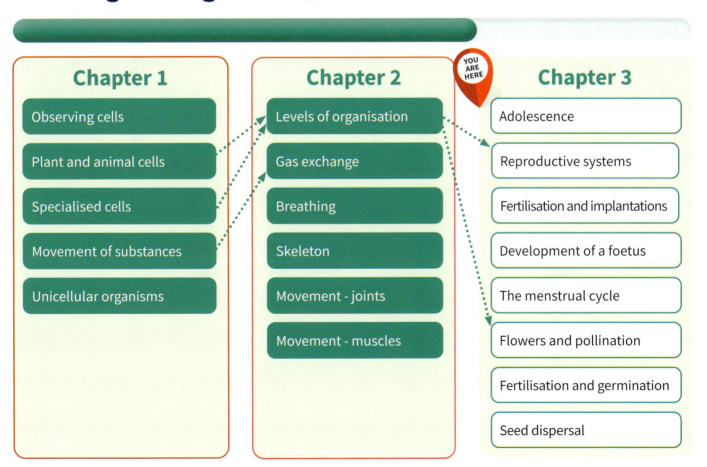

3.1 Adolescence

Learning objectives

After this topic, you will be able to:
- describe the difference between adolescence and puberty
- compare the physical changes in males and females during puberty
- describe the role of sex hormones during puberty.

Reactivate your knowledge

1. What does the reproductive system do?
2. Name some stages in the human life cycle.
3. Name some life processes carried out by all living organisms.

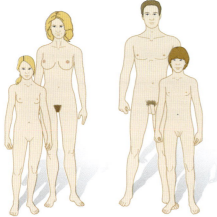

▲ **Figure 1** Physical changes take place during puberty.

Key words

adolescence, puberty, ovaries, testes, penis, sex hormones

▲ **Figure 2** To reduce unwanted body odour, you should wash regularly and use deodorant.

Think about yourself and your body. Do you think of yourself as a child or an adult? Everyone in your year group is at a different stage of their emotional and physical development. The time during which you change from a child to an adult is known as adolescence.

What happens during adolescence?

Adolescence involves both emotional and physical changes. These can cause you to become moody, self-conscious, and angry. Some adolescents' behaviour may also change – they want to experiment with new and risky activities, such as smoking, alcohol, and sex. During adolescence your body goes through physical changes like those shown in Figure 1. This is called **puberty**.

A Describe the difference between adolescence and puberty.

Puberty takes place between the ages of about 9 and 14 in most people. Generally, females start puberty before males, but it differs for everyone. Most of the changes take place in your reproductive system. Your reproductive system develops so that you can have children when you are older, if you choose to.

What happens during puberty?

There are a number of changes that happen to both females and males during puberty. These include:

- your pubic hair grows
- your underarm hair grows, like in Figure 2
- your body smell becomes stronger – this is often called body odour
- you have a growth spurt (get taller).

Reactivate your knowledge answers
1 Produces new offspring 2 Baby, toddler, child, teenager, adult 3 Examples include: moving, growing, reproducing, excreting

B1 Chapter 3: Reproduction

B Describe one other change that both boys and girls experience during adolescence.

What happens to females during puberty?

Some changes only happen to females. These include:

- breasts develop
- **ovaries** start to release egg cells
- periods start
- hips widen.

What happens to males during puberty?

Some changes only happen to males. These include:

- voice breaks – it gets deeper
- **testes** and **penis** get bigger
- testes start to produce sperm
- shoulders widen
- hair grows on the face and chest.

C Give two changes that occur to a male's testes during puberty.

What causes puberty?

All of the changes that take place in your body during puberty are caused by **sex hormones**. These are chemical messengers that travel around your body in the blood. Sex hormones in females are made in the ovaries. Different sex hormones in males are made in the testes. These chemicals trigger different processes, such as egg release in females and pubic hair growth in both males and females. They can also cause spots, called acne. Figure 3 shows a teenager suffering from acne.

▲ **Figure 3** Most teenagers get spots or acne. This is caused by hormones.

Link

You can learn more about periods in B1 3.5 *The menstrual cycle*.

Problem pages

Imagine you are the editor of a magazine for teenagers, called Teen Mag. You receive the letter below from a 12-year-old boy.

Dear Teen Mag,
My voice has started making funny squeaky sounds and my body is changing shape. What is happening to me, and should I do anything to make it stop?
Thanks, Kyle

Write a reply to Kyle that will be published in the magazine.

Summary Questions

1 Copy and complete the following sentences.

The period of time when a person develops from a child into an adult is known as _____. The _____ changes that take place are known as _____. These changes are caused by _____.   (4 marks)

2 List **three** physical changes that occur to both males and females during adolescence.   (3 marks)

3 Compare the roles of male and female sex hormones in puberty.   (4 marks)

57

3.2 Reproductive systems

Learning objectives
After this topic, you will be able to:
- describe the biological function of the male and female reproductive systems
- label the main structures in the male and female reproductive systems
- describe the biological function of the main structures in the male and female reproductive systems.

Reactivate your knowledge
1. Name some changes that happen to males during puberty.
2. Name some changes that happen to both males and females during puberty.
3. What is the function of a sperm cell?

Link
You can learn more about sexual intercourse in B1 3.3 *Fertilisation and implantation*.

Key words
testes, scrotum, semen, sperm duct, urethra, penis, sexual intercourse, ovary, oviduct, uterus, cervix, vagina

You have known since you were small that the male and female body look different. They look different because their bodies perform different jobs, or functions. Their reproductive systems can work together to produce a baby.

The female reproductive system

The biological function of the female reproductive system is to produce egg cells (the female sex cells), and then grow a baby for long enough that it can be born and survive.

Females have two **ovaries** (singular: ovary), which contain egg cells. Each month one egg cell matures and is released from an ovary. You can see the female reproductive system in Figure 1.

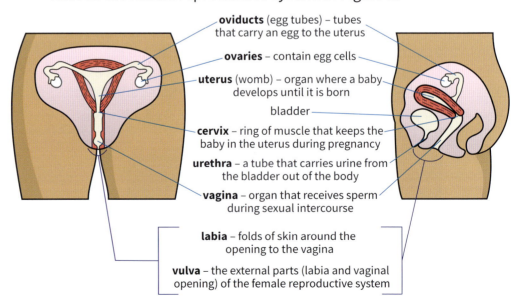

▲ Figure 1 The female reproductive system.

- **oviducts** (egg tubes) – tubes that carry an egg to the uterus
- **ovaries** – contain egg cells
- **uterus** (womb) – organ where a baby develops until it is born
- bladder
- **cervix** – ring of muscle that keeps the baby in the uterus during pregnancy
- **urethra** – a tube that carries urine from the bladder out of the body
- **vagina** – organ that receives sperm during sexual intercourse
- **labia** – folds of skin around the opening to the vagina
- **vulva** – the external parts (labia and vaginal opening) of the female reproductive system

A Name the organ where a male's penis enters the female body.

Reactivate your knowledge answers
1. Examples include: voice breaks, sperm produced, penis enlarges 2. Examples include: growth spurt, underarm/pubic hair growth 3. Transfer genetic material to the egg cell

B1 Chapter 3: Reproduction

The male reproductive system

The biological function of the male reproductive system is to produce sperm cells (the male sex cells) and release them inside the female reproductive system.

Males have two **testes** (singular: testis), which are contained in a bag of skin called the **scrotum**. The testes produce sperm cells and the male sex hormones. You can see the male reproductive system in Figure 2.

Glossary

A glossary provides a definition of key words used in a book. There are many new words on these pages. Make a glossary of the terms you have learnt so far.

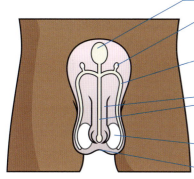

- bladder
- glands – produce nutrients to keep sperm alive. The mixture of sperm and fluid is called **semen**.
- **sperm ducts** – tubes that carry sperm from the testes to the penis
- penis
- **urethra** – tube that carries urine from the bladder out of the body or sperm from the sperm duct
- testis – produces sperm and sex hormones
- scrotum

▲ **Figure 2** The male reproductive system.

> **B** List the structures semen passes through on its way out of the body.

The **penis** is an organ that swells with blood and stiffens. This is known as an erection and allows the male to release sperm into a female's vagina during **sexual intercourse.** Although the bladder can empty when the penis is erect, semen and urine are never released at the same time.

> **C** Name the two body fluids that leave the body through the penis.

Summary Questions

1 Match each structure to its biological function.

penis	contains eggs
vagina	produces sperm
sperm duct	carries an egg to the uterus
oviduct	carries sperm out of the body
testes	carries sperm to the penis
ovaries	where sperm is released during sexual intercourse

(5 marks)

2 Describe the biological function of the female reproductive system. (2 marks)

3 Describe **one** similarity and **one** difference in the biological function of the male and female reproductive systems. (2 marks)

59

3.3 Fertilisation and implantation

Learning objectives
After this topic, you will be able to:
- describe the process of fertilisation
- describe what happens during sexual intercourse
- describe the main steps that must take place for implantation to occur.

Reactivate your knowledge
1. Where are sperm cells produced?
2. Name the tube connecting the ovaries to the uterus.
3. What are the adaptations of an egg cell?

Link
You can learn more about the structure of sperm and egg cells in B1 1.3 *Specialised cells*.

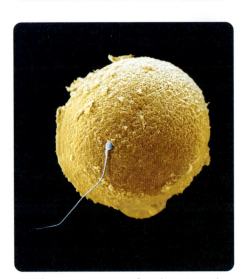

▲ **Figure 1** During fertilisation, the head of the sperm burrows into the egg.

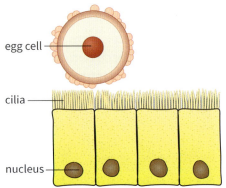

▲ **Figure 2** Cilia in the oviduct waft the egg towards the uterus.

How were you made? Babies are made by a female and a male, but how does this actually happen? During adolescence, your body becomes able to create a baby with someone of the opposite sex.

What are gametes?

Gametes are reproductive cells. They join together to create a new organism. The male gamete is a sperm cell. The female gamete is an egg cell. To create a new organism, the nucleus of the sperm and the nucleus of the egg have to join together – this is known as **fertilisation**. You can see fertilisation occurring in Figure 1. This process takes place in most animals so they can reproduce.

A Name the gametes found in animals.

Where do sperm cells meet an egg cell?

Each ovary is connected to the uterus by an oviduct. An egg cell cannot move by itself. However, the oviduct is lined with **cilia** – these are tiny hairs on the surface of cells. You can see cilia in Figure 2. Every month, an egg is released from an ovary. The cilia then waft the egg along the inside of the oviduct towards the uterus.

The sperm are released into the vagina in semen during sexual intercourse. They then swim towards the egg in the oviduct.

B Describe how an egg cell travels along the oviduct.

What happens during sexual intercourse?

When a male and a female have sex, semen is released into the vagina. People do this to make a baby or to show how much they care for each other. It is a very intimate act that gives many people a lot of pleasure.

Reactivate your knowledge answers
1 Testes 2 Oviduct 3 Fat stores in the cytoplasm, jelly layer to protect cell/attract sperm

B1   Chapter 3: Reproduction

When a male becomes sexually aroused, his penis fills with blood and becomes erect. When a female becomes sexually aroused her vagina becomes moist. This allows the penis to enter her vagina. Figure 3 shows what happens during sexual intercourse.

During intercourse, the male moves his penis backwards and forwards. This increases the pleasure and can stimulate the release of semen into the vagina. This is known as **ejaculation.**

C Describe the biological purpose of sexual intercourse.

▲ **Figure 3** During sexual intercourse, sperm are released into the vagina.

How do sperm cells reach the egg cell?

Figure 4 shows the process of fertilisation within the uterus.

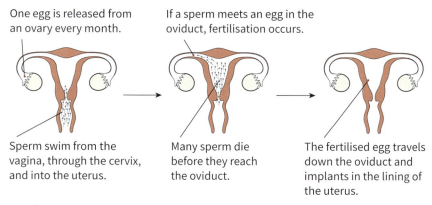

▲ **Figure 4** Sperm cells swim from the vagina to meet the egg cell.

The fertilised egg divides several times to form a ball of cells called an **embryo**. The embryo attaches to the lining of the uterus and begins to develop into a baby. This is called **implantation**.

D Describe the difference between a fertilised egg and an embryo.

Key words

gamete, fertilisation, cilia, ejaculation, embryo, implantation

Summary Questions

1 Match each word to its meaning.

fertilisation	the fertilised egg attaches to the lining of the uterus
ejaculation	the nuclei of the sperm and egg cell join together
implantation	the little hairs that move the egg cell along the oviduct
cilia	semen is released into the vagina
gametes	reproductive cells

(4 marks)

2 Describe what happens during sexual intercourse.

(3 marks)

3 Compare gamete production, release, and movement in males and females.

(3 marks)

61

3.4 Development of a foetus

Learning objectives
After this topic, you will be able to:
- describe what is meant by the term gestation
- describe the function of the placenta, umbilical cord, and fluid sac
- describe the main stages in the process of birth.

Reactivate your knowledge
1. Name the human gametes.
2. Where in the female body does a sperm meet an egg?
3. What is diffusion?

Small children often say that babies 'grow inside their mum's tummy'. A baby actually develops in the uterus, not the stomach.

How long to grow a baby?

In all mammals the time from fertilisation until birth is known as **gestation**, or pregnancy. In humans, it takes around nine months (40 weeks) for a fertilised egg to develop into a baby in the uterus.

During pregnancy a female has regular check-ups with a midwife to check their health and the health of the developing baby. The midwife will advise her to eat a healthy diet, not to smoke, and to avoid alcohol. Smoking can cause babies to be born early, when they are not fully developed. Drinking alcohol can cause problems in the development of the baby's brain.

A Give the gestation time for a human.

Link
You can learn more about the harmful effects of smoking in B2 1.8 *Smoking*.

Elephants
In elephants, gestation lasts for around 22 months. Calculate how many weeks this is and compare it to the gestation of humans.

Where does a baby grow?

A baby develops inside the uterus of its mother, as you can see in Figure 1.

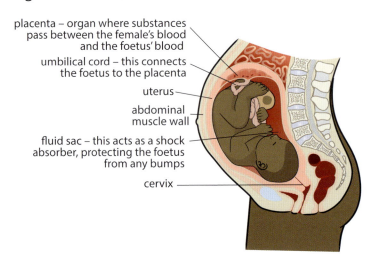

▲ Figure 1 A baby develops inside the uterus.

Reactivate your knowledge answers
1 Sperm and egg cells 2 Oviduct 3 Movement of particles from a place of high concentration to low concentration

B1 Chapter 3: Reproduction

During the early stages of pregnancy, cells in the embryo divide and specialise. After eight weeks of growth the embryo is called a **foetus**.

Inside the placenta, the blood of the mother and the blood of the foetus flow very close to each other. They do not mix. Oxygen and nutrients diffuse across the placenta from the mother to the foetus. Waste substances, such as carbon dioxide, diffuse from the foetus to the mother. The placenta also acts as a barrier. It stops infections and harmful substances from reaching the foetus.

B Name two substances a foetus needs to grow.

How does a baby develop?

Figure 2 shows the main steps in a baby's development.

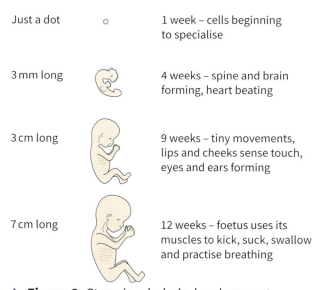

▲ **Figure 2** Steps in a baby's development.

C Describe the movement in a foetus that may be visible at a 12-week scan.

What happens during birth?

After around 40 weeks the baby is ready to be born. The female's cervix relaxes, and muscles in the wall of the uterus contract. This gradually pushes the baby out through the vagina. When the baby is born it is still joined to its mother by the umbilical cord. This needs to be cut. The placenta is then pushed out after birth.

D Name the ring of muscle that must relax for a baby to be born.

Link

You can learn more about diffusion in C1 1.7 *Diffusion* and B1 1.4 *Movement of substances*.

Key words

gestation, placenta, umbilical cord, fluid sac, foetus

Summary Questions

1 Copy and complete the following sentences.

A _____ develops in the _____. This is known as _____. The _____ _____ protects the foetus from bumps. The foetus is attached to the placenta by the _____ _____. Substances transfer between the mother and baby through their _____ in the placenta. After _____ weeks the baby is ready to be born. (7 marks)

2 Describe the process of birth. (3 marks)

3 Explain how substances are transferred between a female and her foetus, using a named example. (4 marks)

63

3.5 The menstrual cycle

Learning objectives
After this topic, you will be able to:
- describe what happens during a period
- describe the main stages in the menstrual cycle
- describe some different methods of contraception.

Reactivate your knowledge
1. Where does a baby develop?
2. What happens during fertilisation?
3. Name some changes that happen to females during puberty.

You may have heard your classmates talking about periods. You may know that only females have them, but what are they and why do they happen?

What are periods?

During puberty, a female's **periods** start. Around once a month, blood from the lining of the uterus leaves the body through the vagina. Each period normally lasts between three and seven days.

The female reproductive system works in a sequence called the **menstrual cycle**. This lasts about 28 days, though the length and timing of each stage in the cycle is different for each female. The cycle is controlled by hormones.

> **A** Estimate how many periods an adult female will have in one year.

What are the main stages in the menstrual cycle?

Figure 1 shows what happens during the menstrual cycle.

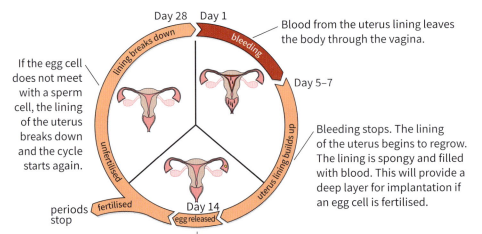

▶ **Figure 1** The stages of the menstrual cycle.

Reactivate your knowledge answers
1 Uterus 2 Sperm and egg cell nucleus join 3 Examples include: periods start, breasts develop, eggs released, hips widen

B1 Chapter 3: Reproduction

B Give the day in the menstrual cycle on which ovulation is likely to occur.

If the egg is fertilised, it attaches to the lining of the uterus and the female becomes pregnant. During pregnancy a female does not have any periods.

What is contraception?

Pregnancy is a result of sexual intercourse. Until you decide to have a baby, there are things you can do to avoid pregnancy. This is called **contraception**. Two of the most common forms of contraception are **condoms** and the **contraceptive pill**.

How do condoms work?

A condom is a thin layer of latex rubber that fits over an erect penis. It is called a 'barrier' method of contraception. It prevents semen from being released into a female's vagina.

When used correctly, condoms are a very effective method of contraception. Condoms, like the one in Figure 2, also prevent the transfer of sexually transmitted infections (STIs), such as HIV and syphilis.

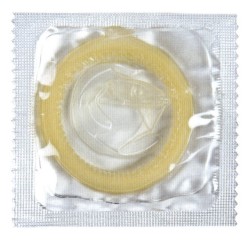
▲ **Figure 2** Condoms are a barrier method of contraception.

C Give two reasons for using condoms during sexual intercourse.

How does the pill work?

The contraceptive pill ('the pill') is a tablet that a female must take daily in order for it to work. The tablet contains hormones that can prevent pregnancy by stopping ovulation. A packet of contraceptive pills is shown in Figure 3.

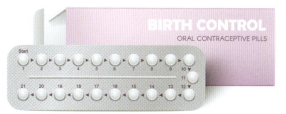
▲ **Figure 3** The contraceptive pill is very effective at preventing pregnancy.

When used correctly, the contraceptive pill is a very effective method of contraception. However, it provides no protection against the transfer of STIs.

Maths Box

Used correctly, condoms are 98% effective.

If 100 couples use a condom as a method of contraception, estimate how many are likely to get pregnant.

Key words

period, menstrual cycle, ovulation, contraception, condom, contraceptive pill

Summary Questions

1 Copy and complete the following sentences.

The female reproductive system works in a cycle called the _____ _____. An egg is released each month. If the egg is not fertilised then the _____ of the uterus breaks down and leaves the body through the _____. This is called a _____. The contraceptive pill and _____ can be used to prevent _____. (6 marks)

2 Describe the key stages that take place during the menstrual cycle. (4 marks)

3 Compare the use of condoms and the contraceptive pill as methods of contraception. (4 marks)

65

3.6 Flowers and pollination

Learning objectives
After this topic, you will be able to:
- describe the function of the main structures in a flower
- describe the process of pollination
- compare the structure of wind-pollinated and insect-pollinated plants.

Reactivate your knowledge
1. What are gametes?
2. Where are egg cells found?
3. Which organ system is found in a flower?

When looking at a flower, you might only notice its colour or its smell. But what is inside a flower and why are flowers important?

What's inside a flower?

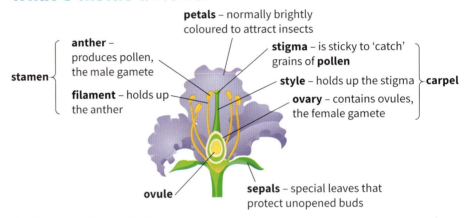

▲ **Figure 1** Parts of a flower.

You can see in Figure 1 that inside a flower there are both male and female parts:

- The stamen is the male reproductive part – it contains an anther and a filament.
- The carpel is the female reproductive part – it contains a stigma, style, and ovary.

A Name the parts of a flower that produce gametes.

How are new plants made?

Just like people, the formation of a new plant begins with fertilisation. Pollen grains, like those in Figure 2, need to fertilise the ovule. For this to happen, pollen from the anther needs to transfer to the stigma. This is called **pollination**. If you suffer from hayfever you may be allergic to some types of pollen grain.

Key words
petal, anther, stigma, pollen, stamen, style, carpel, filament, ovary, ovule, sepal, pollination

▲ **Figure 2** These are pollen grains viewed under a microscope.

Reactivate your knowledge answers
1 Reproductive cells   2 In the ovaries   3 Reproductive system

Pollination can occur between two different plants (cross-pollination) or between the male and female parts of the same plant (self-pollination).

> **B** Identify the type of pollination that occurs between two flowers in a garden.

How does pollination happen?

There are two ways that pollen can be transferred to the stigma:

- By the wind – the pollen from the flower of one plant is blown by the wind and might land on the stigma of another plant's flower.
- By insects – when insects visit the flower, pollen gets stuck to them. When they move to the flowers of another plant, the pollen from the first flower rubs off onto the stigma of the next flower.

Insect-pollinated plants

Most insect-pollinated plants, like the one in Figure 3:

- are brightly coloured and have sweet-smelling petals to attract insects
- contain nectar, a sweet, sugary fluid
- produce small quantities of sticky or spikey pollen which sticks to insects
- have their anthers and stigma held firmly inside the flower, so insects can brush against them easily.

Insect pollination is very important in food production. Plants that make fruit, vegetables, and nuts are pollinated by insects.

> **C** Give two ways flowers attract bees.

Wind-pollinated plants

Most wind-pollinated plants, like the one in Figure 4:

- have small petals that are brown or dull green
- do not produce nectar
- produce large amounts of very light pollen that is easily carried by the wind
- have loosely-attached anthers and stigmas which dangle out of the flower. This makes it easier for the plant to release pollen and to catch pollen from other plants.

▲ **Figure 4** The flowers of an oak tree. Oak trees are wind-pollinated.

> **D** Explain why the pollen from wind-pollinated plants is very light.

B1 Chapter 3: Reproduction

▲ **Figure 3** A bee collecting nectar on an insect-pollinated plant. Bees use nectar to make honey.

Cartoon strip

Produce a cartoon strip showing how a plant is pollinated by an insect. Each frame should contain a caption explaining what is happening.

Summary Questions

1 Match each part of a flower to its function.

anther	holds up the anther
filament	brightly coloured to attract insects
stigma	produces pollen
style	contains ovules
ovary	this is sticky to 'catch' pollen grains
petal	holds up the stigma

(5 marks)

2 Pollination can occur in a number of ways.

a Describe what pollination is. (2 marks)

b Describe the differences between cross-pollination and self-pollination. (2 marks)

3 Explain **two** differences between the structure of insect-pollinated and wind-pollinated plants. (4 marks)

3.7 Fertilisation and germination

Learning objectives
After this topic, you will be able to:
- describe the process of fertilisation in plants
- describe how seeds and fruits are formed
- describe the main steps in germination.

Reactivate your knowledge
1. Which part of a flower produces pollen?
2. What is the function of the stigma?
3. What does a plant need to grow?

Key words
fruit, seed, germination

Have you ever grown a plant from a seed? Seeds need water, oxygen, and a warm enough temperature to start to grow. A plant only needs light once it has grown its first leaf. All the nutrients a seed needs are stored inside the seed.

How do plants make seeds?

Carried by either the wind or an insect, a pollen grain lands on a stigma. If the stigma the pollen lands on is from the correct species, it grows a pollen tube down the style. This allows the pollen nucleus to join with the ovule nucleus. The main steps in fertilisation in plants are shown in Figure 1.

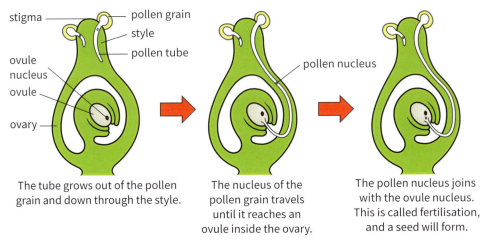

▲ **Figure 1** Fertilisation happens when pollen lands on a stigma.

A Describe what happens during fertilisation in plants.

After fertilisation the ovary develops into the **fruit**, and the ovules become **seeds**. A fruit is normally the sweet and fleshy product of a plant that can be eaten as food. All fruits contain seeds.

B Name the organ in the flower that becomes the fruit.

Reactivate your knowledge answers
1 Anther 2 Catch pollen 3 Light, warmth, water, nutrients, (air)

B1 Chapter 3: Reproduction

What's inside a seed?

Most seeds have a similar structure, which you can see in Figure 2. However, they often have different shapes, sizes, and colours.

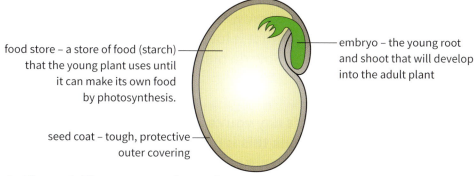

▲ **Figure 2** The structure of a seed.

What do seeds need for growth?

When a seed starts to grow, it is called **germination**. A seed needs three things to germinate:

- Water – this allows the seed to swell up and the embryo to start growing.
- Oxygen – this is used for respiration, transferring energy for germination.
- Warmth – this speeds up reactions in the plant, speeding up germination.

C List the three factors needed for germination.

How does a plant grow?

Figure 3 shows the main steps in germination.

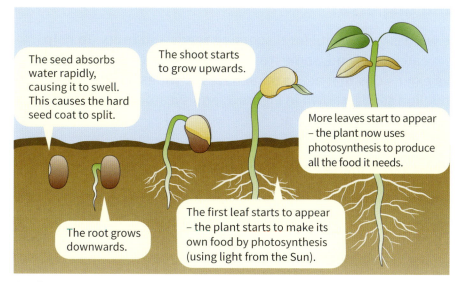

▲ **Figure 3** Seeds need lots of water to grow into a plant.

Investigating germination

Design an investigation to test whether warmth, oxygen, and water are required for germination.
What equipment will you need? What method will you use? What variables will you keep the same, change, and control?

Link

You can learn more about respiration in B2 2.5 *Aerobic respiration*.

Summary Questions

1 Copy and complete the following sentences.

During _____, the nucleus of the _____ grain and the nucleus of the _____ join together. The ovary then develops into the _____, and the ovules become _____. To _____, the seed needs water, _____, and oxygen. (7 marks)

2 Describe what happens after the ovule is fertilised. (2 marks)

3 To produce new plants, seeds have to germinate. Explain **two** ways to maximise the rate of germination in seeds. (4 marks)

69

3.8 Seed dispersal

Learning objectives
After this topic, you will be able to:
- describe the advantages of seed dispersal
- explain how seeds are adapted for their method of dispersal
- describe a method to investigate seed dispersal.

Reactivate your knowledge
1. What is the process of seeds starting to grow?
2. What is found inside a seed?
3. How do plants take in nutrients?

Seed dispersal
A student decided to investigate if the length of a wind-dispersed seed would affect the distance travelled when blown by the wind. State a prediction for this investigation, including a scientific reason.

Key words
seed dispersal

Sometimes on a summer's day you can see lots of things blowing in the air. Many people think this is pollen, but pollen grains are tiny and hard to see. You are probably looking at seeds being moved away from the parent plant. This is known as seed dispersal.

How are seeds dispersed?
Seeds are dispersed away from each other and from the parent plant. This is so they have space to grow and do not compete for resources such as nutrients. Nearly all seeds are found inside fruits. This increases the number of ways they can be dispersed. The main methods of **seed dispersal** are:

- wind
- animal
- water
- explosive.

A Name four methods of seed dispersal.

Wind dispersal
The wind is very useful for dispersing seeds and fruits. To help them catch the wind, some fruits and seeds are very light and have extensions that act as parachutes or wings. Examples include dandelion seeds, shown in Figure 1, and sycamore seeds.

Animal dispersal
Animals can disperse fruits and seeds in two ways:
- Internally – animals eat lots of fruit, including tomatoes, blackberries, and strawberries. Fruits are normally brightly-coloured and taste sweet, which attracts animals to them. These fruits contain seeds with hard coats. This means the seeds pass through the animal without being damaged.

▲ **Figure 1** Dandelion seeds are dispersed by the wind.

Reactivate your knowledge answers
1 Germination 2 An embryo, food store (inside a seed coat) 3 From the soil, into the roots

B1 Chapter 3: Reproduction

When they reach the ground in animal droppings, the seeds might be able to germinate. They are surrounded by waste material, which provides nutrients and helps the plant to grow.
- Externally – some seeds have hooks on them, which help them stick to animals. As an animal brushes past a plant such as goose grass or burdock, the seeds get caught in their fur. They get carried away from the parent plant. The seeds drop off the animal's fur and reach the ground, where they might be able to germinate. Figure 2 shows seeds adapted for external animal dispersal.

B Name two types of seed that are dispersed by animals.

Water dispersal

Many plants that live near water, such as willow trees, produce light seeds that float on water. The seeds are transported away from the parent plant in streams and rivers. They might germinate if they get washed up onto land. Other trees, such as coconut trees, produce woody fruits that are waterproof. They are carried away by the sea and might germinate if they reach another shore.

C Describe the structure of a seed that can be transported by water.

Explosive dispersal

Some fruits burst open when they are ripe, throwing the seeds in all directions. Peapods, shown in Figure 3, and gorse disperse seeds in this way.

▲ Figure 3 Peapods burst open when ripe, dispersing seeds away from the parent plant.

▲ Figure 2 Burdock seeds have little hooks on them to help them stick to animals' fur.

Standard Units

Three quantities which could be measured when investigating seed dispersal are the mass of the seed, the length of the seed, and the time of the flight.

Give the standard units for mass, length, and time.

Summary Questions

1 Copy and complete the following sentences.

Seeds are _____ away from the parent plant and other seeds to reduce _____. This increases their chances of having enough space and _____ to grow. Seeds can be dispersed by the _____, water, _____, and explosion.   (5 marks)

2 Explain **two** ways that animals can disperse seeds.   (4 marks)

3 A student found a small seed that had a smooth hard coat and a relatively high mass. Suggest, giving reasons, the most likely method of seed dispersal for this seed.   (3 marks)

3 Chapter 3 Summary

In this chapter you have looked at both the physical and emotional changes that take place in male and female bodies during adolescence. You have learnt about the structure and function of both the male and female reproductive systems and how a sperm cell is needed to fertilise an egg. You then discovered how a fertilised egg implants into the mother's uterus, where it develops into a baby.

In the second half of the chapter you learnt how plants reproduce. You studied the structure of a flower and the process of pollination, before looking at fertilisation and the conditions needed for germination. Finally, you investigated the different methods a plant uses to disperse its seed to increase their chances of successful germination.

Metacognition and self-reflection task

Flow diagrams are very useful for summarising the main steps in a process such as reproduction. Produce a flow diagram to describe the main steps in human reproduction, and another to describe the main steps in plant reproduction.

Journey through B1

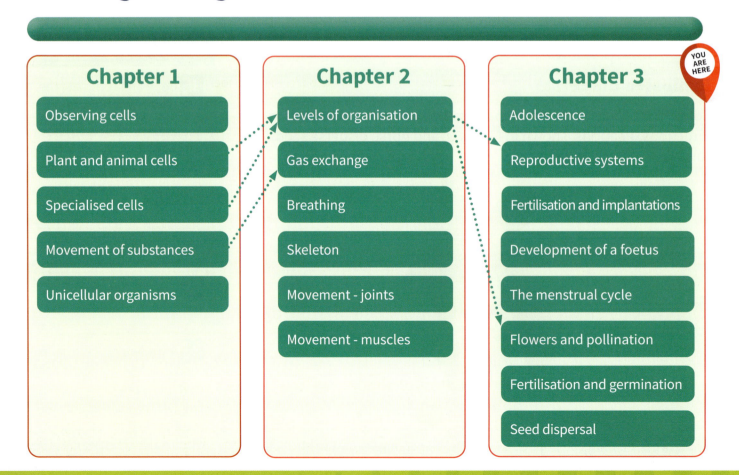

Chapter 3 Summary Questions

1 As people get older, their bodies begin to change.

a Sort the following physical changes based on whether they happen in males, females, or both males and females.

breasts develop
testes produce sperm
pubic hair grows
(3 marks)

b State the name given to the physical changes that take place during adolescence. (1 mark)
(4 marks)

2 Order the statements below to describe how pregnancy begins.

A Sperm may fertilise an egg if present in the oviduct.
B Embryo attaches itself into the uterus lining.
C Sperm swim through the cervix into the uterus.
D Sperm cells are released into the vagina.
E Fertilised egg divides several times to form a ball of cells. **(4 marks)**

3 The diagram shows the main structures in the female reproductive system.

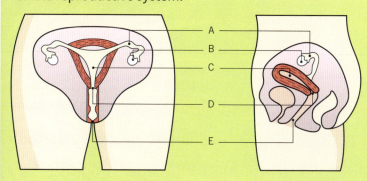

a Name structures A and D. (2 marks)
b State where sperm are released during sexual intercourse. (1 mark)
c State where the baby develops during pregnancy. (1 mark)
d Describe what happens during ovulation. (2 marks)
(6 marks)

4 Flowers are the part of a plant that allows it to reproduce.

a Identify the parts of the flower labelled below. (4 marks)

b Insect-pollinated flowers are normally brightly coloured. Give **one** other way flowers attract insects. (1 mark)
(5 marks)

5 A foetus develops inside the uterus.

During this time it depends on the mother for its growth and development.

a Name the structure that connects the foetus to the placenta. (1 mark)
b Explain how the foetus is protected from bumps. (1 mark)
c Describe what happens during birth. (3 marks)
d Explain the role of the placenta. (3 marks)
(8 marks)

6 Plants can be pollinated by insects or the wind.

a Describe what happens during pollination. (1 mark)
b Explain the differences in the structure of insect-pollinated and wind-pollinated plants. (4 marks)
(5 marks)

Welcome

Chemistry is the study of matter, the stuff that everything is made of. You will learn what matter is made of, and how this explains its properties. You will explore how matter changes when heated or and cooled, and why these changes happen.

1 Chemistry

Chemistry and you

Chemistry is everywhere. It happens in nature and in the laboratory. Nothing and nowhere is chemical-free.

Chemistry is everything you see, smell, and touch. It provides clean water and warm clothes. It makes materials of great beauty, great strength, and flexibility. It makes materials with properties perfect for their purpose, like glass for phones, nylon for clothes, wood for furniture, and explosives for fireworks.

Chemistry cooks and digests food. It makes muscle, bone, and hair. Its smells may make you feel love – or warn of danger. Chemistry keeps you alive.

Chemistry is united by one big idea: that tiny, invisible particles – and their arrangement, rearrangement, movement, and separation – explain the properties of everything and dictate how to make everything else.

Chemistry and the world

Chemistry knowledge helps you to use products safely, take the correct dose of a medicine, and cook the food you eat.

Chemistry helps you to make climate-friendly decisions, and work out what's true and what's not. Will you buy clothes made of cotton or nylon, or only second-hand?

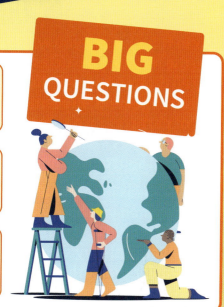

BIG QUESTIONS

What gives materials their properties?
We use models to understand how they are made.

How do chemists make new substances?
By looking at the chemical reactions used to produce them.

What are acids, and how are they useful?
By understanding how they react with other substances.

Journey through C1

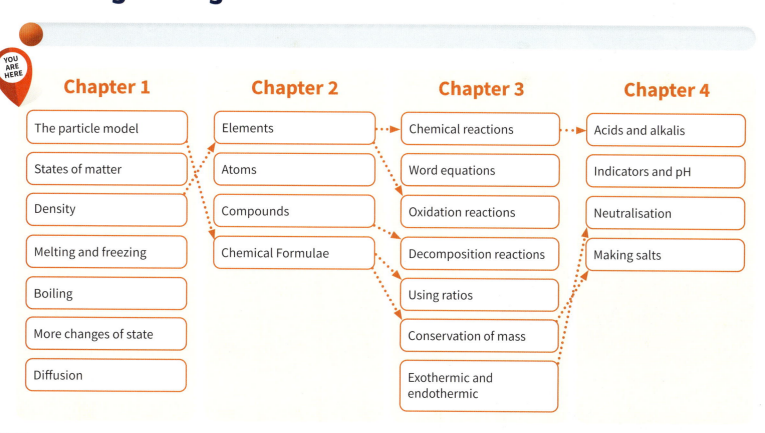

Chapter 1
- The particle model
- States of matter
- Density
- Melting and freezing
- Boiling
- More changes of state
- Diffusion

Chapter 2
- Elements
- Atoms
- Compounds
- Chemical Formulae

Chapter 3
- Chemical reactions
- Word equations
- Oxidation reactions
- Decomposition reactions
- Using ratios
- Conservation of mass
- Exothermic and endothermic

Chapter 4
- Acids and alkalis
- Indicators and pH
- Neutralisation
- Making salts

75

1 Particles and their behaviour

In this chapter you will learn about the invisible particles that make up all matter. You will discover how the arrangement, movement, and separation of particles give substances their properties – as well as what happens when substances melt, boil, or condense.

The ideas in this chapter explain what you see when you boil water or freeze food to preserve it. You'll learn how smells travel, and why some materials are much heavier than others for their size.

Reactivate your knowledge

1. Write a list of materials that are solid at room temperature. Write another list of materials that are liquid at room temperature.

2. Draw pictures of ice, liquid water, and steam. Draw an arrow from ice to liquid water, and label it with one of these words: melting, evaporating, freezing, condensing. Repeat for the other changes of state.

3. State which happens at a lower temperature – ice melting or water boiling.

You already know

Materials can be in the solid, liquid, or gas state.

Some materials change state when they heat up or cool down.

Different materials change state at different temperatures.

 How to interpret a number line using your maths skills.

 How to work scientifically to: Record observations and data in tables.

Journey through C1

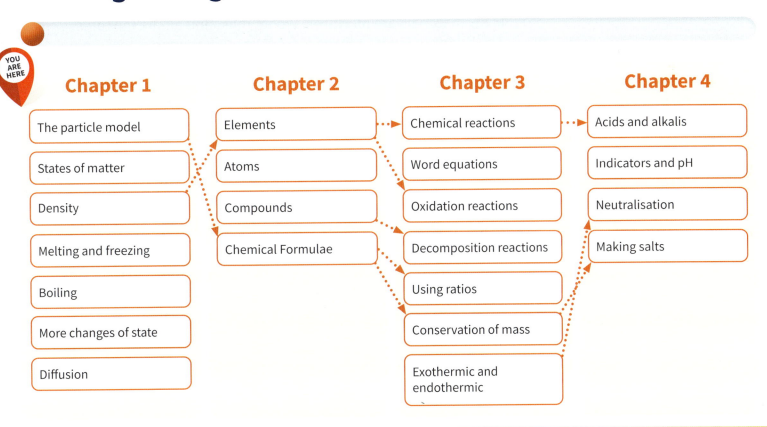

1.1 The particle model

Learning objectives
After this topic, you will be able to:
- use the particle model to explain why different materials have different properties
- state the factors that determine the properties of a substance.

Reactivate your knowledge
1. Name three materials.
2. Give two properties of gold.
3. How are the properties of ice and liquid water different?

Look around you. Can you see things made of wood, plastic, or steel? The different types of stuff that things are made from are called *materials*. There are millions of materials.

What's in a material?

Materials are made up of tiny **particles**. You cannot see the particles because they are too small. There are about 8 400 000 000 000 000 000 000 000 particles in a glass of water.

A Name the tiny things that materials are made up of.

What is a substance?

Many materials are **mixtures**. Wood, milk, and air are mixtures. The bridge in Figure 1 is made from another mixture, steel. Some materials are not mixtures and consist of just one **substance**. A substance is made of one type of material only. It is the same all the way through. Substances include gold, pure water, and oxygen.

Key words
material, particle, mixture, substance, property, particle model

Vital vocabulary
Use the Glossary at the back of this book to find out the meaning of the key words in bold.

Link
You can learn more about the arrangement and movement of particles in C1 1.2 *States of matter*.

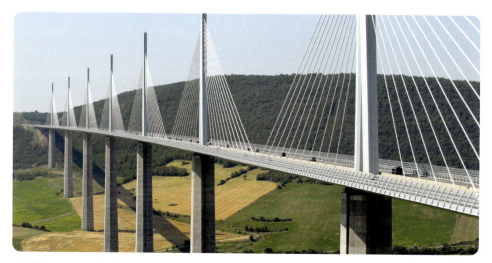

▲ **Figure 1** The bridge cables are made from steel. Steel is a mixture of substances.

Reactivate your knowledge answers
1 For example: wood, plastic, gold 2 Any two, for example: shiny, yellow, conducts electricity 3 For example: liquid water flows, but ice does not; or ice keeps its shape, but liquid water does not

C1 **Chapter 1:** Particles and their behaviour

Particles in substances

In a substance, every particle is the same. In the air, all oxygen particles are identical. One water particle is the same as all other water particles. One gold particle is the same as all other gold particles. The gold ingot in Figure 2 is made of gold particles only.

But gold particles are not the same as oxygen particles. Oxygen particles are not the same as water particles. Every substance has its own type of particle.

> **B** Explain why gold is a substance.

What gives a substance its properties?

The **properties** of a substance describe what it looks like and how it behaves. Every substance has its own properties. The **particle model** describes the movement and arrangement of particles in a substance. You can use the particle model to explain properties of a substance.

The properties of a substance depend on four things, or factors:

- what its particles are like, for example, their shape and size
- how its particles are arranged and separated
- how its particles move
- how strongly its particles hold together.

For example, gold and silver particles are almost the same size, but a gold particle is heavier than a silver particle. This explains why a gold ring is heavier than a silver ring of the same size.

In liquid water, particles slide over each other. In an ice cube, the particles do not move around. This explains why you can pour water from a glass, but you cannot pour water from an ice cube.

The particles in gold are held together less strongly than the particles in diamond. This explains why gold is easier to scratch than diamond.

> **C** Choose one factor from the list of factors that explains why you can pour water, but you cannot pour ice.

▲ **Figure 2** Gold is a single substance. All its particles are the same.

Summary Questions

1 Copy and complete the following sentences.

There are **hundreds/millions** of materials. Materials are made up of **practicals/particles**. In a substance, all the particles are **the same/different**. The particles of different substances are **the same/different**. The properties of a substance describe its **behaviour/particles**. (5 marks)

2 Name **four** factors that give a substance its properties. (4 marks)

3 A material is made up of three types of particle. Explain whether or not the material is a substance. (2 marks)

79

1.2 States of matter

Learning objectives
After this topic, you will be able to:
- compare the properties of a substance in its three states
- describe the particles in the three states of matter
- explain the different properties of a substance in its three states.

Reactivate your knowledge
1. What is the particle model?
2. How many types of particle are in a single substance?
3. Write down the science definition of property.

Do you like ice in cold drinks? The ice cubes in Figure 1 are made up of water particles. Ice is water in the solid state. Now imagine a steaming kettle. Steam is also made up of water particles. It is water in the gas state.

Water can exist in three states: as a **solid**, a **liquid**, or a **gas**. These are the **states of matter**. In each of the three states, the water particles are identical. But the properties of ice, liquid water, and steam are different. These pages explain why.

A Give the state of water when it is steam.

▲ Figure 1 Ice is water in the solid state.

How does state affect a substance's properties?

Most substances can exist in three states. The state of a substance depends on its temperature. At room temperature, gold is solid. But if you make it hot enough, gold exists as a liquid or gas. Table 1 compares the properties of a substance in its three states.

Express particle?

In 2015, a Japanese train set a world record. It reached a speed of 603 km/h (0.168 km/s). In the air, oxygen particles travel at about 500 m/s. Calculate which is faster – the train or the particles.

Hint: 1 km/s is the same as 1000 m/s. You can start by converting the speed of the train from km/s to m/s.

State	Can you compress (squash) the substance in this state?	Does the substance flow in this state?	Shape
solid	no	no	fixed, unless you apply a force
liquid	no	yes	takes the shape of the bottom of its container
gas	yes, a lot	yes	takes the shape of the whole container

▲ Table 1 A comparison of the properties of a substance in its three states.

B Describe two differences between the properties of a substance in the solid and liquid states.

Reactivate your knowledge answers
1. It describes the movement and arrangement of particles in a substance 2. One 3. What a substance looks like and how it behaves

C1 Chapter 1: Particles and their behaviour

How can particles explain properties?

The particles of a substance do not change. All water particles are the same, in all three states. But the arrangement and movement of the particles – and how strongly they hold together – are different in each state.

Key words

solid, liquid, gas, states of matter

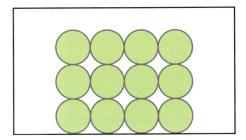

▲ **Figure 2** The arrangement of particles in a solid substance.

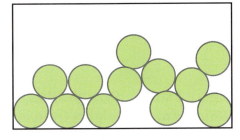

▲ **Figure 3** The arrangement of particles in a liquid substance.

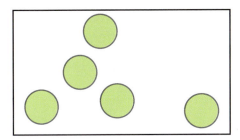

▲ **Figure 4** The arrangement of particles in a gas substance.

The solid state

Figure 2 shows particles of a substance in the solid state. When a substance is in the solid state, its particles touch their neighbours. This explains why you cannot compress it. In the solid state, a substance's particles are arranged in a pattern. This explains why crystals have straight edges and smooth faces.

When a substance is in the solid state, its particles do not move around. Instead, they vibrate on the spot. This explains why solids have a fixed shape and why they cannot flow.

The liquid state

Figure 3 shows particles of a substance in the liquid state. When a substance is in the liquid state, its particles touch their neighbours. This explains why you cannot compress it. The particles move randomly from place to place, sliding over each other. This explains why liquids flow and why they have no fixed shape.

The gas state

Figure 4 shows particles of a substance in the gas state. In the gas state, particles spread out until they are far apart. This makes it easy to compress a gas. The particles move quickly and randomly, everywhere in the container. This explains why gases flow.

> **C** Explain why you can compress a substance in the gas state, but not in the solid or liquid states.

Summary Questions

1 Copy and complete the following sentences.

In the solid state, the shape of a substance is _____ .

In the liquid state, a substance can be compressed only a very _____ .

In the gas state, a substance can be compressed a _____ .

A gas takes the shape of its _____ . (4 marks)

2 Use the particle model to explain why:

a a substance has no fixed shape in the liquid state

b a substance cannot flow in the solid state

c a substance can be compressed a lot in the gas state. (3 marks)

3 Compare **three** properties of a substance in the solid and gas states. (3 marks)

1.3 Density

Learning objectives
After this topic, you will be able to:
- state the meanings of mass, volume, and density
- explain why the same substance has different densities in each of its three states
- explain why different solids have different densities.

Reactivate your knowledge
1. Give the state of matter of ice.
2. In which two states of matter do particles touch their neighbours?
3. Write four factors from the particle model that give a substance its properties.

▲ **Figure 1** Weights are made from iron.

Figure 1 shows a weightlifter, Su. Her weights are made from iron. Why not make weights from another metal, like aluminium?

What is density?

Su's iron weights are heavy. They have a mass of 20 kg. Aluminium barbells of the same size are less heavy. They have a mass of only 7 kg. **Mass** is the amount of matter (stuff) in an object. It is measured in grams, g, or kilograms, kg.

The **volume** of an object is the amount of space it takes up. In Figure 2, the block of iron on the right has the greater volume. Volume is measured in cm^3.

The **density** of a substance is its mass in a certain volume. It tells you how heavy something is for its size. Iron has a greater density than aluminium, so iron barbells are heavier than aluminium barbells of the same size.

▲ **Figure 2** The block on the right has the greater volume.

A Write the definitions for mass, volume, and density.

How does the particle model explain density?

The particle model explains why different substances have different densities. Table 1 shows the densities of aluminium and iron.

Substance	Density in the solid state in g/cm³	Relative mass of one particle of the substance
aluminium	3	27
iron	8	56

▲ **Table 1** The densities of aluminium and iron.

Iron has a greater density than aluminium. This is partly because iron particles have a greater mass than aluminium particles. The density of a substance depends on the mass of its particles.

Reactivate your knowledge answers
1 Solid   2 Solid and liquid   3 What the particles are like, how the particles are arranged, how the particles move, how strongly the particles hold together

C1 Chapter 1: Particles and their behaviour

B Explain why aluminium has a lower density than iron.

How does state affect density?

The same substance has different densities in its three states, even though the particles are identical. Table 2 shows the density of gold in two states.

Substance	Density in the solid state in g/cm³	Density in the liquid state in g/cm³
gold	19	17

▲ **Table 2** The densities of solid and liquid gold.

Solid gold has a greater density than liquid gold. This is because the particles are packed together more tightly in solid gold. In the gas state, the particles are far apart. So gold gas has a lower density than liquid gold.

Most substances are like gold. Their density is greater in the solid state than in the liquid state. Their density in the gas state is lowest of all.

C Which factor explains why solid gold has a greater density than liquid gold: what the particles are like, or how the particles are arranged?

How is water different?

Water is unusual. Below 4 °C, its density is greater in the liquid state than in the solid state. This is because the particles pack together more closely in the liquid state. This densisty difference means that, below 4° C, ice floats on liquid water (Figure 3).

▲ **Figure 3** Solid water (ice) is less dense than liquid water. This is why ice floats.

Density problem

You can calculate density using mass and volume.

density = mass ÷ volume

A block of silver has a mass of 100 g. Its volume is 9.5 cm³. Calculate the density of silver.

Key words

mass, volume, density

Summary Questions

1 Copy and complete the following sentences.

The amount of matter in an object is its _____. The amount of space an object takes up is its _____. The mass of a substance in a certain volume is its _____. (3 marks)

2 Use the particle model to explain why:

a The density of liquid gold is less than the density of solid gold.

b The density of liquid water is less than the density of steam.

c The density of solid gold is greater than the density of solid aluminium. (3 marks)

3 Compare the reasons for:
- different substances in the same state having different densities
- the same substance in different states having different densities.

Use the particle model in your answers. (2 marks)

83

1.4 Melting and freezing

Learning objectives
After this topic, you will be able to:
- describe what happens to the particles in a substance when it melts or freezes
- state the factor in the particle model that explains why different substances have different melting points
- estimate the melting point of a substance from its temperature–time graph.

Reactivate your knowledge
1. Write the definition of substance.
2. Give three properties of a substance in the solid state.
3. How do particles move in the liquid state?

▲ **Figure 1** Ice melts on warm hands.

Imagine ice cubes in your hand, as in Figure 1. What happens?

When a substance changes from the solid to liquid state, it melts. **Melting** is the change from solid to liquid. **Freezing** is the change from liquid to solid.

Melting and freezing are examples of **changes of state**. Changes of state are **reversible**. For example, ice melts to make liquid water, but ice forms again if the water is cooled to 0 °C.

A Name the two states involved in freezing.

Explaining melting and freezing

What happens when an ice cube melts? The surroundings transfer energy to the ice, making its particles vibrate faster. The particles move away from their places in the pattern (Figure 2). The particles continue to move around. As more particles leave the pattern, more ice melts.

When a liquid starts to freeze, its particles move more slowly as they transfer energy to their surroundings. The particles get into a pattern and vibrate on the spot. Eventually, all the liquid freezes.

No particles are added or removed when a substance melts or freezes. This means that its mass does not change. Scientists say that mass is **conserved** when a substance melts.

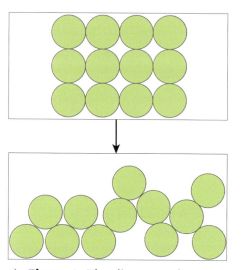

▲ **Figure 2** The diagrams show particles before and after melting. Particles move from their pattern to a random arrangment.

B Describe how particle movement changes when a substance melts.

Reactivate your knowledge answers
1. A single type of material, with identical particles 2. Can compress only a very little, does not flow, fixed shape 3. Move from place to place, sliding over each other

C1 **Chapter 1:** Particles and their behaviour

What is a melting point?

The temperature at which a substance melts is its **melting point**.

Melting points give us information about the states of substances at different temperatures:
- Below its melting point, a substance is in the solid state.
- Above its melting point, a substance may be in the liquid or gas state. You need more data to work out which.

▲ **Figure 3** Gallium is solid at room temperature. On a warm hand, it melts.

Look at the data in Table 1. At room temperature (20 °C), gallium and gold are below their melting points. So at 20 °C, gallium and gold are solid. Above 30 °C, gallium is liquid. This is why gallium will melt in your hand, as shown in Figure 3.

Substance	Melting point in °C
gallium	30
gold	1064
oxygen	−219
water	0

▲ **Table 1** The melting points of different substances.

At 20 °C, oxygen is above its melting point, so it must be in the liquid or gas state. However, from the data in Table 1, you cannot tell which of these two states it is in.

Gold has a higher melting point than water. This means that the particles in solid gold hold together more strongly than the particles in solid water (ice).

C Write the names of the substances in Table 1 in order of increasing melting point, starting with oxygen.

Key words

melting, freezing, change of state, reversible, conserved, melting point

Summary Questions

1 Copy and complete the following sentences.

The change of state from solid to liquid is **freezing**/**melting**. As a substance melts, its particles vibrate **slower**/**faster**. The particles start moving **around**/**upwards**. The substance is now in the **liquid**/**solid** state. The melting point of a substance is the **speed**/**temperature** it melts at. (5 marks)

2 Figure 4 shows some particles of a substance in the solid state.

Draw a diagram showing the same particles after the substance has melted. (2 marks)

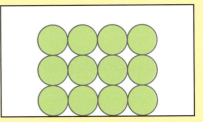

▲ **Figure 4**

3 A substance has a melting point of −7 °C. Yanek says the substance is liquid at 20 °C. Beth says it could be liquid or gas.

Explain who is correct.

(2 marks)

85

1.5 Boiling

Learning objectives
After this topic, you will be able to:
- describe how the arrangement, separation, and movement of particles change when a substance boils
- predict the state of a substance at a given temperature
- give the boiling point of a substance from its temperature–time graph (heating curve).

Reactivate your knowledge
1. Give two properties of a substance in the gas state.
2. How are particles arranged in the gas state?
3. What is mass?

Close your eyes. Imagine water boiling in a kettle or pan. What can you hear? What can you see? *Boiling* is a change of state from liquid to gas. You can use the particle model to explain boiling.

Explaining boiling

When water boils, bubbles of steam form all through the liquid. In the liquid, water particles touch their neighbours. But inside the bubbles, the water particles spread out (Figure 1).

As water boils, the steam bubbles rise to the surface of the liquid. They escape into the air. All the particles still exist, so the total mass of steam and water is the same as the mass of water at the start. The total mass of substance stays the same. Scientists say that mass is conserved in boiling.

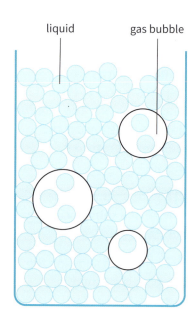

▲ Figure 1 Particles in boiling water (not to scale).

> **A** Use the particle model to explain why mass is conserved in boiling.

What is a boiling point?

Boiling happens if enough energy is transferred to the particles. The particles in some substances hold together more strongly than in others. This means that different substances need different amounts of energy to boil, and different substances boil at different temperatures. The temperature a substance boils at is its **boiling point**.

Measuring boiling point

You can measure the boiling point of a substance like this:
- Pour the liquid into a beaker.
- Heat the liquid and measure the temperature every minute.
- Plot the results on a graph.

Key words
boiling, boiling point

Reactivate your knowledge answers
1 Two from: compresses a lot, flows, takes the shape of its container 2 Randomly and far apart 3 The amount of matter (stuff) in an object

C1 Chapter 1: Particles and their behaviour

Kemal heated liquid water and plotted the graph shown in Figure 2. At first, the temperature increased. At 100 °C, the water bubbled vigorously. It was boiling. The temperature remained at 100°C. This is the boiling point of water.

> **B** Explain how the graph shows that the boiling point of water is 100 °C.

Using boiling points

Identifying substances

You can use data about boiling points to help identify substances.

Lucy has a colourless liquid. Her teacher tells her it could be water, ethanol, or propanol. Lucy finds out the boiling points of these substances. She writes them in Table 1.

Substance	Boiling point in °C
water	100
ethanol	78
propanol	97

▲ **Table 1** The boiling points of water, ethanol, and propanol.

Lucy heats her liquid with an electric heater. She measures its temperature every minute. At 78 °C the liquid bubbles vigorously. It remains at 78 °C for several minutes, so Lucy concludes that the liquid is ethanol.

Predicting states

If you know the melting point and the boiling point of a substance, you can predict its state at different temperatures. Figure 3 shows that the melting point of silver is 961 °C and the boiling point is 2162 °C.

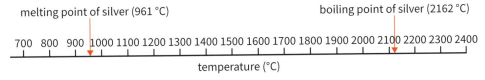

▲ **Figure 3** The melting and boiling points of silver.

At room temperature (20 °C), silver is in the solid state. At 961 °C, its melting point, silver exists as both a solid and a liquid. Between 961 °C and 2162 °C silver is a liquid. At 2162 °C, the boiling point, silver exists as both a liquid and a gas. Above 2162 °C silver exists in the gas state.

> **C** Predict the state of silver at 1000 °C.

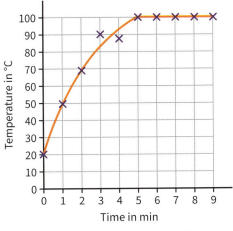

▲ **Figure 2** A temperature–time graph for heating water.

Summary Questions

1 Copy and complete the following sentences.

When a substance boils, it changes state from **liquid/gas** to **liquid/gas**. Bubbles form **at the top of/all the way through** the liquid. A certain substance boils at **any/a certain** temperature. (3 marks)

2 Answer the following questions.

a Draw a particle diagram to show 5 particles of a substance in the liquid state.

b Draw the same 5 particles after the substance has boiled. (2 marks)

3 Use the data below to predict the state of oxygen at −200 °C.

Data for oxygen:
melting point = −219 °C
boiling point = −183 °C
(1 mark)

87

1.6 More changes of state

Learning objectives

After this topic, you will be able to:
- compare evaporating, condensing, and subliming in terms of their before and after states
- describe a substance's particles when it evaporates, condenses, and sublimes
- compare the particles in a substance when it evaporates and boils.

Reactivate your knowledge

1. Give two properties of a substance in the liquid state.
2. Name the starting and finishing states in boiling.
3. Why is mass conserved in boiling?

Key words

evaporating, evaporation, condensing, subliming, sublimation

Key word sentences

Use the glossary to find out the meanings of the five key words in this spread. Then write each word in a sentence.

What happens to the water if you use a hairdryer to dry your hair? It changes state from liquid to gas without boiling. This is *evaporation*. You can use the particle model to explain evaporation.

Explaining evaporation

In a liquid, some particles have more energy than others. The particles with most energy leave the liquid surface. Then they move away from the liquid. The particles spread out, forming a gas. The liquid has evaporated. The mass stays the same, because all the particles still exist – they have just moved.

A substance can change from the liquid to the gas state by **evaporating** or boiling. Table 1 shows some differences between these two processes.

▲ **Figure 1** When you use a hairdryer to dry your hair the water evaporates.

Process	How particles leave the liquid	Temperature	Does the mass change?
evaporating	particles escape from the liquid surface	happens at any temperature	no
boiling	bubbles of the substance form everywhere in the liquid, they rise to the surface and escape	happens only at the boiling point	no

▲ **Table 1** Differences between evaporating and boiling.

A Give two differences between evaporating and boiling.

Reactivate your knowledge answers
1. Two from: flows, compresses a very little, takes the shape of the bottom of its container 2. Starting – liquid; finishing – gas
3. All the particles still exist

C1 **Chapter 1:** Particles and their behaviour

How is evaporating useful?

The person in Figure 2 is sweating. Why do you sweat? Sweating cools you down by evaporation. Sweat comes out of pores in your skin. Water from the sweat then evaporates. The water particles need energy to move away as a gas. They take this energy from your skin. This cools you down.

Why is it quicker to dry your hair with a hairdryer? The hairdryer speeds up evaporation in two ways. It transfers energy to help particles leave the liquid surface. It also moves just-evaporated water particles away from your hair.

▲ **Figure 2** Sweat helps to cool you down by evaporation.

What is condensing?

Is the inside of your bedroom window ever wet after a cold night? At bedtime, water particles in the room were mixed with air particles. They were spread out, as a gas. During the night, water particles hit the cold glass of the window. They moved closer to other water particles, until they were touching. They continued to move, but they stopped moving everywhere in the room and started to slide over each other.

The changes in the arrangement and movement of the particles result in liquid water. This change of state from gas to liquid is called **condensing**. It can happen at any temperature below a substance's boiling point.

B Name the starting and finishing states in condensing.

What is subliming?

Where does stage smoke come from? It comes from solid carbon dioxide. Carbon dioxide is solid at temperatures below −78.5 °C. At this temperature and above, solid carbon dioxide changes state to become a gas. It does not normally exist as a liquid. This change of state from solid to gas is called **subliming** or **sublimation**. Water particles from the air condense around carbon dioxide particles. Tiny drops of liquid water form. It is this liquid water that you see as stage smoke (Figure 3).

▲ **Figure 3** Water particles from the air condense around carbon dioxide particles to produce stage smoke.

C Give the state of carbon dioxide at room temperature, 20 °C.

Summary Questions

1 Write **six** correct sentences using the sentence starters and enders below.

Sentence starters
In boiling…
In condensing…
In evaporating…
In subliming…

Sentence enders
…particles leave from the surface of a liquid.
…particles change from the solid to the gas state.
…substances change from the liquid to the gas state.
…particles leave from all parts of a liquid.
…substances change from the gas to the liquid state.
(5 marks)

2 Describe the changes in the movement and arrangement of particles when a substance condenses. (2 marks)

3 Name the process that occurs when:
a puddles dry up
b a glass of very cold water gets wet on the outside. (2 marks)

89

1.7 Diffusion

Learning objectives

After this topic, you will be able to:
- describe how the movement of the particles changes when a substance diffuses
- use the particle model to explain how temperature, particle size, and state affect how quickly diffusion happens
- use the particle model to explain the observations in a diffusion experiment.

Reactivate your knowledge

1. What are the three states of matter?
2. What are particles?
3. How do particles move in the gas state?

▲ **Figure 1** Bromine diffuses into the upper gas jars.

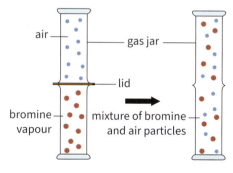

▲ **Figure 2** A particle diagram showing why bromine diffuses into the upper gas jar.

Link

You can learn more about diffusion in *B1 1.4 Movement of substances*.

A teacher fills a gas jar with brown bromine gas. She puts a lid on it and places a gas jar of air on top. This is shown on the left of Figures 1 and 2.

Then the teacher removes the lid. Gradually, bromine gas fills the upper gas jar, as shown on the right of Figures 1 and 2. You can use the particle model to explain why this happens.

> **A** Describe the difference between the 'before' gas jars on the left of the photo and the 'after' gas jars on the right.

What is diffusion?

In the gas jars in Figure 1, bromine particles move from areas where there are many particles to an area where there are fewer particles. In other words, particles move from an area of high **concentration** to an area of low concentration. This is **diffusion**.

Diffusion happens in any substance in the liquid or gas state. It happens because the particles move randomly all the time. When they bump into each other, they change direction. Over time, the moving particles spread out. Diffusion happens by itself. You do not need to shake or stir.

Diffusion explains why you can smell perfume across a room. Perfume particles evaporate from skin. The particles move randomly and bump into other perfume particles and air particles. Over time, they move from where there are many particles (near the skin) to where there are few particles.

> **B** Name the two states of matter in which diffusion can happen.

Reactivate your knowledge answers
1 Solid, liquid, and gas 2 The tiny things that materials are made up of 3 Quickly and randomly, anywhere in the container

C1 Chapter 1: Particles and their behaviour

What factors affect how quickly diffusion happens?

Several factors affect how quickly diffusion happens, including:
- temperature
- particle size
- the state of the diffusing substance.

Temperature

Diffusion happens more quickly at higher temperatures because particles move faster.

Particle size

A teacher sets up the apparatus in Figure 3 to demonstrate diffusion.

Hydrogen chloride particles evaporate from the piece of cotton wool at the left side of the test tube. Ammonia particles evaporate from the piece of cotton wool at the right. The particles diffuse along the tube. The two types of particle meet and form a ring of white solid.

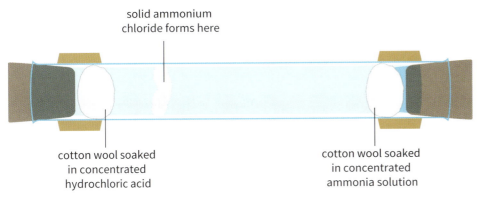

▲ **Figure 3** The apparatus used to demonstrate diffusion in air.

The solid is formed closer to the hydrogen chloride end. This shows that the hydrogen chloride particles diffuse more slowly. Hydrogen chloride particles are bigger and heavier than ammonia particles. Big, heavy particles diffuse more slowly than small, light ones.

State

Diffusion happens more quickly in the gas state than in the liquid state. Diffusion does not happen in solids because the particles cannot move from place to place.

> **C** Suggest why particles diffuse more slowly at lower temperatures.

Key words

concentration, diffusion

Summary Questions

1 Copy and complete the following sentences.

The movement of particles from a region where there are many to a region where there are few is called _____. Diffusion happens in the liquid and _____ states. Diffusion happens more quickly at _____ temperatures. (3 marks)

2 Diffusion can be observed in an experiment.

a Describe an experiment that provides evidence for the diffusion of bromine. (2 marks)

b Explain the observations in your answer to **2a**. (3 marks)

3 The air contains particles of argon, nitrogen, and other substances.

Use the data below to predict which type of particle diffuses faster. Give a reason for your choice.

Relative masses of particles: nitrogen = 28 argon = 40
(2 marks)

91

1 Chapter 1 Summary

In this chapter you have learnt about the invisible particles that make up all matter. You have also discovered how the arrangement, movement, and separation of particles give substances their properties – as well as what happens when substances melt, boil, or condense.

You have seen how the particle model explains boiling water to make hot drinks and freezing food to preserve it. You have also used the particle model to explain why smells travel, and why different materials have different densities.

Metacognition and self-reflection task

Discussing questions with a partner is a useful way of checking your understanding. Make up one question for each learning objective in this chapter, and ask your partner to do the same. Then take turns to ask and answer your questions. If you disagree on an answer, use the information in this chapter to improve it.

Journey through C1

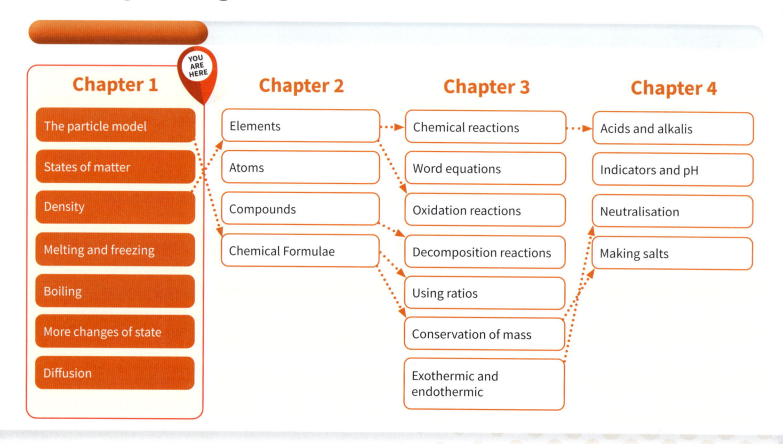

Chapter 1 Summary Questions

1 Copy Table 1 and complete it by writing the word 'yes' or 'no' in each empty box.

State	Can you compress the substance in this state?	Does the substance flow in this state?
Solid		
Liquid		
Gas		

(3 marks)

2 Figure 1 shows some particles in solid gold. Draw another diagram to show the same particles in the gas state.

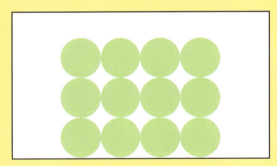

▲ **Figure 1** Gold particles in the solid state.

(2 marks)

3 Describe the arrangement and movement of particles in the liquid state. **(2 marks)**

4 This question is about density.
a Give the definition for density. (1 mark)
b Use the particle model to explain why steam (water in the gas state) has a lower density than liquid water. (1 mark)
(2 marks)

5 Table 2 shows the melting points and boiling points of six substances.

Substance	Melting point in °C	Boiling point in °C
bromine	−7	59
krypton	−157	−152
mercury	−39	357
neon	−249	−246
platinum	1769	4530
silver	961	2210

a Write down the name of the substance with the highest boiling point. (1 mark)
b Write down the names of the substances in order of increasing melting point, lowest first. (5 marks)
c Name **one** substance in the table that is in the gas state at 20 °C. (1 mark)
d Name **two** substances in the table that are in the liquid state at 20 °C. (2 marks)
e Name **one** substance in the table that is in the liquid state at 100 °C. (1 mark)
(10 marks)

6 Read the following statements about particles in a substance in the solid state.

A The particles touch other particles.
B The particles are in a pattern.
C The particles do not move around from place to place.
D The particles vibrate.

a Write down the letter of the statement that best explains why you cannot pour a solid. (1 mark)
b Choose **one** of the other statements and explain why it does not explain why you cannot pour a solid.
(1 mark)
(2 marks)

7 Compare the processes of boiling and evaporating.
(4 marks)

2 Elements, atoms, and compounds

In this chapter you will learn about elements and use an international code to identify them. You will find out about the invisible particles – atoms – that make up elements, and how they join together in different combinations to make up all the substances on Earth and in the Universe.

Just six of the elements mentioned in this chapter make up nearly 99% of your body mass. Every new material is made from atoms of one or more of the hundred or so elements that exist.

Reactivate your knowledge

1 Write down three properties of gold, three properties of water, and three properties of salt.

2 Draw an object that is made from gold. Explain why the properties of gold make it suitable for this object.

3 Draw a diagram showing the arrangement of 12 particles in a substance that is in the solid state.

4 Gold particles have a greater mass than silver particles. Predict which has the greater density, gold or silver.

You already know

- Different materials have different properties.
- The uses of materials depend on their properties.
- Everything is made up of particles.
- Three factors give a substance its properties: what its particles are like, how its particles are arranged, and how its particles move.

 How to add numbers using your maths skills.

 How to work scientifically to: interpret data in tables.

Journey through C1

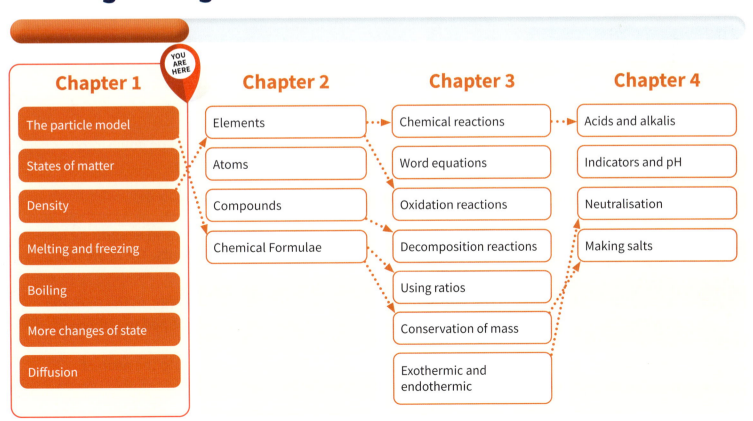

Chapter 1
- The particle model
- States of matter
- Density
- Melting and freezing
- Boiling
- More changes of state
- Diffusion

Chapter 2 (YOU ARE HERE)
- Elements
- Atoms
- Compounds
- Chemical Formulae

Chapter 3
- Chemical reactions
- Word equations
- Oxidation reactions
- Decomposition reactions
- Using ratios
- Conservation of mass
- Exothermic and endothermic

Chapter 4
- Acids and alkalis
- Indicators and pH
- Neutralisation
- Making salts

95

2.1 Elements

Learning objective
After this topic, you will be able to:
- state the definition of an element and list some examples of elements
- describe what the Periodic Table shows and use it to find a named element.

Reactivate your knowledge
1. What is a substance?
2. Name three substances.
3. What are properties?

Look at the pictures in Figures 1, 2, and 3. What do the objects have in common?

▲ **Figure 1** Jewellery.

▲ **Figure 2** A catalytic converter.

▲ **Figure 3** A heart pacemaker.

Key words
element, Periodic Table, chemical symbol

Link
You can learn more about the Periodic Table in C2 1.2 *Groups and periods*.

Name the elements
Listen to your teacher read the names of the elements in the row of the Periodic Table that starts with sodium. In pairs, take it in turns to practise pronouncing the words correctly.

All of these objects contain platinum. Catalytic converters change harmful car exhaust fumes into less harmful ones. Pacemakers are used to help the heart beat regularly.

Platinum is a shiny substance that is not damaged by air or water. It is easy to make platinum into different shapes. These properties make platinum suitable for the uses in Figures 1, 2, and 3.

Platinum is an example of an **element**. An element is a substance that cannot be broken down into other substances. You may have heard of some elements, including gold, silver, oxygen, chlorine, and helium.

> **A** Predict whether or not platinum can be broken down into other substances. Explain how you decided.

How many elements?

There are millions of materials. Every material, and everything in the Universe, is made up of one or more elements. There are about 100 elements.

The **Periodic Table** (Figure 4) lists all the elements. In the Periodic Table, elements with similar properties are grouped together.

> **B** Give the approximate number of elements, to the nearest hundred.

Reactivate your knowledge answers
1 A material that is not a mixture 2 For example: gold, pure water, oxygen 3 What a material/substance looks like and how it behaves

							H hydrogen										He helium
Li lithium	Be beryllium											B boron	C carbon	N nitrogen	O oxygen	F fluorine	Ne neon
Na sodium	Mg magnesium											Al aluminium	Si silicon	P phosphorus	S sulfur	Cl chlorine	Ar argon
K potassium	Ca calcium	Sc scandium	Ti titanium	V vanadium	Cr chromium	Mn manganese	Fe iron	Co cobalt	Ni nickel	Cu copper	Zn zinc	Ga gallium	Ge germanium	As arsenic	Se selenium	Br bromine	Kr krypton
Rb rubidium	Sr strontium	Y yttrium	Zr zirconium	Nb niobium	Mo molybdenum	Tc technetium	Ru ruthenium	Rh rhodium	Pd palladium	Ag silver	Cd cadmium	In indium	Sn tin	Sb antimony	Te tellurium	I iodine	Xe xenon
Cs caesium	Ba barium	La lanthanum	Hf hafnium	Ta tantalum	W tungsten	Re rhenium	Os osmium	Ir iridium	Pt platinum	Au gold	Hg mercury	Tl thallium	Pb lead	Bi bismuth	Po polonium	At astatine	Rn radon
Fr francium	Ra radium	Ac actinium	Rf rutherfordium	Db dubnium	Sg seaborgium	Bh bohrium	Hs hassium	Mt meitnerium	Ds darmstadtium	Rg roentgenium	Cn copernicium	Nh nihonium	Fl flerovium	Mc moscovium	Lv livermorium	Ts tennessine	Og oganesson

Ce cerium	Pr praseodymium	Nd neodymium	Pm promethium	Sm samarium	Eu europium	Gd gadolinium	Tb terbium	Dy dysprosium	Ho holmium	Er erbium	Tm thulium	Yb ytterbium	Lu lutetium
Th thorium	Pa protactinium	U uranium	Np neptunium	Pu plutonium	Am americium	Cm curium	Bk berkelium	Cf californium	Es einsteinium	Fm fermium	Md mendelevium	No nobelium	Lr lawrencium

▲ **Figure 4** The Periodic Table lists all the elements.

What are chemical symbols?

Every element has its own **chemical symbol**. This is a one- or two-letter code for the element. Scientists all over the world use the same chemical symbols, no matter what language they speak or write in.

Table 1 shows some chemical symbols. The first letter of a chemical symbol is a capital letter. The second letter is lowercase.

Name of element	Chemical symbol
carbon	C
nitrogen	N
chlorine	Cl
gold	Au
iron	Fe
tungsten	W

▲ **Table 1** Elements and their chemical symbols.

For some elements, their chemical symbol is the first letter of its English name. For others, the chemical symbol is the first and second or first and third letters of its name.

The chemical symbols of some elements come from their Latin names, for example, *aurum* for gold and *ferrum* for iron. The chemical symbol of tungsten comes from its German name, *Wolfram*.

C Write down the chemical symbols of the elements carbon, chlorine, gold, and iron.

Summary Questions

1 Copy and complete the following sentences.

A substance that cannot be broken down into other substances is called an ______ . There are about ______ elements. The elements are listed in the ______ ______ . Every element has its own one- or two-letter code, called its chemical ______ . (4 marks)

2 Find these elements in the Periodic Table: carbon, calcium, cobalt, copper, xenon, praseodymium. Write down the chemical symbol of each element in the list. (6 marks)

3 Identify the three elements in this list of substances: argon, air, carbon dioxide, methane, nitrogen, water, krypton. Explain your answers. (3 marks)

2.2 Atoms

Learning objective
After this topic, you will be able to:
- state the meaning of 'atom'.
- state the meaning of 'element' (in terms of its atoms).

Reactivate your knowledge
1. What is an element?
2. What are particles?
3. How are the particles arranged in a substance in the solid state?

Look at Figures 1 and 2. What do you think they show?

▲ Figure 1

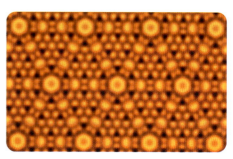

▲ Figure 2

Both pictures show the element silicon. Figure 1 was taken with a normal camera. Figure 2 was taken with a special type of microscope. It shows the surface of a silicon crystal at a magnification of ×10 000 000 (ten million).

Silicon is an important element. It holds the tiny electric circuits in every computer, tablet, and phone.

What are atoms?

The spheres in Figure 2 are atoms. Atoms are particles. An **atom** is the smallest part of an element that can exist.

Every element is made up of just one type of atom. All the atoms of an element are the same as each other. The atoms of one element are different to the atoms of all other elements. There are about 100 elements, so there are about 100 types of atom.

You can now give a better definition of an **element**: a substance that cannot be broken down into other substances. It contains just one type of atom.

A Give the number of types of atom in a piece of silicon.

Key words
atom, element

Reactivate your knowledge answers
1. A substance that cannot be broken down into other substances
2. The tiny things that materials are made from
3. In patterns, touching their neighbours

C1 **Chapter 2:** Elements, atoms, and compounds

All silicon atoms are the same. But silicon atoms are different to gold atoms. For example, gold atoms are bigger.

Gold atoms are also heavier than silicon atoms. This difference explains the data in Table 1.

> **B** Describe two differences between gold and silicon atoms.

Element	Mass of 1 cm³ of the element in g
gold	19.30
silicon	2.33

▲ **Table 1** The masses of gold and silicon.

Just one atom?

One atom on its own does not have the properties of its element. A gold atom is not yellow. It is not shiny. It is not in the solid, liquid or gas state.

The properties of an element are the properties of very many atoms joined together, like those in Figure 3. The block of gold in Figure 4 has a mass of 1000 g. It is made up of about 3 000 000 000 000 000 000 000 000 atoms. Together, these atoms make the gold yellow and shiny.

How many particles?

There are 3 000 000 000 000 000 000 000 000 atoms in a 1000 g gold bar. A gold ring has a mass of 10 g.

Calculate the number of atoms in the ring.

▲ **Figure 3** The circles represent a few atoms in solid gold. One atom on its own has no colour.

▲ **Figure 4** When many gold atoms are arranged into a block of gold, the resulting substance has properties, like colour.

In a gold block, the atoms are touching each other in rows. They vibrate on the spot. The gold in Figure 4 is in the solid state. If you heat gold to 1063 °C its atoms start moving around. The gold is melting. One atom of gold cannot melt. Only a group of many atoms can melt.

> **C** Describe two differences between a gold atom and a block of gold.

Summary Questions

1 Copy and complete the following sentences.

The smallest part of an element that can exist is called an _____ . All the atoms of an element are the _____ . The atoms of one element are _____ to the atoms of all other elements. An atom on its own does not have the properties of the _____ . (4 marks)

2 An Olympic bronze medal is made up of three elements – copper, zinc, and tin.

Give the number of types of atom in the medal. Explain your answer. (2 marks)

3 A student says that a gold atom is yellow and shiny, and that it is in the solid state at 20 °C. Explain why the student is incorrect. (2 marks)

99

2.3 Compounds

Learning objective
After this topic, you will be able to:
- state the meaning of 'compound'
- explain whether a molecule diagram shows an element or a compound
- explain why a compound has different properties to the elements whose atoms are in it.

Reactivate your knowledge
1. What is an atom?
2. How many types of atom are there in an element?
3. How are the particles arranged in a substance in the gas state?

▲ **Figure 1** A water meter measures the amount of water used in a home.

Key words
compound, molecule

How much water have you used today? A water meter, like that in Figure 1, can tell you.

Water is vital. But what is water? Water is made from the atoms of two elements, hydrogen and oxygen. This means that water is a **compound**. A compound is a substance made up of atoms of two or more elements, with the atoms joined together strongly. The properties of a compound are different to the properties of the elements whose atoms are in it.

A Explain why water is a compound.

Why is water different to its elements?

Hydrogen, oxygen, and water particles are all different. This explains why the three substances have different properties.

Hydrogen is a gas at room temperature. If mixed with air, and ignited with a spark, hydrogen explodes.

Hydrogen atoms go round in pairs, as shown in Figure 2. These two-atom particles are molecules of hydrogen. A **molecule** is a group of two or more atoms strongly joined together.

Oxygen is a gas at room temperature. You cannot see or smell it. Oxygen exists as molecules. Each molecule is made up of two oxygen atoms (see Figure 3). In the air, oxygen molecules spread out. They move quickly from place to place.

Molecular maths

One oxygen molecule is made up of two oxygen atoms.

Calculate the number of oxygen atoms in 25 oxygen molecules.

▲ **Figure 2** A hydrogen molecule consists of two hydrogen atoms.

▲ **Figure 3** An oxygen molecule consists of two oxygen atoms.

Reactivate your knowledge answers
1 The smallest part of an element that can exist 2 One 3 Far apart, moving around quickly and randomly

Chapter 2: Elements, atoms, and compounds

Water particles are three-atom molecules, as shown in Figure 4. Each water molecule is made up of one oxygen atom and two hydrogen atoms. This means that water is a compound.

One property that is different for hydrogen, oxygen, and water is boiling point. In liquid hydrogen, weak forces hold the molecules close to each other. In liquid water, stronger forces hold the molecules close to each other. This means that it takes less energy to separate hydrogen molecules from each other than to separate water molecules from each other. Hydrogen has a lower boiling point than water.

B Explain why a compound has different properties to the elements whose atoms it is made from.

▲ **Figure 4** A water molecule has one oxygen atom joined to two hydrogen atoms. The atoms are not actually different colours in reality.

Link

You can learn more about boiling points in C1 1.4 *Boiling*.

What is salt?

Do you add salt to food? (Figure 5).

▲ **Figure 5** Some people add salt to food.

Salt is a compound. Its scientific name is sodium chloride. It contains particles of two elements, sodium and chlorine.
- Sodium is a shiny silver-coloured metal that fizzes in water.
- Chlorine is a smelly, green poisonous gas at room temperature.

So why doesn't salt smell? Or poison you? Or fizz in your mouth?

In salt, sodium and chlorine particles are not just mixed up. They are joined together to make one substance – sodium chloride. The compound has different properties to the elements whose atoms are in it.

C Describe one difference in properties between sodium chloride and sodium.

Summary Questions

1 Copy and complete the following sentences.

A compound is a substance made up of atoms of **one/two or more** elements. The properties of a compound are **the same as/different to** the properties of the elements it is made of. A molecule is a group of **two/three or more** atoms **weakly/strongly** joined together. (4 marks)

2 Look at Figure 6. For each diagram, write down whether it shows an element or a compound. Explain your answers. (4 marks)

　　　A　　　　　　B

▲ **Figure 6** A water molecule (left) and an oxygen molecule (right).

3 Suggest why water has a higher boiling point than oxygen. (2 marks)

101

2.4 Chemical formulae

Learning objectives
After this topic, you will be able to:
- name a familiar two-element compound.
- determine the chemical formula of a compound, given the relative numbers of atoms of the elements in it.

Reactivate your knowledge
1. What is a molecule?
2. What is a compound?
3. Name the change of state from gas to liquid.

▲ **Figure 1** A carbon dioxide molecule has one carbon atom and two oxygen atoms.

▲ **Figure 2** A carbon monoxide molecule has one carbon atom and one oxygen atom.

Are the windows closed? If so, there is probably more carbon dioxide in the room now than there was 10 minutes ago. Every cell in your body makes carbon dioxide, which you breathe out. Carbon dioxide is a compound. It is made up atoms of two elements – carbon and oxygen.

Carbon monoxide is another compound. It also consists of atoms of carbon and oxygen. But carbon monoxide is poisonous. It can be deadly if you breathe it in.

Why are carbon–oxygen compounds different?

You already know that the properties of a compound depend on the elements whose atoms are in it. The numbers of atoms of each element also make a difference.

Carbon dioxide has two oxygen atoms for every carbon (Figure 1)
Carbon monoxide has one oxygen atom for every carbon (Figure 2).

> **A** Give the number and types of atoms in one carbon dioxide molecule.

Name that substance

Give the correct names for the compounds with these chemical formulae. Choose from the list of names below.
a CO_2 **b** SO_3 **c** CO **d** SO_2
List of names: carbon monoxide, carbon dioxide, sulfur dioxide, sulfur trioxide.

How do we name compounds?

Compounds made up of oxygen and one other element have two-word names. The second word is oxide. Table 1 gives some examples.

Elements in compound	Name of compound
aluminium and oxygen	aluminium oxide
zinc and oxygen	zinc oxide

▲ **Table 1** The names of some compounds containing oxygen.

Reactivate your knowledge answers
1 A group of two or more atoms, strongly joined together 2 A substance made up of atoms of two or more elements, with the atoms strongly joined together 3 Condensing / condensation

C1 **Chapter 2:** Elements, atoms, and compounds

As you know, some elements form more than one oxide. Table 2 gives some examples.

Compound molecule made up of…	Name of compound
1 carbon atom and 1 oxygen atom	carbon monoxide
1 carbon atom and 2 oxygen atoms	carbon dioxide
1 sulfur atom and 2 oxygen atoms	sulfur dioxide
1 sulfur atom and 3 oxygen atoms	sulfur trioxide

▲ **Table 2** The names of some oxides.

▲ **Figure 3** A sulfur dioxide molecule has one sulfur atom and two oxygen atoms. You can represent it with a 2-D or a 3-D diagram.

▲ **Figure 4** A sulfur trioxide molecule has one sulfur atom and three oxygen atoms. You can represent it with either a 2-D or 3-D diagram.

The compound of sodium and chlorine is called sodium chloride. Chlor**ine** becomes chlor**ide**. In any compound of a metal with a non-metal, the end of the name of the non-metal becomes **-ide**.

> **B** Name the compound that has molecules with one sulfur atom joined to three oxygen atoms.

What is a chemical formula?

Every element and compound has its own chemical formula. The **chemical formula** for a substance shows the **relative number** of atoms of each element that are in it. 'Relative number' means how many atoms of one type there are compared to another type.

For example:
- The chemical formula of oxygen gas is O_2. This shows that its molecules have two oxygen atoms.
- The chemical formula of carbon dioxide is CO_2. This shows that there is one carbon atom for every two oxygen atoms.
- The chemical formula for carbon monoxide is CO. This shows that there is one carbon atom for every oxygen atom.

When you are writing chemical formulae, write the numbers:
- to the right of their chemical symbol, just below the line.
- smaller than the chemical symbols.

> **C** A compound has one sulfur atom for every two oxygen atoms. Write the formula of the compound, with the chemical symbol for sulfur first.

Key words

chemical formula, relative number

Summary Questions

1 Copy and complete the following sentences.

A compound is made up of atoms of sodium and chlorine. Its name could be **sodium chloride/sodium oxide.** A compound has one atom of nitrogen to two atoms of oxygen. Its name is **nitrogen dioxide/nitrogen trioxide.**
(2 marks)

2 Figure 3 shows one molecule of a compound. Write its formula. (2 marks)

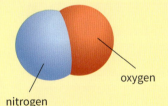

▲ **Figure 3**

3 Paracetamol is a painkiller. Its molecules are made up of these atoms: 8 carbon atoms, 9 hydrogen atoms, 1 nitrogen atom, and 2 oxygen atoms. Write the chemical formula of paracetamol. (4 marks)

103

Chapter 2 Summary

In this chapter you have learnt about elements and used an international code to identify them. You have found out about the invisible particles - atoms - that make up elements, and how they join together in different combinations to make up all the substances on Earth and in the Universe.

Just six of the elements mentioned in this chapter (carbon, oxygen, hydrogen, nitrogen, calcium, and phosphorus) make up nearly 99% of your body mass. And every new material is made from atoms of one or more of the hundred or so elements that exist.

Metacognition and self-reflection task

It is important to use key words correctly. Write each key word in this chapter on a separate card. Then use the glossary in this book to write the definition of each key word on the back of the card. Next, use the cards to test yourself. Start by reading a definition, and writing the key word on scrap paper. Make sure your spelling is correct. Repeat for all your cards. Then turn the cards over and write a definition for each key word.

Journey through C1

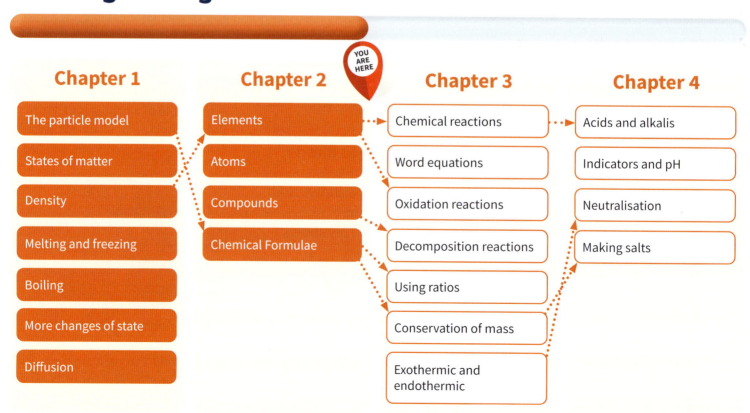

Chapter 2 Summary Questions

1 Give the definitions for these key words:
 a element (1 mark)
 b atom (1 mark)
 c compound (1 mark)
 d molecule (1 mark)
 (4 marks)

2 Mobile phones store electrical charge in capacitors. Capacitors contain a mixture of tantalum and tantalum oxide. Tantalum is an element.
 a Give the number of types of atom in tantalum. (1 mark)
 b Tantalum oxide is a compound of two elements. One of the elements is tantalum. Name the other element. (1 mark)
 c Write down the number of types of atom in tantalum oxide. (1 mark)
 d Copy and complete the sentences below.

The formula of tantalum oxide is Ta_2O_5. This means that there are _____ atoms of tantalum for every five atoms of _____. (2 marks)
 (5 marks)

3 Figure 1 shows a molecule of sulfur dioxide. Each sphere represents one atom. Different coloured spheres represent atoms of different elements.

▲ **Figure 1** A sulfur dioxide molecule.

 a Give the total number of atoms in the molecule. (1 mark)
 b Give the number of different types of atom in the molecule. (1 mark)
 c State whether sulfur dioxide is an element or a compound. Explain your decision. (2 marks)
 d Copy and complete Table 1. (3 marks)

Name of element	Number of atoms of this element in one sulfur dioxide molecule
sulfur	

▲ **Table 1**

 e Write the formula of sulfur dioxide. (2 marks)
 (9 marks)

4 Table 2 shows data for six elements. Figure 2 shows their positions in the periodic table.

Name of element	Chemical symbol	Melting point (°C)
lithium	Li	180
sodium	Na	98
potassium	K	64
neon	Ne	-249
argon	Ar	-189
krypton	Kr	-157

▲ **Table 2**

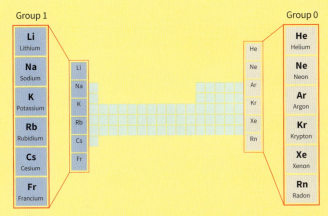

▲ **Figure 2** The positions of six elements in the periodic table.

 a Draw a bar chart to display the melting point data for the group 1 elements. (3 marks)
 b Compare the melting point patterns for the group 1 and group 0 elements. (4 marks)
 (7 marks)

105

3 Reactions

In this chapter you will learn about chemical reactions. You will discover how atoms rearrange and join together differently to make new substances, and why the total mass does not change. You will learn to write word equations, classify chemical reactions, and use patterns to make predictions.

Reactivate your knowledge

1 Describe what you can see before, during and after wood burns.

2 When wood has burnt, you cannot get the wood back again. In other words, burning wood is not reversible. Explain whether baking a cake is reversible or not.

3 Give the number of different types of atom in: a piece of copper, oxygen gas, a piece of copper oxide.

You already know

- Some changes, like burning, make new materials.
- Changes that make new materials are not usually reversible.
- An atom is the smallest part of an element that can exist.
- Compounds are substances made up of atoms of two or more elements, strongly joined together.

 How to divide numbers using your maths skills.

 How to work scientifically to: make observations in experiments.

Journey through C1

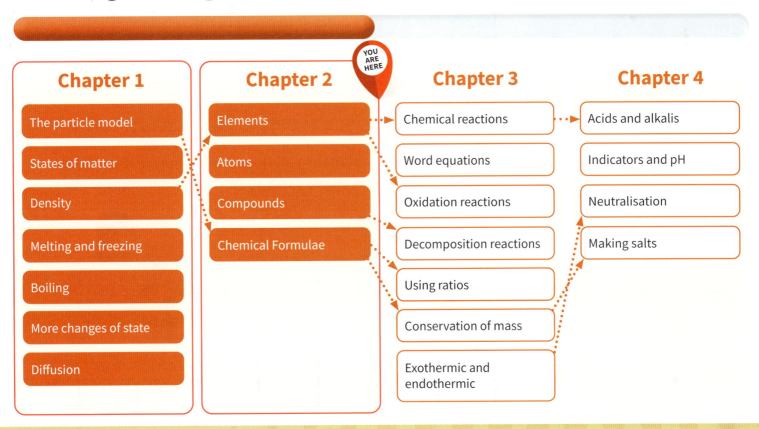

107

3.1 Chemical reactions

Learning objectives
After this topic, you will be able to:
- state what chemical reactions are
- explain how chemical reactions are useful
- compare chemical reactions to physical changes.

Reactivate your knowledge
1. What is an atom?
2. Name three changes of state.
3. What does reversible mean in science?

▲ **Figure 1** A distress flare.

▲ **Figure 2** A rusting bike chain.

Key words
chemical reaction, catalyst, physical change

Describing observations
Think of a chemical reaction you have observed, at school or elsewhere. Describe your observations to your partner. You could tell them what you saw, heard and smelt. Try to be clear and accurate.

Magnesium burns brightly in a distress flare (Figure 1). An old iron bike rusts (Figure 2). An egg cooks over burning gas. What do these changes have in common? They are all chemical reactions.

What are chemical reactions?

A **chemical reaction** is a change in which atoms rearrange and join together differently to make new substances. The atoms are joined together in one way before the reaction and in a different way after the reaction. Elements and compounds can take part in chemical reactions.

All chemical reactions:
- make new substances
- transfer energy to or from the surroundings.

Most chemical reactions are not easily reversible. At the end of the reaction it is very difficult to get back the substances you started with.

A Describe what happens to the atoms in a chemical reaction.

How do you know if it's a chemical reaction?

You do an experiment in the lab. How do you know if it involved chemical reactions? Figures 3 to 6 show the clues to look for.

▲ **Figure 3** You might see huge flames, or tiny sparks.

▲ **Figure 4** You might notice a sweet smell, or a foul stink.

Reactivate your knowledge answers
1. The smallest part of an element that can exist. 2. Three from: freezing, melting, evaporating, boiling, condensing, subliming 3. The original substance can easily be got back again.

C1 **Chapter 3:** Reactions

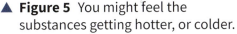

▲ **Figure 5** You might feel the substances getting hotter, or colder.

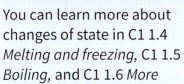

▲ **Figure 6** You might hear a loud bang, or gentle fizzing.

> **B** Describe three pieces of evidence that may suggest that a chemical reaction is happening.

Why are chemical reactions useful?

Chemical reactions make useful things, including:

- medicines, such as paracetamol
- fabrics, such as polyester
- building materials, such as cement
- tissues in your body, such as muscle and bone.

Chemical reactions also transfer energy. This transfer can be useful. Burning gas cooks food. Burning petrol makes vehicles go. Chemical reactions in your cells provide energy for biological processes.

Some chemical reactions are not useful. Rusting may damage bicycles, boats, and bridges. Chemical reactions make food rot.

> **C** Describe two ways that chemical reactions are useful, and one way they are not useful.

How fast are chemical reactions?

Some reactions happen quickly. Others are slow. Chemists use **catalysts** to speed up slow reactions if they want to make a product more quickly. Different reactions need different catalysts. A catalyst is not used up in a reaction.

Are all changes chemical reactions?

Not all changes involve chemical reactions. If you warm chocolate, it melts. But you still have chocolate afterwards. Melting is a physical change.

Physical changes are changes that do not make new substances. They are reversible, so you can get back what you started with. All changes of state, and dissolving, are physical changes.

> **D** Give four examples of physical changes.

Link

You can learn more about changes of state in C1 1.4 *Melting and freezing,* C1 1.5 *Boiling,* and C1 1.6 *More changes of state.*

Summary Questions

1 Copy and complete the following sentences.

Chemical reactions involve re-arranging **atoms/states** and joining them together **the same/differently**. Chemical reactions **always/sometimes** make new substances. They **are/are not** easily reversible. They **always/never** involve energy transfers. Physical changes include changes of **substance/state**. They **are/are not** reversible. (7 marks)

2 Compare chemical reactions to physical changes. Include two examples in your answer. (4 marks)

3 Some chemical reactions are useful, but some are not. Give the letters of the **three** useful reactions below. Explain your choices. (6 marks)

A Breaking down food in your stomach.
B Wood rotting in a fence.
C Making ethanoic acid, a substance in vinegar, from ethanol and oxygen.
D Sodium hydrogencarbonate making carbon dioxide gas when a cake bakes.

109

3.2 Word equations

Learning objectives
After this topic, you will be able to:
- identify reactants and products in word equations
- write word equations for chemical reactions
- explain how atoms rearrange and join together differently in a chemical reaction.

Reactivate your knowledge
1. What is a chemical reaction?
2. What two things happen in all chemical reactions?
3. What is a molecule?

▲ Figure 1 Burning charcoal.

Figure 1 shows charcoal burning on a barbecue. What happens when substances burn?

Charcoal is a form of carbon. At 20 °C, it is a black solid. When carbon burns, it reacts with oxygen from the air. The chemical reaction makes a new substance, carbon dioxide, which forms as an invisible gas. In this chemical reaction, two elements join together to make a compound.

A Name the two elements that react to make carbon dioxide.

Representing reactions

Many other pairs of elements join together in chemical reactions. Figure 2 shows a mixture of iron filings and sulfur powder. If you heat the mixture, it glows red. A chemical reaction happens. A new substance, iron sulfide, forms. Figure 3 shows iron sulfide.

▲ Figure 2 A mixture of iron and sulfur. ▲ Figure 3 Iron sulfide.

In chemical reactions, the starting substances are the **reactants**. The substances that are made are the **products**. In the reaction of iron with sulfur:

- The reactants are iron and sulfur
- The product is iron sulfide.

B Name the reactants and product in the reaction of carbon and oxygen to make carbon dioxide.

Key words
reactant, product, word equation

Link
You can learn more about the numbers of particles that react together in C1 3.5 *Using ratios*.

Reactivate your knowledge answers
1. A change in which atoms are rearranged and joined together differently to make new substances. 2. New substances are made; energy is transferred 3. A group of two or more atoms, strongly joined together.

C1 Chapter 3: Reactions

Word equations show reactions in a simple way. A word equation shows:

- reactants on the left of the arrow
- products on the right of the arrow.

The arrow means 'reacts to make'. It is different to an equals sign (=) used in a maths equation.

The word equation for the reaction of iron and sulfur is:

iron + sulfur ⟶ iron sulfide

C Carbon and oxygen react to make carbon dioxide. Write a word equation for the reaction.

Rearranging atoms

In every chemical reaction, atoms are rearranged to make new substances. The atoms are joined together in one way before the reaction and in a different way after the reaction. The numbers of each type of atom do not change.

At very high temperatures, nitrogen reacts with oxygen:

nitrogen + oxygen ⟶ nitrogen oxide

In the air, nitrogen exists as molecules. Each molecule is made up of two nitrogen atoms, so its formula is N_2. Oxygen gas also exists as molecules, O_2.

In the chemical reaction of nitrogen and oxygen, their molecules split up. The atoms join together differently to make nitrogen monoxide molecules, NO. Figure 4 shows how the atoms rearrange and join together differently in the chemical reaction. The numbers of nitrogen and oxygen atoms do not change.

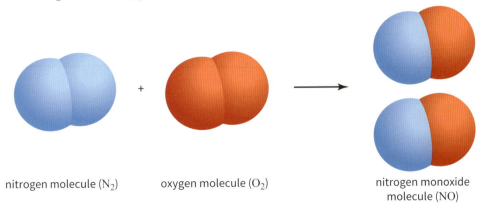

nitrogen molecule (N_2)　　oxygen molecule (O_2)　　nitrogen monoxide molecule (NO)

▲ **Figure 4** How the atoms rearrange and join together differently in the reaction of nitrogen and oxygen.

Literacy

Look at Figure 4. Write two or three sentences to describe what the diagram shows about how the atoms rearrange and join together differently when nitrogen reacts with oxygen.

Summary Questions

1 Copy the word equation below. Circle and label the reactants, then circle and label the products.

methane + oxygen ⟶ carbon dioxide + water　(2 marks)

2 Write word equations for the reactions described below.

a Nitrogen reacts with oxygen to make nitrogen monoxide.
(2 marks)

b Magnesium reacts with oxygen to make magnesium oxide.
(2 marks)

c Sodium reacts with chlorine to make sodium chloride.
(2 marks)

3 Draw a particle diagram to show how the atoms rearrange and join together differently in the reaction described below. Show hydrogen atoms as white circles and oxygen atoms as red circles. Description: Two hydrogen molecules (H_2) react with one oxygen molecule (O_2) to make two water molecules (H_2O).
(4 marks)

111

3.3 Oxidation reactions

Learning objectives
After this topic, you will be able to:
- state the meanings of combustion and oxidation
- write word equations for oxidation reactions
- predict the products of the combustion of fuels.

Reactivate your knowledge
1. What does the arrow mean in a word equation?
2. In a word equation, are the products on the left or right of the arrow?
3. Name a greenhouse gas.

▲ **Figure 1** This facility makes methane from waste.

How do you heat your home? Some central-heating systems burn methane gas. Methane comes from under the ground or sea. It was formed from tiny plants and animals that lived millions of years ago.

If you live in Poundbury, Dorset, your methane might come from another source. The facility in Figure 1 makes methane from food waste in just a few weeks.

What are fuels?

Methane is a fuel. A **fuel** is a material that burns to transfer energy by heating. Fuels include methane, petrol, diesel, hydrogen, and waste cooking oil.

> **A** A methane molecule has one atom of carbon joined to four atoms of hydrogen. Write its chemical formula.

What happens when fuels burn?

Fuels burn in chemical reactions. Burning is also called combustion. In a **combustion reaction**, a substance reacts with oxygen. Energy is transferred to the surroundings as heat and light.

Methane is a compound of carbon and hydrogen. Its chemical formula is CH_4. When methane burns, it reacts with oxygen from the air. The chemical reaction makes two products — carbon dioxide and water:

$$\text{methane} + \text{oxygen} \longrightarrow \text{carbon dioxide} + \text{water}$$

The particle diagram in Figure 2 represents this chemical reaction. It shows that one molecule of methane reacts with two molecules of oxygen to make one molecule of carbon dioxide and two molecules of water.

Link
You can learn more about climate change in C2 4.7 *Climate change.*

Key words
fuel, combustion reaction, fossil fuel, non-renewable, oxidation reaction

Reactivate your knowledge answers
1 Reacts to make 2 Right 3 For example, carbon dioxide

Chapter 3: Reactions

▲ **Figure 2** The reaction of methane and oxygen.

Petrol is a mixture of compounds made up of carbon and hydrogen atoms. Petrol makes mainly carbon dioxide and water when it burns in engines.

Petrol, diesel, and methane from under the ground or sea, are **fossil fuels**. They are **non-renewable**. They cannot be replaced once they have been used, so they will run out.

> **B** Name the products of the combustion reactions of petrol.

What are the alternatives to fossil fuels?

In a few years, factories will stop making cars fuelled by petrol and diesel. This is because the combustion of petrol and diesel makes carbon dioxide. Extra carbon dioxide in the air causes climate change.

Electric cars do not make carbon dioxide directly. They are starting to replace petrol and diesel cars.

Scientists and engineers are also developing hydrogen vehicles, like the bus in Figure 3. Some hydrogen vehicles burn hydrogen in their engines. This combustion reaction has one harmless product, water.

hydrogen + oxygen ⟶ water

But where does the hydrogen come from? Companies may make hydrogen from methane or water. Some of these processes make harmful waste products.

> **C** In one combustion reaction, hydrogen reacts with oxygen. The product is water. Write a word equation for the reaction.

What are oxidation reactions?

Combustion reactions are examples of **oxidation reactions**. An oxidation reaction is any reaction in which a substance reacts with oxygen.

▲ **Figure 3** This bus uses hydrogen fuel.

Summary Questions

1 Copy and complete the following sentences.

Any reaction in which a substance reacts with oxygen is an **oxidation/rusting** reaction. Oxidation reactions in which substances react quickly with oxygen and give out heat and light are **combustion/rusting** reactions. In the combustion reaction of methane, the products are water and **nitrogen monoxide/carbon dioxide**. (3 marks)

2 Diesel contains compounds of carbon and hydrogen. Predict **two** products of its combustion. (2 marks)

3 Petrol is a mixture of compounds. One compound in the mixture is octane. The combustion reaction of octane makes carbon dioxide and water. Write a word equation for this reaction. (3 marks)

117

3.4 Decomposition reactions

Learning objectives
After this topic, you will be able to:
- state the meaning of decomposition reaction
- write word equations for decomposition reactions
- from data in a table, identify the substance that starts to decompose first.

Reactivate your knowledge
1. What do reactant and product mean?
2. What is a compound?
3. What is a combustion reaction?

▲ **Figure 1** This person has blond hair.

The person in Figure 1 has blond hair. What made it blond?

A hairdresser put hydrogen peroxide in her hair. Hydrogen peroxide is a compound. Its molecules have atoms of two elements: hydrogen and oxygen. Its formula is H_2O_2.

You cannot bleach hair with old hydrogen peroxide. This is because hydrogen peroxide molecules break up over time. When this happens there are two products – water and oxygen.

$$\text{hydrogen peroxide} \longrightarrow \text{water} + \text{oxygen}$$

The particle diagram in Figure 2 represents this reaction. The number of atoms of each element in the reactants is the same as the number of atoms of each element in the products.

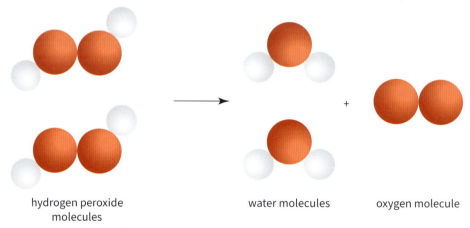

hydrogen peroxide molecules　　water molecules　　oxygen molecule

▲ **Figure 2** Two molecules of hydrogen peroxide break down, making two molecules of water and one molecule of oxygen.

The reaction in Figure 2 is a **decomposition** reaction. In a decomposition reaction, one compound breaks down into two or more products. The products may be elements or compounds.

A Describe how Figure 2 shows how the atoms rearrange and join together differently when hydrogen peroxide decomposes.

Key words
decomposition, thermal decomposition, discrete

Reactivate your knowledge answers
1. Reactant – the starting substances in a chemical reaction; product – the substances that are made in a chemical reaction.
2. A substance made up of the atoms of two or more elements, with the atoms joined together strongly.
3. A reaction with oxygen in which energy is transferred as heat and light.

C1 Chapter 3: Reactions

Thermal decomposition reactions

Copper carbonate is a green compound. It is made up of atoms of three elements – copper, carbon, and oxygen.

If you heat copper carbonate in a test tube, it breaks down. The reaction makes copper oxide and carbon dioxide. Copper oxide is black and remains in the test tube. Carbon dioxide forms as a gas.

copper carbonate → copper oxide + carbon dioxide

You can show that the gas is carbon dioxide by bubbling it through limewater. The limewater goes cloudy, which you can see in Figure 3.

Other carbonates decompose on heating:

lead carbonate → lead oxide + carbon dioxide

zinc carbonate → zinc oxide + carbon dioxide

When a substance breaks down when heated, the reaction is a **thermal decomposition** reaction. All decomposition reactions start with just one reactant.

> **B** Predict the products of the thermal decomposition reaction of aluminium carbonate.

Comparing reactions

Sara compares thermal decomposition reactions. She heats different carbonates in the apparatus in Figure 4. She measures the time before the limewater starts to look milky.

Sara recorded her results in Table 1.

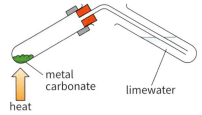
▲ Figure 4 Sara's apparatus.

Compound	Time for limewater to look cloudy in minutes
copper carbonate	0.5
zinc carbonate	2.5
lead carbonate	1.0

▲ Table 1 Sara's results.

Sara decides to present her results on a bar chart. This is because the variable she changes is **discrete**. A discrete variable is described by words, or by numbers that can only have certain values, like shoe sizes.

> **C** State which substance in the table starts to decompose first.

▲ Figure 3 Limewater goes cloudy when you bubble carbon dioxide through it.

Summary Questions

1 Copy and complete the following sentences.

In a decomposition reaction, **a compound/an element** breaks down to make two or more **reactants/products**. On heating, copper carbonate decomposes to carbon dioxide and **carbon/copper** oxide. You can use **limewater/a splint** to test for the gas. (4 marks)

2 When heated, magnesium nitrate decomposes to make magnesium oxide, nitrogen dioxide, and oxygen. Predict the products of the thermal decomposition reaction of calcium nitrate. (3 marks)

3 Look at the four reactions below.

A calcium + oxygen
→ calcium oxide

B zinc carbonate
→ zinc oxide + carbon dioxide

C sodium hydrogencarbonate
→ sodium carbonate + carbon dioxide + water

D aluminium + iodine
→ aluminium iodide

Give the letters of the **two** decomposition reactions. Explain your choices. (3 marks)

115

3.5 Using ratios

Learning objectives

After this topic you will be able to:
- show information using ratios
- simplify ratios
- use ratios to calculate values.

Reactivate your knowledge

1. How many carbon and oxygen atoms are in one carbon dioxide molecule, CO_2?
2. What is a combustion (burning) reaction?
3. What happens to the atoms in a chemical reaction?

Figure 1 shows Zac's pets. He has two dogs and three cats. You can show this information with a ratio. A *ratio* is a way of comparing values. The ratio of the number of dogs to the number of cats is 2:3. In a ratio, the order of the numbers is important. For the ratio of dogs to cats, write the number of dogs first.

▲ **Figure 1** Zac's pets.

A What is the ratio of the number of cats to the number of dogs?

Ratios are useful in science. For example:

- A carbon dioxide molecule (Figure 2) has one carbon atom and two oxygen atoms. Its formula is CO_2. The ratio of carbon atoms to oxygen atoms in carbon dioxide is 1:2.
- In carbon monoxide (Figure 3) the ratio of carbon atoms to oxygen atoms is 1:1.

Simplifying ratios

Amal has three apples and six strawberries, shown in Figure 4.

carbon dioxide

▲ **Figure 2** A carbon dioxide molecule.

carbon monoxide

▲ **Figure 3** A carbon monoxide molecule.

Key word

ratio

▲ **Figure 4** Three apples and six strawberries.

Reactivate your knowledge answers
1. 1 carbon atom, 2 oxygen 2. A reaction in which a substance reacts with oxygen, and energy is transferred to the surroundings as heat and light 3. They are rearranged and join together differently.

The ratio of apples to strawberries is 3:6. You can simplify the ratio by dividing both numbers in the ratio by the smaller number:

3 ÷ 3 = 1   6 ÷ 3 = 2

The simplified ratio is 1:2. This means that, for every one apple, there are two strawberries.

It is useful to simplify ratios in science. The formula of glucose sugar is $C_6H_{12}O_6$. The ratio of carbon atoms to hydrogen atoms to oxygen atoms is 6:12:6. In short:

C:H:O = 6:12:6

You can simplify the ratio by dividing all the numbers in the ratio by the smallest number:

6 ÷ 6 = 1   12 ÷ 6 = 2   6 ÷ 6 = 1

The simplified ratio is 1:2:1. This means that, for every one carbon atom, there are two hydrogen atoms and one oxygen atom.

> **B** Vinegar contains ethanoic acid, formula $C_2H_4O_2$. Give the ratio of carbon to hydrogen to oxygen atoms. Then simplify the ratio.

Calculating values with ratios

The flower in Figure 5 has five petals. You can write this as a ratio:

number of flowers : number of petals = 1:5

You can use this ratio to calculate the number of petals in different numbers of flowers:

number of petals in 100 flowers = 100 × 5 = 500

> **C** Calculate the number of petals in seven flowers.

Ratio calculations are useful in science. When burnt, one methane molecule reacts with two oxygen molecules (Figure 6). The ratio of methane molecules to oxygen molecules is 1:2.

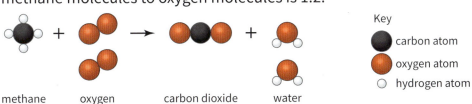

methane   oxygen   carbon dioxide   water

Key
● carbon atom
● oxygen atom
○ hydrogen atom

▲ **Figure 6** Burning methane.

You can use this ratio to calculate the number of oxygen molecules needed to burn different numbers of methane molecules. For example, the number of oxygen molecules involved in burning five methane molecules = 5 × 2 = 10.

C1 Chapter 3: Reactions

▲ **Figure 5** This flower has five petals.

Summary Questions

1 Write the definition of ratio. (1 mark)

2 Nat has three sheep and nine hens.
a Write the ratio for the number of sheep to the number of hens. (1 mark)
b Simplify the ratio you wrote in **a**. (1 mark)

3 In a camping stove, one propane molecule reacts with five oxygen molecules when it burns.
a Write the ratio for the number of propane molecules to the number of oxygen molecules. (1 mark)
b Calculate the number of oxygen molecules used to burn three propane molecules. (1 mark)

117

3.6 Conservation of mass

Learning objectives
After this topic, you will be able to:
- explain why mass is conserved in a chemical reaction
- calculate the masses in a chemical reaction
- describe what a balanced formula equation shows.

Reactivate your knowledge
1. What is mass?
2. What happens to the atoms in a chemical reaction?
3. What are physical changes?

Figure 1 shows a campfire. What happens when wood burns?

Wood is a mixture of many substances. When burnt, the substances react with oxygen. The reactions make many products, including ash and carbon dioxide. The total mass of wood and oxygen at the start is equal to the mass of ash and all the other products at the end.

mass of wood + mass of oxygen = total mass of all products

In any chemical reaction, atoms rearrange and join together differently. No atoms are added, and no atoms are removed. The number and mass of each type of atom does not change. This explains why – in every chemical reaction – the total mass of reactants is equal to the total mass of products. This is called **conservation of mass**. Mass is also conserved in physical changes, such as dissolving and melting.

▲ **Figure 1** When wood burns, its substances react with oxygen.

A Explain why mass is conserved in chemical reactions.

Calculating masses

Tariq and Sam have some magnesium. They find its mass. They burn the magnesium in the apparatus in Figure 2. They find the mass of the product.

mass of magnesium = 0.24 g
mass of product = 0.40 g

▲ **Figure 2** Investigating burning magnesium.

They wonder why the mass appears to have increased. The word equation helps them to work out the answer.

magnesium + oxygen ⟶ magnesium oxide
0.24 g   0.40 g

Magnesium has reacted with oxygen gas from the air. The oxygen has its own mass. The total mass of magnesium and oxygen at the start of the reaction is equal to the mass of magnesium oxide made.

Key words
conservation of mass, balanced formula equation

Reactivate your knowledge answers
1. The amount of matter in an object. 2. They are rearranged and join together differently. 3. Changes that do not make new substances.

Tariq and Sam calculate the mass of the oxygen that reacted:

total mass of reactants = total mass of products
0.24 g + mass of oxygen = 0.40 g
mass of oxygen = 0.40 g − 0.24 g
mass of oxygen = 0.16 g

B Calculate the total mass of magnesium and oxygen at the start of the students' reaction. Show your working.

Writing balanced equations

Word equations show the reactants and products in chemical reactions. **Balanced formula equations** give extra information:

- The formulae of the reactants and products
- The ratios of the amounts of reactants and products.

A balanced formula equation shows the atoms in the reactants and products, and how they are rearranged.

Follow the steps shown in the example below to write balanced formula equations for chemical reactions.

- First, write a word equation:

magnesium + oxygen ⟶ magnesium oxide

- Write the chemical formula for each reactant and product. You cannot guess these.

Mg + O_2 ⟶ MgO

Now balance the equation. There must be the same number of atoms of each element on each side of the equation.

- Balance the amounts of oxygen. There are two atoms on the left of the arrow, and one on the right. Write a big 2 to the left of the MgO. Do not add or change any little numbers:

Mg + O_2 ⟶ 2MgO

The big 2 applies to both Mg and O in magnesium oxide. It doubles the number of magnesium atoms and the number of oxygen atoms.

- Now balance the amounts of magnesium. The partly balanced equation above shows one magnesium atom on the left of the arrow, and two on the right. Write a big 2 to the left of the Mg.

2Mg + O_2 ⟶ 2MgO

The equation is balanced. It shows two atoms of magnesium in both the reactants and products. It also shows two atoms of oxygen in both the reactants and the products.

C1 Chapter 3: Reactions

Link

You can learn more about word equations in C1 3.2 *Word equations*. You can learn more about ratios in C1 3.5 *Using ratios*.

Masses

12 g of carbon reacts with 32 g of oxygen. There is one product, carbon dioxide. Calculate the mass of carbon dioxide made.

Summary Questions

1 Copy and complete the following sentences. Choose from these words:

products, conservation, rearranged, removed

In chemical reactions, the atoms are _____ and join together differently. Atoms are not added or _____ . This means that the total mass of reactants is equal to the total mass of _____ . This is called _____ of mass.

(4 marks)

2 Kezi heats 12.5 g of zinc carbonate. It decomposes to make 8.1 g of zinc oxide and some carbon dioxide. Calculate the mass of carbon dioxide.

(2 marks)

3 Copper carbonate ($CuCO_3$) decomposes to make copper oxide (CuO) and carbon dioxide (CO_2). Write a balanced equation for the reaction.

(3 marks)

3.7 Exothermic and endothermic

Learning objectives
After this topic, you will be able to:
- describe the energy changes in exothermic and endothermic changes
- predict whether a given change is exothermic or endothermic
- identify endothermic and exothermic changes from temperature data.

Reactivate your knowledge
1. What are combustion reactions?
2. What are decomposition reactions?
3. What are the before and after states for these changes: melting, boiling, freezing, condensing?

Key words
endothermic change, exothermic change

Have you ever used a cold pack on an injury (Figure 1)? How did the pack get cold?

▲ **Figure 1** A cold pack on an injury.

One type of cold pack has two substances. An outer bag contains liquid water. An inner bag contains solid ammonium nitrate. When you break the inner bag, the water and the solid mix. The solid dissolves in the water, and the mixture cools.

The warm injured body part transfers energy to the cold mixture. The injury cools and feels better. The mixture in the bag slowly warms to the temperature of the surroundings.

What is an endothermic change?

The process in the cold pack is an **endothermic change**. In an endothermic change, energy is transferred *from* the surroundings to the substances that are reacting, changing state, or dissolving.

Endothermic changes include:
- Some chemical reactions, for example thermal decomposition
- Melting and boiling
- Dissolving some substances in water.

Temperature Change
Some water has a temperature of 20 °C. A substance dissolves in the water, and the temperature increases to 36 °C. Calculate the temperature change.

Reactivate your knowledge answers
1 A reaction in which a substance reacts with oxygen, and energy is transferred as heat and light. 2 A reaction in which one compound breaks down into two or more products. 3 Melting – solid to liquid; boiling – liquid to gas; freezing – liquid to solid; condensing – gas to liquid.

C1 Chapter 3: Reactions

Marcus has some citric acid crystals. Their temperature is 20 °C. He adds sodium hydrogen carbonate powder. There is a chemical reaction. The reacting mixture feels cold. Its temperature goes down to 10 °C. The temperature decrease shows that it is an endothermic reaction. Figure 2 shows this reaction.

When the reaction is complete, Marcus leaves the mixture of products in the lab. After a while its temperature returns to 20 °C.

A Give two changes of state that are endothermic.

What is an exothermic change?

Some changes are exothermic. In an **exothermic change**, energy is transferred *to* the surroundings from the substances that are reacting, changing state, or dissolving.

Exothermic changes include:

- Some chemical reactions, for example combustion (Figure 3)
- Freezing and condensing
- Dissolving some substances in water.

B Give one type of physical change that may be endothermic or exothermic, depending on the substance.

Zoe has some dilute sulfuric acid and some sodium hydroxide solution. The temperature of both solutions is 20 °C. Zoe mixes them. There is a chemical reaction. She measures the temperature again. It is 30 °C. The temperature increase shows that it is an exothermic reaction.

When the reaction is complete, Zoe leaves the mixture of products in the lab. After a while its temperature returns to 20 °C.

C Explain how the arrows in Figure 3 show that combustion is an exothermic change.

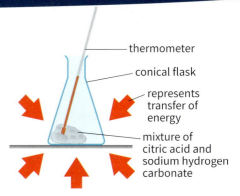

▲ **Figure 2** The reaction of sodium hydrogen carbonate with citric acid is endothermic. Energy is transferred *from* the surroundings.

▲ **Figure 3** Combustion reactions are exothermic. Energy is transferred *to* the surroundings.

Summary Questions

1 Copy and complete the following sentences.

All chemical reactions involve **colour/energy** transfers. An endothermic change transfers energy **to/from** the surroundings. The temperature of the substances **decreases/increases** at first. An exothermic change transfers energy **to/from** the surroundings. The temperature of the substances **decreases/increases** at first.
(5 marks)

2 Adam dissolves calcium chloride in some water. He finds that the water is hotter after the calcium chloride has dissolved. Explain whether this reaction is exothermic or endothermic.
(2 marks)

3 Predict whether each of these changes is exothermic or endothermic.

  a The thermal decomposition of copper carbonate.
  b Carbon dioxide subliming.
  c Making toast.   (3 marks)

121

Chapter 3 Summary

In this chapter you have learnt about chemical reactions. You have discovered how atoms rearrange and join together differently to make new substances, and why the total mass of substances in a chemical reaction does not change. You have learnt to write word equations, to classify chemical reactions, and use patterns to make predictions.

You have seen that chemical reactions are vital. They make substances used in medicines, fabrics, phones, and everything else. You have seen that we use the energy transferred in chemical reactions to keep us warm, or to travel from place to place.

Metacognition and self-reflection task

To learn about different types of the same thing, it is helpful to make comparisons. To compare oxidation reactions and decomposition reactions, draw two overlapping circles. Label one circle 'oxidation' and the other 'decomposition'. In the overlap, list things that are true for both types of chemical reaction. In the other part of each circle, list things that are true for oxidation or decomposition reactions only. Repeat the process to compare *chemical reactions* and *physical changes*.

Journey through C1

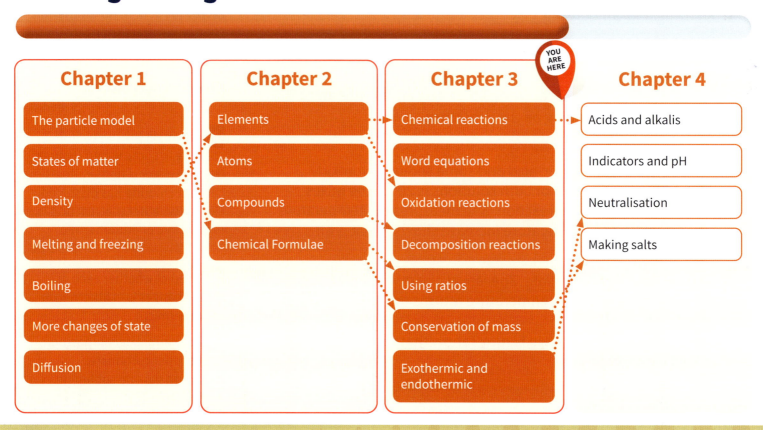

Chapter 3 Summary Questions

1 Izzy heats some magnesium in a Bunsen burner. It burns with a bright flame. A white ash forms.

a Describe **two** observations that show this is a chemical reaction. (2 marks)
b State what happens to the atoms in a chemical reaction. (1 mark)
(3 marks)

2 Marcus plans an investigation to find out which fuel makes water hotter, ethanol, or propanol. Marcus burns each fuel in turn to heat water. He measures how hot the water gets.

a State whether the burning reactions are exothermic or endothermic. Explain your decision. (2 marks)
b Name the independent variable in the investigation. (1 mark)
c Name **two** variables that Marcus must keep the same. (2 marks)
d Explain why he must keep these variables the same. (1 mark)
(6 marks)

3 Sze-Kie heats some calcium carbonate in a test tube. There is a chemical reaction:

calcium carbonate → calcium oxide + carbon dioxide

a State what type of reaction the word equation shows. Choose from the list below. (1 mark)
  • combustion
  • oxidation
  • thermal decomposition
  • exothermic
b Name the product(s) of the reaction. (1 mark)
c Sze-Kie started with 100 g of calcium carbonate. At the end of the reaction, there was 56 g of calcium oxide in the test tube. Calculate the mass of carbon dioxide made. Show your working. (2 marks)
(4 marks)

4 Burning methane is a chemical reaction. Here are some ways of representing this reaction.

Equation X
methane + oxygen → carbon dioxide + water

Equation Y
$CH_4 + 2O_2 \rightarrow CO_2 + 2H_2O$

Diagram Z

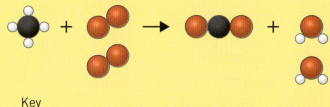

Key
● carbon atom ● oxygen atom ○ hydrogen atom

a Explain how Equation X, Equation Y, and Diagram Z all show that burning methane is a chemical reaction. (2 marks)
b Compare the advantages and disadvantages of representing the reaction with Equation X, Equation Y, and Diagram Z. (4 marks)
(6 marks)

4 Acids and alkalis

In this chapter you will learn about acids, bases, and alkalis. You'll also cover how to use indicators and the pH scale to find out how acidic or alkaline a solution is, and how to work safely with these solutions. Towards the end of the chapter, you'll learn about neutralisation reactions and how you can use these to make beautiful crystals.

Reactivate your knowledge

1 Describe what happens when you add sugar to water and stir.

2 State three things that are true of all chemical reactions.

3 Write a word equation to show the reaction of iron with sulfur to make iron sulfide.

You already know

Some materials dissolve in liquid to make a solution.

A substance can be obtained from its solution by evaporation.

Chemical reactions are changes that make new substances.

Word equations show chemical reactions simply.

 How to compare numbers using your maths skills.

 How to work scientifically to: manipulate apparatus in experiments.

Journey through C1

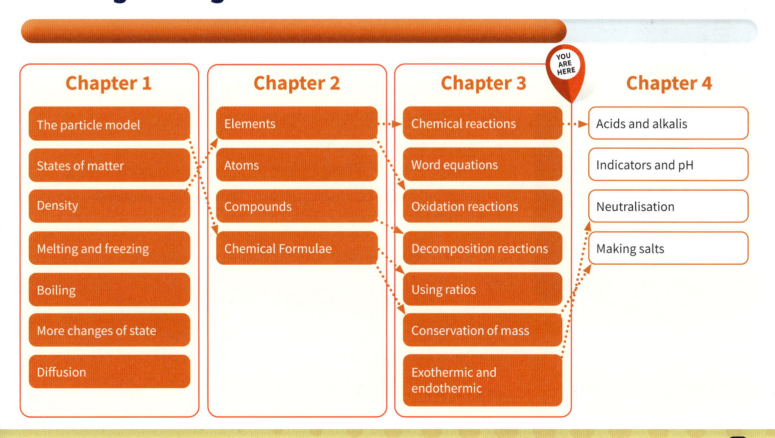

4.1 Acids and alkalis

Learning objectives
After this topic, you will be able to:
- describe the hazards of using acids and alkalis
- state how to control the risks of using acids and alkalis
- compare concentrated and dilute solutions.

Reactivate your knowledge
1. Describe the movement of particles in a liquid.
2. Describe how to protect your eyes during an experiment.
3. Name a food that is sour.

What do vomit, vinegar, and lemons have in common?

They all taste sour. This is because they contain acids. Vomit includes an **acid** from the stomach that helps digest foods. Vinegar contains ethanoic acid and lemons contain citric acid.

Alkalis are the chemical opposite of acids. Soap solutions and toothpaste are alkalis. Most alkalis feel soapy. You must never taste or touch solutions in the lab.

A Write the chemical names of two acids.

Using acids and alkalis safely

It is safe to eat the acid in lemons, and to use alkaline soap. But there are hazards linked to some acids and alkalis.

The bottle in Figure 1 has a hazard symbol. The symbol shows that the solution in the bottle is **corrosive**. It could burn your skin and eyes.

You can control risks from corrosive solutions by:
- wearing eye protection
- keeping the solution off your skin.

If a solution is very corrosive, a teacher might wear protective gloves when using it.

B Describe two hazards of using a corrosive solution.

▲ **Figure 1** This solution is corrosive.

Concentrated or dilute?

Pure ethanoic acid causes severe burns. It catches fire easily. Vinegar contains ethanoic acid. It is safe to eat, and does not catch fire. Why is there a difference? Pure ethanoic acid contains no water. Dissolving in water changes some properties.

Reactivate your knowledge answers
1. Move from place to place, sliding over each other 2. Wear eye protection 3. Any sour food, for example, lemons

C1 Chapter 4: Acids and alkalis

The amount of water makes a difference, too. Both the bottles in Figure 2 contain hydrochloric acid. Hydrochloric acid is a solution of hydrogen chloride in water.

▲ **Figure 2** Two bottles of acid.

- The acid in bottle A has 370 g of hydrogen chloride in 1 litre of solution.
- The acid in bottle B has 3.70 g of hydrogen chloride in 1 litre of solution.

Acid A has more hydrogen chloride per litre than acid B. Acid A is **concentrated**. Acid B is **dilute**. The concentrated acid burns skin and eyes. The dilute acid hurts if it gets into a cut, and might make your skin slightly red, but has no other hazards.

Figure 3 shows some particles in concentrated and dilute solutions of the same acid.

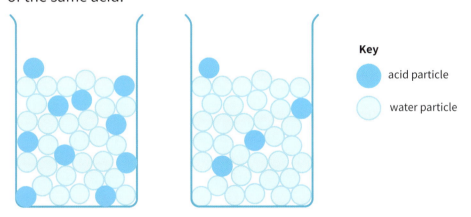

▲ **Figure 3** The acid on the left is more concentrated. It has more acid particles per litre. *Particles not to scale*.

An alkali may also be concentrated or dilute. The hazards of using acids and alkalis depend on:

- the acid or alkali you are using
- whether the solution is concentrated or dilute.

> **C** Describe one difference between a concentrated solution of an acid and a dilute solution of the same acid.

Safe handling

A teacher has a solution of an alkali. The solution is corrosive – it causes severe burns to skin and eyes. Describe how to control the risks from these hazards. Do you think the teacher should allow your class to use the alkali? Explain your decision.

Key words

acid, alkali, corrosive, concentrated, dilute

Summary Questions

1 Copy and complete the following sentences.

Acids **taste sour/feel soapy**. Some acid and alkali solutions are **corrosive/correlated**. A concentrated acid is **more/less** corrosive than a dilute acid. A concentrated acid has **fewer/more** acid particles per litre than a dilute acid. (4 marks)

2 Acids can be hazardous.

a Describe **two** hazards of using the acid in Figure 1. (2 marks)

b Describe how to control the risks from these hazards. (2 marks)

3 Calculate which is the more concentrated alkali:

- alkali X (20 g of alkali in 250 cm^3 of water)
- alkali Y (10 g of the same alkali in 500 cm^3 of water) Show your working. (2 marks)

127

4.2 Indicators and pH

Learning objectives

After this topic, you will be able to:
- determine whether a solution is acidic or alkaline, given its colour in indicator
- identify acids, alkalis, and neutral solutions on the pH scale
- use universal indicator to measure pH.

Reactivate your knowledge

1. Give one property of an acid.
2. Which has the greater number of alkali particles per litre – a concentrated or dilute solution?
3. How can you control the risks of using a corrosive solution?

A student has two beakers. One contains an acid and the other contains an alkali. How can they find out which is which?

You can use an **indicator** to find out whether a solution is acidic or alkaline. An indicator contains a dye. The dye turns a different colour in acidic and alkaline solutions.

Which plants make good indicators?

You can make indicators from plants. Table 1 gives the colours of juices from three plants in acidic and alkaline solutions.

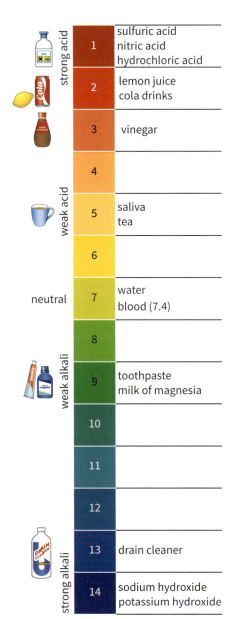

▲ **Figure 2** Universal indicator changes colour depending on the pH.

Juice extracted from…	Colour in dilute hydrochloric acid	Colour in dilute sodium hydroxide (an alkali)
red cabbage	red	yellow/green
hibiscus flower	dark pink/red	dark green
beetroot	red/purple	yellow

▲ **Table 1** The colours of some plant indicators in acidic and alkaline solutions.

A A student adds beetroot juice to an alkaline solution. Predict the colour of the mixture.

At school, you might use **litmus** indicator. Litmus is a solution of dyes from lichens. Paper can be soaked in litmus solution to make litmus paper.

- Red litmus turns blue in alkaline solutions.
- Blue litmus turns red in acidic solutions (Figure 1).

▲ **Figure 1** Using litmus paper.

Reactivate your knowledge answers
1 Tastes sour (but you must never taste or touch solutions in the lab) 2 Concentrated 3 Wear eye protection/do not touch

C1 Chapter 4: Acids and alkalis

B A student adds a solution to litmus paper. There is a colour change from red to blue. State whether the solution is acidic or alkaline.

How acidic? How alkaline?

Which is more acidic, vinegar, or stomach acid? How can you find out? You cannot use blue litmus paper. Both acids would make it red.

Instead, you need **universal indicator**. Universal indicator is a mixture of dyes. It changes colour to show how acidic or alkaline a solution is. Figure 2 shows these colours.

What is the pH scale?

The **pH scale** is a measure of how acidic or alkaline a solution is. On the pH scale:

- An acid has a pH of less than 7. The lower the pH, the more acidic the solution.
- An alkaline solution has a pH of more than 7. The higher the pH, the more alkaline the solution.

Some solutions are **neutral**. This means they are neither acidic nor alkaline. The pH of a neutral solution is exactly 7.

Universal indicator is a different colour at each pH. The scale in Figure 2 shows the colours of universal indicator in solutions of different pH.

C Look at Figure 2. Name two useful things that are acidic, and two that are alkaline.

Acidity

Amie collected the data in Table 2. Use the data to list the names of the solutions in order of increasing acidity, starting with the least acidic.

Solution	pH
milk	6.6
urine	6.1
orange juice	3.2
black coffee	5.5
lemon juice	2.3
vinegar	2.8

▲ **Table 2** The pH values of six solutions.

Key words

indicator, litmus, universal indicator, pH scale, neutral

Summary Questions

1 Copy and complete the following sentences.

Adding an acid to red litmus paper makes the litmus paper go **red/blue**. On the pH scale, acids have a pH of **less/more** than 7. The higher the pH, the **more/less** acidic the solution. A solution is alkaline if its pH is **more/less** than 7. A neutral solution is of pH **7/0**. (5 marks)

2 Universal indicator gives the pH of a solution.

a A student adds universal indicator to solution X. The resulting mixture is purple. State whether solution X is acidic, alkaline, or neutral. (1 mark)

b A solution has a pH of 4. Is the solution acidic, alkaline, or neutral? (1 mark)

3 John has a solution. It turns yellow when he adds juice. Predict the colour of the solution if he added hibiscus flower juice. Explain your answer. (2 marks)

129

4.3 Neutralisation

Learning objectives

After this topic, you will be able to:
- state the meanings of base and alkali
- describe how pH changes in neutralisation reactions
- give examples of useful neutralisation reactions.

Reactivate your knowledge

1. What is a chemical reaction?
2. What is an indicator?
3. What is the pH of a neutral solution?

Link

You can remind yourself about chemical reactions in C3.1 *Chemical reactions*.

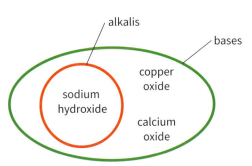

▲ **Figure 1** Alkalis are bases that dissolve in water.

Key words

neutralisation, base, alkali

Volume of sodium hydroxide added in cm³	pH
0	1
1	2
2	2
3	2
4	3
5	4
6	5
7	7

▲ **Table 1** Gwil's data.

Have you ever had stomach ache? Did you take an indigestion tablet?

Extra stomach acid makes your stomach hurt. If you take an indigestion tablet, there is a chemical reaction in your stomach. The chemical reaction removes the excess stomach acid, making new substances as it does so.

The chemical reaction of stomach acid with an indigestion tablet is an example of a **neutralisation** reaction. In a neutralisation reaction, an acid reacts with a substance that cancels it out. The pH gets closer to 7.

Which substances neutralise acids?

A **base** is a substance that neutralises an acid. Look at Figure 1 – bases include sodium hydroxide, calcium oxide, and copper oxide. Some bases dissolve in water. A base that dissolves is an **alkali**.

A Describe one difference between a base and an alkali.

pH changes in neutralisation reactions

Gwil has 10 cm³ of acid. He adds universal indicator. He compares the colour of the mixture to the indicator colour chart. The pH is 1. He writes this result in Table 1.

Gwil adds 1 cm³ of sodium hydroxide solution to the acid. The pH increases. Gwil writes the new pH in the table. He continues to add sodium hydroxide solution. The pH gets closer to 7. The alkali is neutralising the acid. Gwil stops adding alkali when the pH is 7. The mixture is neutral.

B Look at the data in Table 1. Describe how the pH changes in the neutralisation reaction.

Reactivate your knowledge answers

1 A change in which atoms rearrange and join together differently to make new substances 2 A dye that is a different colour in acid and alkaline solutions 3 7

C1 Chapter 4: Acids and alkalis

How is neutralisation useful?

Soil for crops

Some soils are more acidic than others. Every plant has a favourite soil pH. Some are shown in Table 2.

Anchali lives in Thailand. She has a farm and wants to grow tea. She tests the soil. Its pH is 4.5. The soil is too acidic to grow tea.

▲ Figure 2 Tea plants grow best in soil of pH 5.0 to 6.0.

Plant	Soil pH range that the plant grows best in
apple tree	5.0–6.8
cabbage	6.0–7.0
onion	6.0–6.5
tea	5.0–6.0
tomato	5.5–7.0

▲ Table 2 Different plants grow best in soils of different pH.

Anchali adds a base to the soil. The base neutralises some of the acid in the soil. The soil pH increases to pH 5.0. It is now suitable for growing tea.

Acidic lakes

In some places, gases from burning coal make sulfur dioxide gas. The gas dissolves in rainwater to make acid rain. The rain falls in lakes, making them more acidic. Some water animals and plants cannot live in these lakes.

Environmental organisations may add bases to acid lakes, as in Figure 3. The pH of the lake water increases.

▲ Figure 3 Adding a base to an acidic lake.

C Describe two situations in which neutralisation reactions are useful.

Data logger details

Ralph has a solution. He adds acid to the solution. A pH probe measures the pH. The probe is attached to a data logger, which sends the data to a computer. The computer draws a graph of the data. Describe in detail what the graph shows.

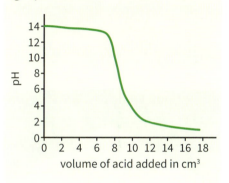

Summary Questions

1 Copy and complete the following sentences.

A base is a substance that neutralises an _____ . A base that dissolves in water is called an _____ . An alkaline solution has a pH that is greater than _____ . (3 marks)

2 Yana has an alkaline solution. Its pH is 14. She adds acid to make a neutral solution. Describe how the pH changes. (2 marks)

3 Explain **one** use of a neutralisation reaction. (2 marks)

4.4 Making salts

Learning objectives
After this topic, you will be able to:
- state the meaning of salt in chemistry
- predict the salt that forms when an acid reacts with a metal or base
- describe how to make a given salt from an acid and a metal or insoluble base.

Reactivate your knowledge
1. What is the chemical symbol of hydrogen?
2. Is the pH of an acid below or above 7?
3. Give the names of two acids.

Key word

salt

▲ Figure 1 Sodium chloride.

▲ Figure 2 Copper sulfate.

▲ Figure 3 Bolivian salt flats.

Here are the formulae of three acids. What do they have in common?

- HCl – hydrochloric acid
- HNO_3 – nitric acid
- H_2SO_4 – sulfuric acid

The formulae show that the acids are compounds. They all include hydrogen atoms.

What are salts?

A **salt** is a compound that forms when an acid reacts with a metal element or compound. The hydrogen atoms of the acid are replaced by atoms of the metal element. Figures 1 and 2 show two salts.

Sodium chloride is the salt you may add to food. Its formula is NaCl. A sodium atom (chemical symbol Na) has replaced the hydrogen of hydrochloric acid.

Farmers use copper sulfate to kill fungus. Its formula is $CuSO_4$. Copper atoms (chemical symbol Cu) have replaced the hydrogen atoms of sulfuric acid.

A Write the definition for a salt.

Which reactions make salts?

Many salts exist naturally. Sodium chloride makes the sea salty. It also exists underground. Figure 3 shows the salt flats of Bolivia. These contain huge amounts of salts.

You can also make salts in chemical reactions.

Reactivate your knowledge answers
1 H 2 below 3 for example: hydrochloric acid, sulfuric acid

Acids and metals

The chemical reaction of an acid with a metal makes two products – a salt, and hydrogen. For example:

- Magnesium reacts with hydrochloric acid to make magnesium chloride (a salt) and hydrogen:

magnesium + hydrochloric acid ⟶ magnesium chloride + hydrogen

- Zinc reacts with sulfuric acid to make zinc sulfate (a salt) and hydrogen:

zinc + sulfuric acid ⟶ zinc sulfate + hydrogen

> **B** Predict the name of the salt made when zinc reacts with hydrochloric acid.

Acids and bases

Reacting an acid with a base also makes a salt. The products are a salt, and water. For example:

sodium hydroxide + hydrochloric acid ⟶ sodium chloride + water

copper oxide + nitric acid ⟶ copper nitrate + water

> **C** Predict the name of the salt made when sodium hydroxide reacts with nitric acid.

How can you make salt crystals?

The reactions of acids with metals or bases make salt solutions. Removing water makes salt crystals. Figure 4 shows how to make copper sulfate crystals.

Summary Questions

1 Copy and complete the following sentences.

A salt is **an element/a compound**. In a salt, the **hydrogen/oxygen** atoms of an acid are replaced by metal atoms. (2 marks)

2 Predict the name of the salt made when magnesium reacts with sulfuric acid. (1 mark)

3 Predict the name of the salt made when potassium hydroxide reacts with hydrochloric acid. (2 marks)

4 Describe the steps in making copper chloride crystals from a base and an acid. Include the names of the acid and the base. (6 marks)

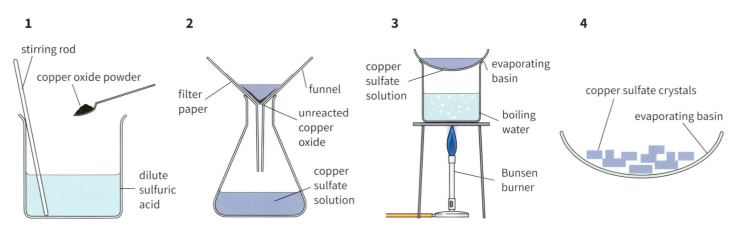

▲ **Figure 4** Steps for making copper sulfate crystals.

4 Chapter 4 Summary

In this chapter you learnt about acids, bases, and alkalis. You studied how to use indicators and the pH scale to find out how acidic or alkaline a solution is, and how to work safely with these solutions. Lastly, you learnt about neutralisation reactions and how to use these to make crystals.

You found out about the vital role of acids in your stomach. You also discovered how environmental scientists use bases to neutralise unwanted acids in soils and lakes.

Metacognition and self-reflection task

You can use flow diagrams to summarise the steps in processes. Make a flow diagram to show the main steps in these processes: using universal indicator to find the pH of a solution; using an acid to neutralise an alkaline solution; making copper sulfate crystals from copper oxide powder and sulfuric acid.

Journey through C1

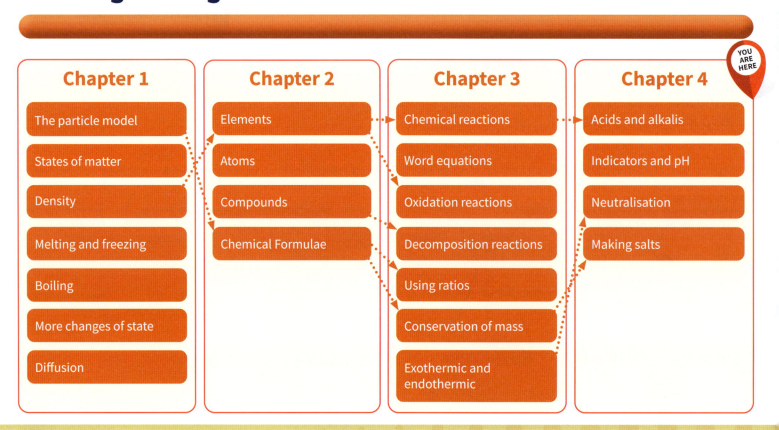

134

Chapter 4 Summary Questions

1 Give the definitions of the following key words.

a acid (1 mark)
b base (1 mark)
c alkali (1 mark)
d neutralisation (1 mark)
(4 marks)

2 A scientist measures the pH of samples of sweat, blood, and urine from one person. Copy the table. Write down whether each sample is acidic, alkaline, or neutral.

Name of mixture	pH	Acidic, alkaline, or neutral?
sweat	5.3	
blood	7.4	
urine	6.8	

(3 marks)

3 Joe wants to make a red-cabbage indicator. He has the apparatus below.

a First, Joe heats a mixture of chopped red cabbage and water. Write the letter of the best apparatus for this. (1 mark)
b Next, Joe filters the mixture. He keeps the solution. Write the letters of the best two pieces of apparatus for this. (2 marks)
c Lastly, Joe adds the red-cabbage solution to acidic and alkaline solutions. Write the letter of the best apparatus for this. (1 mark)
(4 marks)

4 Look at Figure 1. The darker blue circles represent alkali particles, and the light blue circles represent water particles.

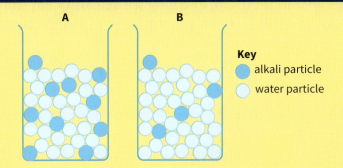

▲ **Figure 1** Particles in two alkaline solutions.

a Give the letter of the more concentrated alkaline solution. (1 mark)
b Explain your decision in question (a). (1 mark)
(2 marks)

5 The table below gives the preferred soil pH of some fruit plants.

Fruit plant	Preferred soil pH
blueberry	1.0–5.0
sweet cherry	6.0–7.5
cranberry	4.2–5.0
pineapple	5.0–6.0
strawberry	5.0–6.5

a Name the plant in the table that can grow well in alkaline soil. (1 mark)
b Name the plant in the table that can grow in the most acidic soil. (1 mark)
c The soil pH in Andy's garden is 6.0. Name three fruit plants that might grow well in this soil. (3 marks)
d The soil pH in Clare's garden is 8.0. She wants to grow strawberry plants. State the type of substance she should add to the soil so that the pH is suitable. Explain your answer. (2 marks)
(7 marks)

6 Describe and explain the stages in making magnesium chloride crystals from an acid and a metal. Include the names of the acid and the metal. (6 marks)

Welcome

Physics is the study of the physical world. You will find out about forces and where they come from, and how they explain motion. You will learn about light and sound and ways we model them, and why we see and hear things as we do. You will learn about our place in the Universe.

1 Physics

Physics and you

Physics affects you every day, even while you are asleep. It's how you interact with objects in the world, like your bed. It's how we design objects to make our lives easier, cleaner, and faster. It's how transport works, so we can get to school or to other countries. It's why music sounds the way it does and how we can see inside the human body without surgery. It's how the objects in sports work, from football to skiing. Studying physics will help you to understand how things work in the world and how you can make a difference.

Did you know that even though we have only looked at about 3% of the sky we've already discovered thousands of planets, some of which are like Earth? Are aliens using their telescopes to observe us?

Scientists use ideas about light to make sense of observations, and ideas about forces to send probes to planets, moons, comets, asteroids, and out beyond our Solar System.

Gravity is pulling everything in the Universe together but we also know that the Universe is expanding faster than it should. What will happen to it in the future?

We still don't know what most of the Universe is made of. There are lots of questions in physics that we still need to answer.

Physics and the world

From microphones and lightbulbs to Wi-Fi and mobiles, lots of technology relies on physics. We also use it in medical technology to look after and repair our bodies. If you learn to drive when you're older, understanding how cars speed up, slow down, and change direction can help keep you safe. Physics lets us launch rockets to take people to the Moon, robots to Mars, and spacecraft beyond the Solar System.

BIG QUESTIONS

How do we know what's in the Universe?
We build models of the Solar System and the Universe from observations we make using telescopes in space and on Earth.

Why is the sky blue?
Sunlight is a mixture of different colours. They get scattered in different ways when the sunlight arrives in our atmosphere. The blue light gets scattered more than the other colours so the sky looks blue most of the time.

What is the ultimate speed limit?
Light travels at 186 000 miles per second. That's 300 000 kilometers per second. There is nothing faster than light!

Journey through P1

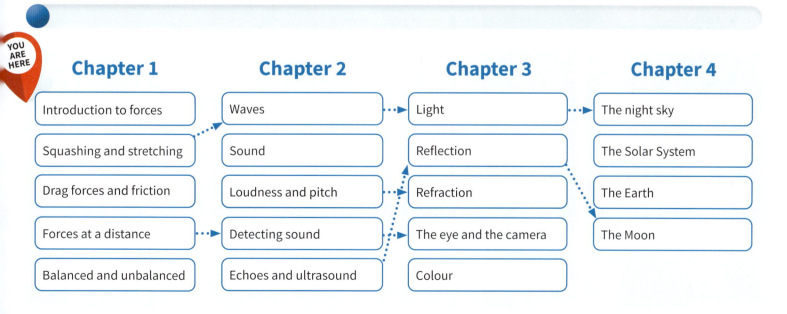

1 Forces

In this chapter you will learn about different types of forces and where they come from. You will find out about contact forces and non-contact forces, and how you know forces are there. You will also learn to explain the motion of objects using forces.

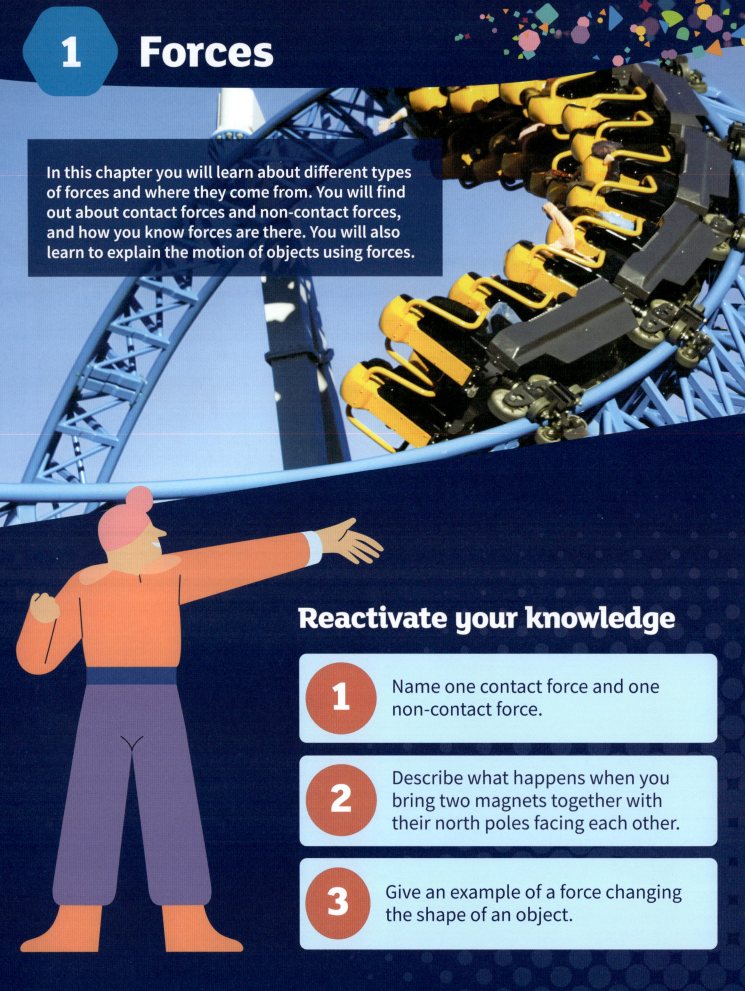

Reactivate your knowledge

1. Name one contact force and one non-contact force.

2. Describe what happens when you bring two magnets together with their north poles facing each other.

3. Give an example of a force changing the shape of an object.

You already know

- Forces can change the shape of objects.
- Some forces act at a distance, but other forces act while objects are in contact.
- Magnets repel or attract each other, and some types of metal.
- Forces affect the motion of objects.
- How to multiply numbers.
- How to work scientifically to: make repeat measurements in an investigation and plot simple graphs.

Journey through P1

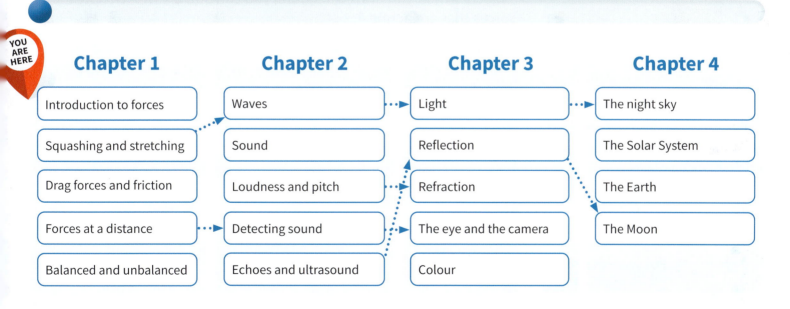

Chapter 1
- Introduction to forces
- Squashing and stretching
- Drag forces and friction
- Forces at a distance
- Balanced and unbalanced

Chapter 2
- Waves
- Sound
- Loudness and pitch
- Detecting sound
- Echoes and ultrasound

Chapter 3
- Light
- Reflection
- Refraction
- The eye and the camera
- Colour

Chapter 4
- The night sky
- The Solar System
- The Earth
- The Moon

139

1.1 Introduction to forces

Learning objectives
After this topic, you will be able to:
- explain what forces, do and how they are represented
- compare different types of forces
- describe how to measure forces and give the unit of force.

Reactivate your knowledge
1 What two things can a force be?
2 Name a force that needs contact.
3 Name a force that does not need contact.

You may think you have nothing in common with a rocket, but both you and a rocket are affected by forces. Forces act on all objects, no matter how big or small they are.

What do forces do?

The rocket in Figure 1 is going to Mars. It moves away from the surface of the Earth very quickly. There is a force pushing the rocket up and a force pulling it down. A force can be a **push** or a **pull**.

Forces explain why objects move the way they do, or why they don't move — but that's not all. Forces can also change the direction that an object is moving in, or change its shape.

How do you describe forces?

You can't see forces, but you can see the effects they have on objects. When you draw a diagram, you can add arrows to show the forces that are acting.

You do this using 'force arrows'. These show the direction and the size of the force. Forces act on objects, so the arrow must touch the object in the diagram, like in Figure 2.

▲ **Figure 1** This rocket took the Perseverance rover to Mars.

a a ball falling

force exerted by the Earth on the ball (due to gravity)

b a ball resting on a table

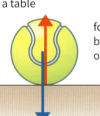

force exerted by the table on the ball

force exerted by the Earth on the ball (due to gravity)

▲ **Figure 2** The force arrows show the forces acting on a tennis ball.

A Draw a force diagram of you sitting on a table and label the force arrows.

Link
You can learn more about non-contact forces in P1 1.4 *Forces at a distance*.

Reactivate your knowledge answers
1 Push, pull 2 Air resistance/water resistance/friction 3 Gravity/magnetism

P1 Chapter 1: Forces

What are the different types of force?

Some forces act when you are touching something. These are called **contact forces**. **Friction** and **air resistance** are contact forces. Support forces, like upthrust, are also contact forces.

The force of **gravity** acts on a tennis ball travelling through the air. The Earth pulls the ball down even though it is not touching it. Gravity is a **non-contact force**. The force between magnets is another non-contact force.

> **B** Name two contact forces acting on you when you are swimming.

What is an interaction pair?

Forces always come in pairs, called **interaction pairs**. In Figure 3:

- Gravity pulls the child down. This is the force of the *Earth* on the *child*.
- The child pulls the Earth up. This is the force of the *child* on the *Earth*.

There is another interaction pair of forces acting on the child.

- The bar supports the child. This is the force of the *bar* on the *child*.
- The child pulls on the bar. This is the force of the *child* on the *bar*.

> **C** During a rocket's takeoff, the Earth exerts a force on it. Describe the other force in this interaction pair.

How do you measure forces?

You can measure force with a **newtonmeter** (sometimes called a spring balance), shown in Figure 4. All forces are measured in **newtons (N)**.

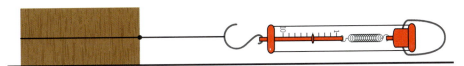

▲ **Figure 4** A student is pulling the block with a force of 5 N.

Key words

push, pull, contact force, friction, air resistance, gravity, non-contact force, interaction pair, newtonmeter, newton (N)

▲ **Figure 3** Forces act on the child hanging from the bar.

Summary Questions

1 Copy and complete the following sentences.

You can sort forces into _____ and _____-_____ forces. We can show the forces acting on an object using force _____. Forces come in pairs, called _____ pairs. To measure force, you use a _____. Force is measured in _____. (6 marks)

2 Describe the forces in **one** of the interaction pairs acting on an apple hanging from the branch of a tree. (2 marks)

3 You are probably sitting on a chair as you read this.

Explain why the two forces that are acting on you are *not* in the same interaction pair. (4 marks)

141

1.2 Squashing and stretching

Learning objectives
After this topic, you will be able to:
- describe how forces deform objects
- explain how solid surfaces provide a support force
- use Hooke's Law.

Reactivate your knowledge
1. What are the four ways you can apply forces to a solid?
2. How do you change the length of a spring?
3. What happens to a mattress when you lie on it?

Why don't you fall through the chair you're sitting on? The chair changes shape when you sit on it. This produces the force that pushes you up.

How do forces affect solid objects?

When a golf club hits a golf ball, like in Figure 1, the ball changes shape, or **deforms**. Forces can **compress** (squash), **stretch**, twist, or bend objects. When you apply forces to an object, you can deform it. Even solid objects can change shape.

▲ **Figure 1** Even a solid golf ball is deformed when it is hit hard enough.

> **A** Suggest what happens to the strings of a tennis racquet when you hit a tennis ball.

How can the floor push you up?

The floor pushes up on you when you stand on it. It seems strange to talk about the floor exerting a force on you because you can't see anything happening.

The model of a solid, shown in Figure 2, can help to explain what is happening. In this model, the particles are held together with springlike bonds. You will use a different version of this model when you talk about solids in chemistry.

Link
You can learn more about particles in solids, liquids, and gases in C1 1.1 *The particle model*.

How long?
You have a spring that is 4 cm long. When you exert a force of 3 N on it, it stretches to a length of 6 cm.

What is the extension?

Key words
deform, compress, stretch, reaction, normal, extension, tension, elastic limit, Hooke's law, linear

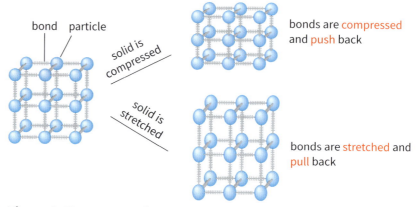

▲ **Figure 2** Two or more forces on a solid compress or stretch it.

Reactivate your knowledge answers
1 Bending/stretching/squashing/twisting 2 Stretch it or compress it/apply forces to each end 3 It squashes/changes shape

P1 **Chapter 1:** Forces

Solid materials, like a chair or the floor, are only compressed a very small amount when you apply a force to them. The support force from a chair or the floor is called the **reaction** force or the **normal** force.

> **B** Compare the compression of the floor when you stand on it with the compression of your bed when you lie on it.

What happens when objects stretch?

Bungee cords, as shown in Figure 3, springs, and even lift cables all stretch when you apply a force to them. The amount that they stretch is called the **extension**.

A bungee cord stretches as the jumper falls. When the bungee cord has stretched as far as it will go, it pulls them back up. This force is called **tension**.

> **C** Compare tension and compression in terms of the directions that the forces act in.

What happens when you stretch a spring?

Springs are special. If you double the stretching force acting on a spring the extension will double as well. This is **Hooke's Law**. You can use the length of the spring to measure the size of a force. When you remove the force, the spring goes back to its original length.

At some point the spring will *not* go back to its original length when you remove the force. This point is called the spring's **elastic limit**.

Not all objects behave like a spring when you stretch them. If you double the force on an elastic band the extension may *not* double. Figure 4 shows graphs for a spring and polythene.

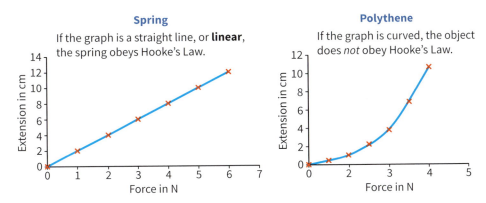

▲ **Figure 4** A graph of extension against force shows whether the object obeys Hooke's Law.

▲ **Figure 3** The shape of a bungee cord changes when you stretch it

Summary Questions

1 Copy and complete the following sentences.

When objects deform, their _____ changes. In a model of a solid we can say solids are made of _____ connected by spring-like bonds. The bonds _____ back on you when you compress them. This produces a force called the _____ force. Springs obey _____ Law. If you double the force, the extension _____.
(6 marks)

2 Describe how your chair pushes you up. (2 marks)

3 Look at the straight-line graph in Figure 4. Find the extension when the force applied is 3 N and when it is 6 N.

Does this spring obey Hooke's Law? Explain your answer.
(2 marks)

143

1.3 Drag forces and friction

Learning objectives
After this topic, you will be able to:
- describe the effects of drag forces and friction
- explain how drag forces and friction arise
- describe how drag forces and friction can be reduced.

Reactivate your knowledge
1. What is the force that affects objects moving through air?
2. What is the force that affects objects moving through water?
3. What does friction do to moving objects?

Slide your finger along the desk. Does the surface feel smooth or rough? Even really smooth surfaces apply a force, allowing things to move across them.

What is friction?

Surfaces like a metal slide in a playground look and feel really smooth. However, if you look closely, they are actually rough, as you can see in Figure 1.

When a book is resting on the table, you can push on it, but it may not move. **Friction** grips objects and makes it more difficult to move them. As you increase the force by pushing harder, the book will start to move. If you remove the force the book slows down and stops. The force of friction also slows down moving objects.

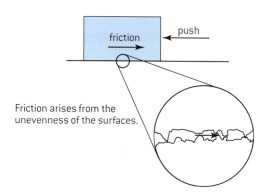

Friction arises from the unevenness of the surfaces.

▲ **Figure 1** Even an object that seems smooth can be uneven close up. This can cause friction.

A Compare the friction on a slide with the friction on the road.

Is friction useful?

Friction can be a good thing. You need friction to walk, as the friction between your foot and the road produces the force needed to move you forward. The brakes on your bike and in a car work because of friction.

How can you reduce friction?

One way to reduce friction is by using oil or grease. This is called **lubrication**. When you oil the chain of your bike, the surfaces move past each other more easily. Snowboarders wax their boards to reduce the friction between their board and the snow.

B Suggest why the hinges of a door need to be lubricated.

Key words
friction, lubrication, water resistance, air resistance, drag force, streamlined

Reactivate your knowledge answers
1 Air resistance 2 Water resistance 3 It slows them down

P1 Chapter 1: Forces

What are drag forces?

A dolphin swimming through the water and a surfer paddling through the water will both experience **water resistance** as shown in Figure 2.

▲ **Figure 2** When you move through water you experience water resistance.

As a snowboarder jumps through the air, she will experience **air resistance**. Water resistance and air resistance are **drag forces**. If you think about the particles in the air and in the water you can explain drag forces, as shown in Figure 3. Figure 3 shows how particles in air and water cause drag.

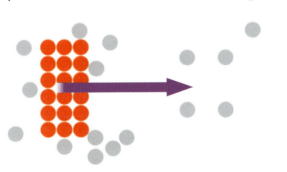
A solid moves through a gas.

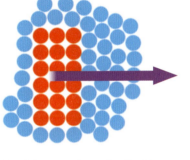
A solid moves through a liquid.

▲ **Figure 3** A moving object is in contact with air or water particles.

As an object moves through air or water, the particles are pushed out of the way. This produces a drag force, which slows it down.

C Name the drag force acting on an aeroplane in flight.

Are drag forces useful?

Parachutes are used to slow down drag-racing cars and skydivers. The contact between the parachute and the air produces a drag force.

How can you reduce drag forces?

Olympic cyclists will tuck their arms in close to their body as they cycle. They will even make sure that their thumbs are as close to the handlebars as possible. This makes them more **streamlined**, which reduces the force of air resistance.

Testing a parachute

A company wants to compare different materials they could use to make parachutes. Name three ways that they could make it a fair test.

Summary Questions

1 Copy and complete the following sentences.

The force of **air resistance/ friction** acts between two touching solid surfaces that are sliding across each other. When the surfaces are **rough/smooth** they will grip each other. There are two drag forces: **air resistance/gravity**, and **magnetism/water resistance**. Drag forces are produced when objects push **bonds/particles** out of the way. (5 marks)

2 Explain why you do not lubricate the brakes on a bicycle. (2 marks)

3 Explain why diving birds pull their wings in when they are about to enter the water. (3 marks)

145

1.4 Forces at a distance

Learning objectives
After this topic, you will be able to:
- describe the effects of fields
- describe the difference between weight and mass
- calculate weight.

Reactivate your knowledge
1. What do unsupported objects do?
2. What is the force that acts on falling objects?
3. Is gravity a contact or non-contact force?

▲ **Figure 1** A magnet picks up metal filings, and a balloon rubbed on a jumper can attract a baby's hair.

Link
You can learn more about electrostatic forces in P2 1.1 *Charging up*.

If you let go of your pen and it moved upwards, you'd be very surprised. We are so familiar with the force of gravity that sometimes we don't even think of it as a force.

Which forces act 'at a distance'?

A gravitational force acts on your pen when you hold it up and let it go. Gravity is a non-contact force, and it is always attractive. There are other types of non-contact force.

Magnets exert a **magnetic force** on magnetic materials or other magnets without touching them. If you rub a balloon, you can pick up bits of paper with it or make your hair stand on end, like in Figure 1. This is an electric or **electrostatic force**. Magnetic and electrostatic forces are non-contact forces that can be attractive or repulsive.

> **A** Compare the force of gravity acting on you when you lie in bed and when you sit on a chair.

What is a field?

In physics, a **field** is a special region in which something experiences a force. In a magnetic field, magnetic things experience a force. In a gravitational field, things with mass experience a force.

Gravitational, magnetic, and electrostatic fields have something in common. As you get further away from the mass, magnet, or charge, the field gets weaker.

Contact forces only act when objects are touching each other. Non-contact forces act at any distance, if the objects are touching or if they are *not* touching.

> **B** Explain how you know that there is a gravitational field around you.

Reactivate your knowledge answers
1 Fall/move towards the Earth 2 Gravity 3 Non-contact

P1 Chapter 1: Forces

What do I weigh?

You can use a newtonmeter to find the **weight** of an apple. The Earth pulls the apple downwards. Measuring the weight of the apple means measuring the force of the Earth on it.

What is the difference between weight and mass?

Weight is a force, so it is measured in newtons (N). **Mass** is the amount of 'stuff' something is made up of, and is a measure of how hard it is to get something to move. Mass is measured in **kilograms (kg)**. One way to measure weight is shown in Figure 2.

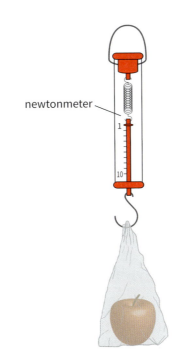

▲ **Figure 2** An apple has a weight of about 1 N.

You can calculate weight using an equation.

weight (N) = mass (kg) × **gravitational field strength**, g (N/kg)

On Earth, the gravitational field strength is about 10 N/kg. This means that the force acting on one kilogram is 10 N. If your mass is 50 kg, for example, then your weight on Earth is:

weight = 50 kg × 10 N/kg
= 500 N

Gravitational field strength is different on other planets and stars. Your weight would be different on different planets because g would be different.

The Apollo astronauts could jump much higher on the Moon because g on the Moon is about one sixth of g on Earth.

What would happen to my weight in space?

Imagine blasting off from the Earth in a spacecraft. As you move away from the Earth its gravitational field gets weaker. If you stood on scales in the spacecraft, the reading would be less than it would be on Earth. Eventually the scale would read zero, but the amount of 'you' would not change — your mass stays the same. It is the force of the Earth on you, your weight, that gets smaller.

C Compare your mass on the Earth with your mass on the Moon.

Units of mass

Smaller masses are measured in grams (g). There are 1000 g in 1 kilogram (kg).

Convert these masses into grams: **a** 2 kg **b** 3.5 kg **c** 0.4 kg

Convert these masses into kilograms: **d** 4700 g **e** 250 g

Key words

magnetic force, electrostatic force, field, weight, mass, kilogram (kg), gravitational field strength

Summary Questions

1 Copy and complete the following sentences.

The force of gravity acts on things that have _____. Rubbing a balloon causes it to exert an _____ force. You can feel a _____ force between two magnets. Your weight is a _____ and is measured in _____. Your _____ is the amount of stuff you are made up of and is measured in _____.
(7 marks)

2 Give **one** reason why your weight on Jupiter is 2.5 times your weight on Earth. (1 mark)

3 Use the information on this page to:

a calculate the mass of an apple (2 marks)

b calculate the weight of the same apple on the Moon.

147

1.5 Balanced and unbalanced

Learning objectives
After this topic, you will be able to:
- describe the difference between balanced and unbalanced forces
- explain why objects are in equilibrium
- explain the changing motion of objects.

Reactivate your knowledge
1. What can a force do to a moving object?
2. What is the effect of air resistance on a falling object?
3. What is the natural object in orbit around the Earth?

Key words
balanced, equilibrium, unbalanced, driving force, resistive force

When you wake up in the morning, you need a force to get you out of bed and moving.

What are balanced forces?

When the forces acting on an object are the same size but act in opposite directions, we say that they are **balanced**. You can think of balanced forces as two teams in a tug of war. If each team pulls with the same force, the rope doesn't move because the forces cancel out. The object is in **equilibrium**.

A Name an object shown on these pages that is in equilibrium.

All stationary objects are in equilibrium. There has to be a support force acting on them to balance out their weight. The person in Figure 1 is in equilibrium when they lie in bed. The support force and their weight are balanced.

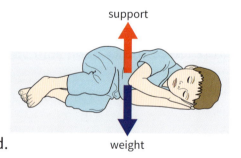

▲ **Figure 1** You are in equilibrium when lying down.

B Draw a diagram showing the forces acting on a stationary mass hanging on a spring.

Equal and opposite...?

Isaac Newton said 'For every action there is an equal and opposite reaction'. The forces in an interaction pair are equal and opposite. Is lying in bed an example of this law? No, it is not. Each of the forces acting on you comes from a *different* interaction pair.

What are unbalanced forces?

Figure 2 shows a rocket-powered car. The forces acting on it are **unbalanced** – they are not the same size, so they do not cancel out. The **driving force** from the engine is shown in blue. The **resistive forces** from air resistance and friction are shown in red.

C Describe a situation where the forces on your pen are unbalanced.

Reactivate your knowledge answers
1 Speed it up, slow it down, stop it 2 Slows it down 3 The Moon

P1 Chapter 1: Forces

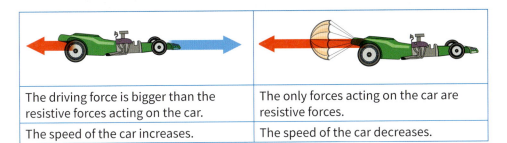

The driving force is bigger than the resistive forces acting on the car.	The only forces acting on the car are resistive forces.
The speed of the car increases.	The speed of the car decreases.

▲ **Figure 2** The car will change speed depending on what direction the unbalanced force is in.

How do unbalanced forces cause changes in speed?

When the car's rocket-powered engine starts moving, the driving force will become very big very quickly and the car will speed up. When the driver wants to stop, she will fire a parachute to slow the car down. In both cases the forces acting on the car are unbalanced.

The driver uses a parachute to slow the car down because it creates a much bigger resistive force than using the brakes alone. This means the car will slow down much faster and stop in a much shorter time.

How do unbalanced forces cause changes in direction?

Isaac Newton worked out that the Earth exerts a force on the Moon. The force of gravity acting on the Moon keeps the Moon in orbit around the Earth, as you can see in Figure 3. The force that keeps the Moon orbiting the Earth is the same force that acts on an apple and pulls it to the ground. It changes the direction of motion, but not the speed.

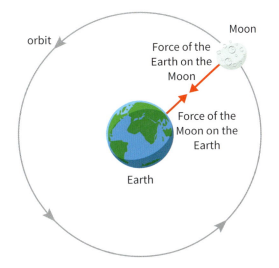

▲ **Figure 3** The force of gravity keeps the Moon in orbit around the Earth.

Just like the Moon orbiting the Earth, every time you go around a corner in a car the friction between the tyres and the road changes the direction of the car.

Summary Questions

1 Copy and complete the following sentences.

If the forces on an object are the same **direction/size** but act in opposite **directions/sizes** they are balanced. This is called **equilibrium/tension**. The forces acting on any stationary object are **balanced/unbalanced**. If the forces on an object are unbalanced the object's **mass/speed** will change. If the **driving/resistive** force is bigger than the **driving/resistive** force the object speeds up. If the **driving/resistive** force is bigger than the **driving/resistive** force the object slows down. (9 marks)

2 A cyclist is slowing down as she is cycling along a road.

  a Draw a diagram to show the forces acting on the cyclist. (2 marks)

  b Label the forces using the words 'resistive' and 'driving'. (2 marks)

  c Explain why her speed is decreasing. (1 mark)

3 Explain how the forces on an object can be unbalanced even though it is moving at a steady speed. (2 marks)

149

Chapter 1 Summary

In this chapter you have learnt that forces act when objects interact. Forces come in pairs. You have seen how to explain contact forces like drag forces, friction, and tension using particles. Non-contact forces such as gravity and magnetism are explained using fields. You have seen how balanced and unbalanced forces explain motion. If there is no unbalanced force an object's speed or direction of motion does not change. An unbalanced force produces acceleration or deceleration, or a change in direction.

Metacognition and self-reflection task

Mind maps help you to see the connections between different concepts. Write down all the key words on pieces of paper and make a mind map by organising them on a big piece of paper. Draw lines between them and write down the reason why they are connected next to the line. Are there more connections than you thought there would be? Are there any places that you couldn't find a connection? Try going back to the key words in the book to see if you can find one.

Journey through P1

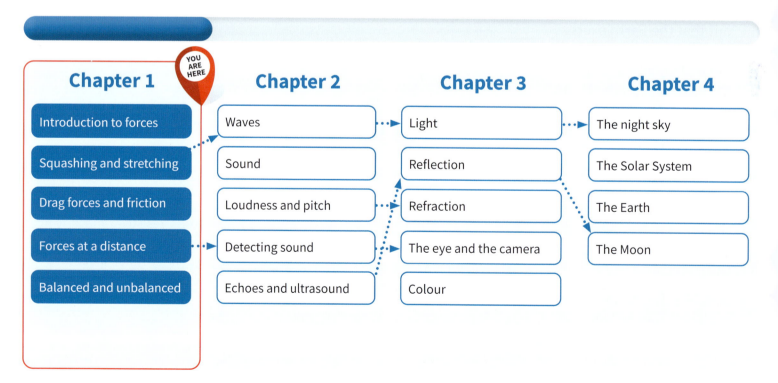

Chapter 1 Summary Questions

1 Sort these forces into contact forces and non-contact forces.

magnetic force   friction   air resistance
gravitational force   electrostatic force   upthrust
(2 marks)

2

a Match the words to the definitions.
Mass   force due to a planet or moon
Weight   region where object experiences a force
Field   amount of stuff
(2 marks)

b Identify which of the statements below is Hooke's Law.
  i The force on an object always makes it longer.
  ii If you double the force the extension doubles.
  iii If you double the force the extension halves.
(1 mark)
(**3 marks**)

3 For each object below state whether the forces on it are balanced or unbalanced.

a a boat that is speeding up. (1 mark)
b a boy who is floating in a swimming pool. (1 mark)
c a cyclist going around a roundabout at a steady speed. (1 mark)
(**3 marks**)

4 A student is investigating friction. They put a block of wood on a ramp and tilt the ramp until the block starts to move. They repeat the experiment using ramps with different types of surface.

a Name the independent variable and dependent variables. (2 marks)
b Name **one** control variable. (1 mark)
c Complete this conclusion for this experiment:
The smoother the surface of the ramp, the _____ the tilt before the block starts to move. (1 mark)
d Explain why the surface exerts a force on the block. (1 mark)
e Explain why the student should plot a bar chart when they have collected their results. (1 mark)
(**6 marks**)

5 Scientists are planning a mission to take astronauts to Mars. Suppose an astronaut has a mass of 65 kg on Earth. The gravitational field strength on Earth is 10 N/kg. On Mars it is 3.8 N/kg.

a Calculate her weight on Earth. (2 marks)
b Describe and explain what will happen to her weight and mass when she goes to Mars. (2 marks)
(**4 marks**)

6 A student has a spring that is 3 cm long. When they exert a force of 2 N the spring length changes to 4 cm.

a Calculate the extension. (1 mark)
b Calculate the extension when the force is doubled. (1 mark)
c Describe the law that you have used to answer part (b). (1 mark)
(**3 marks**)

7 A student wants to make a newtonmeter. He coils a piece of wire around his pencil to make a spring. He puts a 100 g mass on the spring. A 100 g mass has a weight of 1 N. He measures the extension.

a Describe how to measure the extension of a spring. (2 marks)
b Explain the difference between a mass of 100 g and a weight of 1 N. (2 marks)

The student measures the extension for different forces and plots his results on a graph. The line on the graph is a straight line.

c Use the shape of the graph to explain why the spring obeys Hooke's Law. (2 marks)
(**6 marks**)

8 Another student decides to use an elastic band as a newtonmeter and plots these results. She hangs masses on an elastic band and measures the extension. This is her graph.

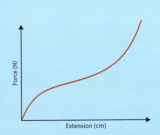

a Use the graph to explain why the elastic band cannot be used as a newtonmeter but a spring can. (3 marks)
b Describe how the graph would change if the experiment was done in a place where the gravitational field strength was lower. Explain your answer. (2 marks)
(**6 marks**)

2 Sound

In this chapter you will learn about sound. You will learn how it is produced, how it travels, and its speed. You will learn how the wave properties of sound explain how we hear, and some of the ways that we can use sound and ultrasound to help us in everyday life.

Reactivate your knowledge

1 Name two objects in your house that produce sound.

2 Name the part of the human body that detects sound.

3 Describe two ways that sounds made on a guitar can be different from each other.

You already know

Vibrating sources emit sound.

Sounds have pitch that can be high or low, and loudness that can be loud or soft.

Sound can travel through materials, like the air, water, and the ground.

 How to multiply numbers when calculating distance using echoes.

 How to work scientifically to: Measure how long it takes for an echo to travel a known distance.

Journey through P1

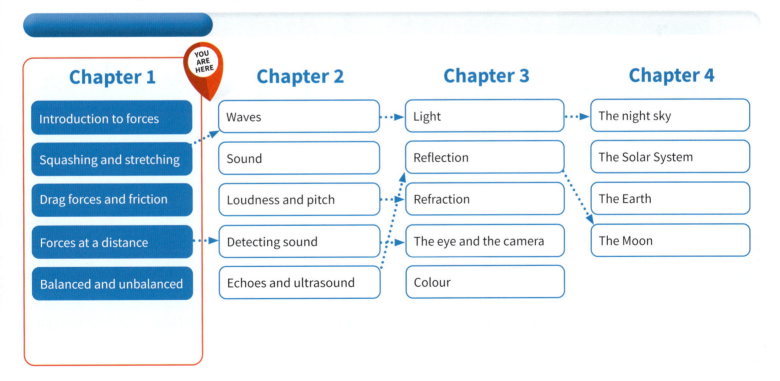

2.1 Waves

Learning objectives
After this topic, you will be able to:
- describe the properties of waves
- describe how waves are superposed and reflected.

Reactivate your knowledge
1. Where do you see waves?
2. What kinds of waves can you hear?
3. How can you make waves in a bath?

Key words
oscillation, vibration, energy, undulation, amplitude, frequency, wavelength, peak, crest, trough, transverse, longitudinal, compression, rarefaction, reflection, incident wave, reflected wave, superpose

What do the ripples across a pond and the sound of a guitar have in common? They are both waves. But what is a wave?

What is a wave?

In science, a wave is an **oscillation** or **vibration** that transfers **energy** or information. A wave can also be an **undulation** on the surface of water. Matter does not get transferred by waves. Waves have many uses. For example, microwaves cook food and sound waves help you communicate.

What are the features of a wave?

All waves have three important features: **amplitude**, **frequency**, and **wavelength**. These are shown in Figure 1.

Frequency is the number of waves that pass a particular point per second. Wavelength is the distance from one point on a wave to the same point on the next wave.

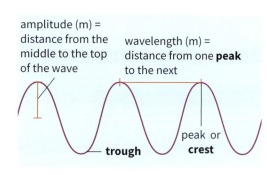

▲ **Figure 1** Features of a wave.

A Name two features of a wave you could measure with a ruler.

What are the two types of wave?

You can send pulses down a slinky spring in two different ways.

1. You can move your hand at right angles to the spring. This produces a **transverse** wave, as shown in Figure 2.

the oscillation is at 90° to the direction of energy transfer

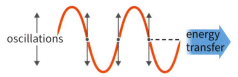

▲ **Figure 2** You can make a transverse wave on a slinky.

Reactivate your knowledge answers
1 Sea waves, people waving 2 Sound (waves) 3 By moving your hand up and down or side to side

154

P1 **Chapter 2:** Sound

2 You can also push and pull the spring. This produces a **longitudinal** wave, as shown in Figure 3. There are **compressions** and **rarefactions** in a longitudinal wave.

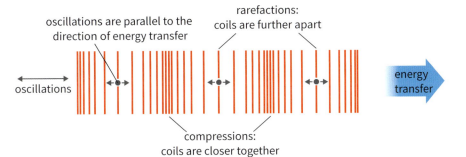

▲ **Figure 3** You can also make longitudinal waves on a slinky spring

Sound waves are longitudinal and light waves are transverse.

B Explain why waves you make in the bath are transverse.

What happens when waves hit a barrier?

Waves bounce off surfaces and barriers, just like a ball bounces off a wall. Figure 4 shows water waves bouncing off a barrier. This is called **reflection**.

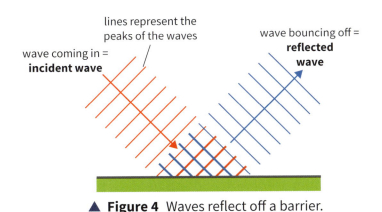

▲ **Figure 4** Waves reflect off a barrier.

C State the angle between the direction a wave is moving and a line from the middle of the wave to the top of a peak.

What happens when waves superpose?

When two waves are put together, they **superpose**. This means that they add up or cancel out. If the waves are in step, they will add together. You get a single wave with *more* height than you had before. If they are not in step, then they cancel each other out. The height of the single wave is *less* than you had before.

Spot the word

Write the word that matches to each of these definitions:
a the distance from the peak to the middle of a wave.
b where the links of a spring are squashed together.

Summary Questions

1 Copy and complete the following sentences.

A wave is an oscillation or vibration that transfers **energy/matter**. The distance from the centre of the wave to the top of the wave is called the **amplitude/wavelength**. The distance between one crest of a wave and the next crest is called the **amplitude/wavelength**. Waves can **reflect/superpose** when they hit a barrier. When two waves meet each other, they will **reflect/superpose**.
(5 marks)

2 Describe the difference between a compression and a rarefaction in a longitudinal wave on a spring. (2 marks)

3 A microwave oven has a turntable which rotates food through areas where microwaves superpose. Suggest what would happen if the turntable breaks. (2 marks)

155

2.2 Sound

Learning objectives
After this topic, you will be able to:
- describe how sound is produced and travels
- use the particle model to explain why the speed of sound is different in different materials.

Reactivate your knowledge
1. What type of wave is a sound wave?
2. What must an object do to produce a sound wave?
3. What can sound waves travel through?

If you very gently press the front of your throat while you are talking, you will feel a vibration. This is your vocal cords vibrating. These vibrations produce the sound waves that travel through the air from your mouth when you speak.

motion of air molecules   motion of sound wave

▲ **Figure 1** Sound is caused by vibrations, such as the vibrations at the ends of a tuning fork which move air molecules backwards and forwards.

What is a sound wave?

All speakers, including the ones inside headphones, have a part that moves backwards and forwards. This part vibrates or oscillates, which makes nearby air molecules move backwards and forwards. This vibration produces a sound wave as you can see in Figure 1. Some people think that sound just 'dies away'. It doesn't. It spreads out as it moves away from the source.

> **A** Name a household object that produces sound when it vibrates.

What does sound travel through?

Dolphins, shown in Figure 2, and whales use sound waves to communicate underwater. Elephants stamp their feet when a predator comes near them. This warning sound travels through the ground to other elephants. Sound needs a **medium** like a solid, liquid, or gas to travel through. It cannot travel through empty space (known as a **vacuum**), because there are no particles to vibrate.

How fast does sound travel?

The **speed of sound** in a medium depends on the arrangement of particles in that medium. Table 1 shows the speed of sound in different types of medium. The particle arrangements help us to explain the different speeds of sound. For example, the particles in a solid are very close together, so vibrations are passed along more quickly than in a gas.

▲ **Figure 2** Dolphins communicate underwater.

Reactivate your knowledge answers
1 Longitudinal 2 An object needs to vibrate 3 Solids, liquids, or gases

P1 **Chapter 2:** Sound

State	solid	liquid	gas
Particle arrangement			
Speed of sound (example)	5000 m/s in steel	1500 m/s in water	340 m/s in air

▲ **Table 1** The speed of sound in different types of medium.

B The speed of sound in a substance is 4000 m/s. Suggest whether the substance is a solid, liquid, or gas.

People sometimes talk about the 'sound barrier'. There is no difference between travelling at the speed of sound or faster than it. Chuck Yeager found this out in 1947, when he became the first human to travel faster than the speed of sound in an aircraft. Figure 3 shows Felix Baumgartner, who was the first person to travel faster than the speed of sound in free fall. He jumped from a balloon 24 miles above the surface of the Earth. There is very little air at that height.

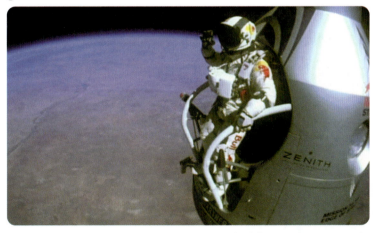

▲ **Figure 3** Felix Baumgartner travelled faster than sound.

C When Felix jumped, he accelerated very quickly. Suggest why this was the case.

Which is faster: sound or light?

Light travels much faster than sound. The **speed of light** is 300 000 000 m/s. This is almost one million times faster than sound. You can notice this difference during a thunderstorm. Thunder and lightning are produced at the same time. You see the lightning almost immediately, but it takes a longer time for the sound of thunder to reach you. Light can also travel through a vacuum. This is because it doesn't need a medium to travel through.

Link
You will learn about particles in C1 1.2 *States of matter*.

Key words
medium, vacuum, speed of sound, speed of light

Stormy night
A girl sees a flash of lightning and then hears the thunder four seconds later.
a How far away is the storm? State your answer in kilometres.
b What would she notice about the thunder and lightning when the storm is directly overhead?

Summary Questions

1 Copy and complete the following sentences.

Sound is produced by objects that _____ . This makes the air molecules _____ and produces a sound wave. Sound travels fastest in _____ and slowest in _____ . Sound cannot travel through a _____ . (5 marks)

2 Explain why sound travels slower in a gas than in a liquid. (2 marks)

3 Compare the amount of time it would take light to travel 10 metres from your teacher to your eye with the time it would take sound to travel the same distance. (3 marks)

157

2.3 Loudness and pitch

Learning objectives
After this topic, you will be able to:
- describe the link between loudness and amplitude of sound waves
- describe the link between the frequency and pitch of sound waves.

Reactivate your knowledge
1. What is the 'frequency' of a sound wave?
2. What is the 'amplitude' of a sound wave?
3. What is the pitch of a sound related to?

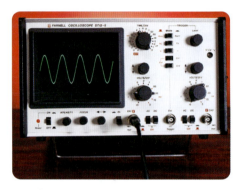

▲ **Figure 1** An oscilloscope shows a visual representation of a sound wave.

If you play a loud note of exactly the right pitch, even if it is not very loud, then you can shatter a glass. What's the difference between loudness and pitch?

Seeing sound

You can plug a **microphone** into an **oscilloscope**, like the one in Figure 1, to see what the sound of your voice looks like. The microphone produces an electrical signal that represents the sound wave. The wave that appears on the screen is transverse, but the sound waves you make when you talk are longitudinal.

What affects the loudness of a sound?

If a drummer hits a drum harder the sound is louder.

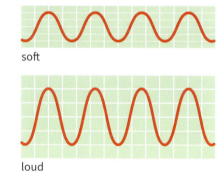

soft

loud

What protection?
Two companies make ear defenders. Plan an experiment to find out which pair is better at reducing sound intensity.

▲ **Figure 2** You can see on an oscilloscope that a loud sound has a larger amplitude than a soft sound.

You can bang a drum harder or pull harder on a guitar string to produce a louder sound. A loud sound has a larger amplitude than a soft sound. It also transfers more energy. To make a louder sound, you need to make the amplitude bigger.

Key words
microphone, oscilloscope, loudness, decibel, pitch, hertz, kilohertz

A Explain why the drawings of waves in Figure 2 do not show what a sound wave is actually like.

Reactivate your knowledge answers
1 The number of sound waves passing a particular point per second 2 The distance from the middle to the top or bottom of a sound wave 3 How fast the object making the sound is vibrating

P1 Chapter 2: Sound

How do you measure loudness?

Sounds made by volcanic eruptions are so loud that they can be heard thousands of miles away. Sound intensity determines **loudness** and is measured in **decibels** (dB). The decibel scale shown in Table 1 is not like a ruler. Each increase of 10 dB increases the intensity of sound by 10 times.

0 dB	20 dB	40 dB	60 dB	80 dB	100 dB	120 dB	140 dB
cannot be heard	leaves rustling	talking quietly	normal speech	heavy traffic	jet engine	causes pain	gun shot

▲ **Table 1** Some examples of sounds and their loudness in decibels.

A 40 dB sound is 100 times more intense than a 20 dB sound. The volcanic eruption of Krakatoa in 1883 produced a sound of 180 dB.

> **B** Using Table 1, suggest the loudness of a person shouting.

What affects the pitch of a sound?

Some singers can produce higher-pitched notes than others. The **pitch** of a note depends on the frequency of the sound wave. High-pitched sounds have a high frequency and low-pitched sounds have a low frequency. Frequency is measured in **hertz** (Hz) or **kilohertz** (kHz), and 1000 Hz = 1 kHz.

To make a higher-pitched sound you need to make something vibrate faster. Faster vibration means there are more waves per second. You can see the difference in frequency between a high-pitched and low-pitched sound in Figure 3.

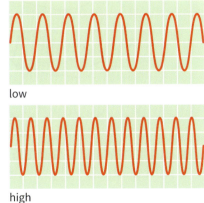

low

high

▲ **Figure 3** A high sound has a higher frequency than a low sound. A whistle produces a sound with a high frequency.

You can have a loud, high-pitched sound or a loud, low-pitched sound. Changing the frequency of a wave, such as sound, does not affect its amplitude.

> **C** Describe what happens to the wavelength of a wave as its frequency increases.

Link

You can learn more about ultrasound in P1 2.5 *Echoes and ultrasound*.

Summary Questions

1 Copy and complete the following sentences.

The loudness of a sound depends on the **amplitude/frequency** of the sound wave. The pitch of a sound depends on the **amplitude/frequency** of the sound wave. Frequency is measured in **decibels/hertz**. Loudness is measured in **decibels/hertz**. (4 marks)

2 A singer produces a soft, low note. Describe what their vocal chords would do to produce:

a a higher note.
b a louder note. (2 marks)

3 Compare the sound intensity of the eruption of Krakatoa with the sound intensity of a gun shot. (2 marks)

159

2.4 Detecting sound

Learning objectives
After this topic, you will be able to:
- describe how the ear works
- compare the range of human and animal hearing
- describe how a simple microphone works.

Reactivate your knowledge
1 Which types of medium can sound travel through?
2 How do particles in a medium move when a sound wave travels through it?
3 What does a sound with a high frequency sound like?

Key words
ear, pinna, auditory canal, eardrum, ossicle, amplify, oval window, cochlea, auditory nerve, semi-circular canal, outer ear, middle ear, inner ear, audible range, infrasound, ultrasound, microphone, diaphragm

Humans do not hear the same sounds as other animals. How does the ear detect sound, and what sounds can a dog hear that you cannot?

How do you hear?

The **ear** detects sound waves. The part of the ear that you can see is called the **pinna**. The different parts of the ear are shown in Figure 1 and Table 1.

Outer ear	Middle ear	Inner ear
pinna, auditory canal, eardrum	ossicles, oval window	cochlea, semi-circular canals

▲ Table 1 Parts of the ear.

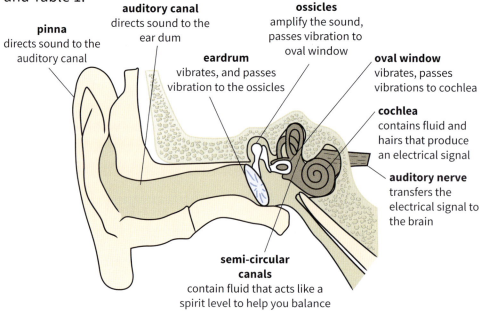

▲ Figure 1 The ear has lots of parts that help to convert sound into electrical signals that get interpreted by the brain.

As the fluid inside the cochlea moves, the hairs inside the cochlea also move. Specialised cells at the base of the hairs shown in Figure 2 convert this movement into electrical signals. When these signals reach the brain, they are turned into sounds.

▲ Figure 2 Without these tiny hairs inside your cochlea, you would not be able to hear.

A Name the first part of the ear to vibrate when a sound wave enters the ear.

Reactivate your knowledge answers
1 Solids, liquids, gases 2 Oscillate/vibrate backwards and forwards 3 High-pitched

What frequencies can you hear?

Most people can only hear a particular range of frequencies, called the **audible range**. You have the largest audible range when you are young: 20–20 000 Hz. Your audible range changes as you get older. You will find it more difficult to hear high-frequency sounds.

> **B** Write down your audible range in kilohertz (kHz).

What frequencies can other animals hear?

Bats, dogs, and goldfish all have completely different audible ranges to humans. These are shown in Table 2. Lots of animals can hear frequencies that are much higher than the frequencies we can hear.
- Frequencies below 20 Hz are called **infrasound**.
- Frequencies above 20 000 Hz are called **ultrasound**.

Animal	Range in Hz
Bat	3000–110 000
Dog	67–45 000
Goldfish	20–3000

▲ **Table 2** Different animals have different hearing ranges. Some can hear a larger range than humans!

How can you damage your hearing?

Your hearing can be damaged if a sharp object makes a hole in your eardrum. However, your eardrum will grow back. A build-up of ear wax can also be damaging. Very loud sounds or head injuries can permanently damage your hearing.

How does a microphone work?

Figure 3 shows what happens when a singer sings into a **microphone**. You can use an amplifier to make the sound louder.

Loudspeakers convert the electrical signals back into sound when they vibrate.

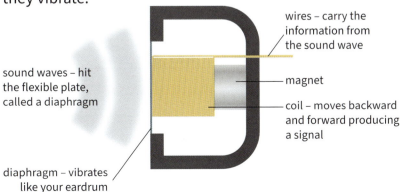

▲ **Figure 3** A microphone detects sound in a similar way to your ear.

Link

You can learn more about specialised cells in B1 1.3 *Specialised cells*.

Conversions

a Using Table 2, convert the audible range for dogs into kilohertz.

b Using Table 2, convert the audible range for goldfish into kilohertz.

Summary Questions

1 Copy and complete the following sentences.

When a sound wave enters your ear, it makes the _____ vibrate. This makes the _____ vibrate. The _____ vibrates and this makes the liquid inside your _____ vibrate. Cells at the base of the _____ produce an electrical signal that travels along your _____ to your brain. Your hearing can be _____ by loud sounds. In a microphone, a _____ vibrates, which produces electrical signals. (8 marks)

2 Compare the audible ranges of:

a a human and a goldfish

b a young human and an older human. (2 marks)

3 Give **two** similarities and two differences between the ear and a microphone. (4 marks)

2.5 Echoes and ultrasound

Learning objectives
After this topic, you will be able to:
- explain how echoes are used to find distance
- describe the uses of ultrasound
- compare sound and ultrasound.

Reactivate your knowledge
1. What happens to waves when they hit a barrier?
2. What is sound with a frequency higher than 20 000 Hz called?
3. How does the speed of sound in water compare with the speed of sound in air?

Key words
echo, transmitter, receiver, sonar

Where is the quietest place in the world? Scientists have designed a room so quiet that you can hear your own heartbeat (Figure 1). The surfaces are designed to absorb sounds. There are no echoes.

What is an echo?

When sound reflects off a surface it produces an **echo**. Sound takes time to travel. There is a time delay between making a sound and hearing an echo. Soft surfaces like curtains, or specially designed surfaces, can reduce echoes.

A Suggest one place where echoes might be a nuisance.

Measuring distances

Imagine someone is standing a long distance from a building as shown in Figure 2. They clap and hear an echo two seconds later. The time delay depends on the distance.

▲ Figure 1 These walls are designed to produce no echoes.

How deep?

A ship's sonar detects an echo 1.6 s after it sends the pulse. The speed of sound in water is 1500 m/s.
Work out how deep the water is.

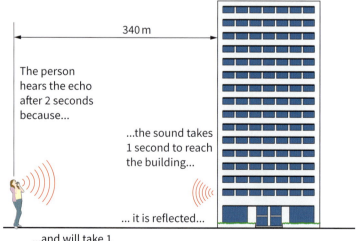

340 m

The person hears the echo after 2 seconds because…

…the sound takes 1 second to reach the building…

…it is reflected…

…and will take 1 second to get back

▲ Figure 2 A sound will bounce off objects nearby to make an echo. This can be used to measure the distance to those objects.

Reactivate your knowledge answers
1 They are reflected 2 Ultrasound 3 It is faster in water than in air

P1 Chapter 2: Sound

You can use the time taken to hear an echo to work out how far away objects are from the source of the sound.

> **B** Describe what happens to the time for an echo to be heard if the person moves closer to the building.

What are the uses of ultrasound?

Ultrasound is sound with a frequency above 20 000 Hz. An ultrasonic **transmitter** produces a beam of pulses of ultrasound. You can produce a narrow beam of ultrasound pulses more easily than a narrow beam of sound pulses.

When radiographers make images of unborn babies (Figure 3), a pulse of ultrasound travels through the body and reflects off the foetus. The ultrasonic **receiver** detects the echo. It uses the time taken for the echo to return to build up an image of the foetus.

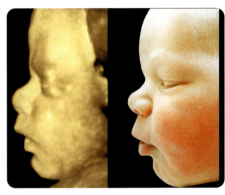

▲ **Figure 3** An ultrasound image (left) of a baby (right).

> **C** Suggest whether ultrasound travels faster in bone or tissue.

Physiotherapists can use ultrasound to reduce the pain and swelling of a damaged tendon. Doctors can use ultrasound to detect cancer. You can also use ultrasound to clean dirty objects.

Where is ultrasound used to measure distance?

Figure 4 shows ultrasound being used on ships at sea. This is called **sonar**. A transmitter under the ship sends out a beam of ultrasound pulses. These travel through the water and reflect off the seabed. A receiver detects the reflection and uses the time taken to work out the depth of the water.

Animals also use ultrasound. Bats and dolphins use ultrasound to find their prey. They use sound and ultrasound to communicate with each other.

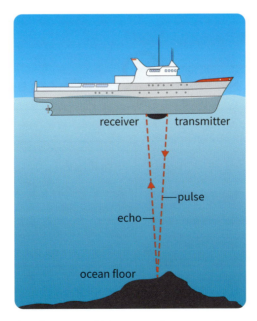

▲ **Figure 4** Ships use ultrasound to work out the depth of the ocean below them.

Summary Questions

1 Copy and complete the following sentences.

An echo is a _____ of sound. You can use the _____ between making a sound and hearing its echo to calculate the _____ to an object. Soft materials _____ sound and so reduce echoes. Some animals use ultrasound to locate their _____ and _____ . Ultrasound is used to make an _____ of a foetus. Sailors can also use ultrasound to find the _____ of the ocean.

(8 marks)

2 Describe how to use sound to calculate how far away a building is. (3 marks)

3 A fishing boat owner uses an ultrasonic transmitter and detector to find fish. The transmitter sends out pulses. Suggest why the captain might think the fish were below where they actually are. Explain your answer. (2 marks)

163

Chapter 2 Summary

In this chapter you have learnt about wave properties – that waves have a wavelength, a frequency, and an amplitude, and travel at different speeds. You saw that vibrating objects produce sound, which travels fastest in a solid because the particles are closer together than in a gas. Sound cannot travel through a vacuum. You learnt how the ear detects sound to produce a signal that is sent to the brain, and that a microphone does a similar thing. You saw how we can use the time of reflection of sound, or an echo, to measure distance, and that this is how ultrasound images are produced. Understanding how sound is made and detected means we can use it for lots of different things, from playing instruments and listening to music to looking inside the human body and treating patients in hospital.

Metacognition and self-reflection task

Writing questions is a great way of seeing how well you understand something you have been learning about. Try this:

- Pick out a key word from each spread in this chapter.
- For each one, write a question where the key word is the answer.
- Now test out your questions by asking someone else in the class to answer them.
- Check that they give you the key word as the answer. Which questions did you find the easiest to write? How could you have made the question harder?

Journey through P1

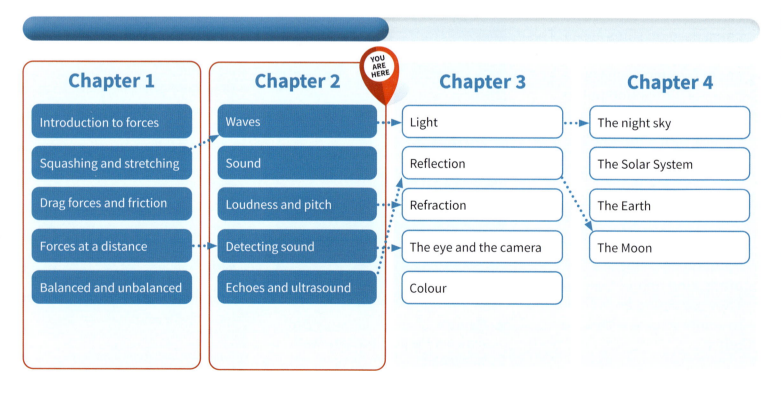

Chapter 2 Summary Questions

1

a Circle the words that can be used to describe waves:
   oscillating   balancing   vibrating   repelling
   (2 marks)

b Choose the correct word to put in these sentences.
   wavelength   frequency   amplitude
   The distance from the middle to the top of a wave is the
   _____
   The distance from one trough to the next trough is the
   _____
   The number of waves per second is the
   _____
   (3 marks)
   (5 marks)

2 A sound wave travels through water and bounces off the sea floor.

Choose the correct words.

a The sound wave is **attached to/reflected by** the sea floor.
b The sound wave travels **faster/slower** in air than it does in water.   **(2 marks)**

3 A tuning fork produces this wave on an oscilloscope:

a Draw the wave you would see if the sound was louder. (1 mark)
b Draw the wave you would see if the sound had a higher pitch. (1 mark)
c A note has a frequency of 400 Hz. State how many sound waves pass a point per second. (1 mark)
   (3 marks)

4 A friend calls your name. Describe:

a how the sound wave is produced   (1 mark)
b how it travels to your ear   (1 mark)
c how it produces a signal that reaches your brain.
   (4 marks)
   (6 marks)

5 This question is about waves travelling through a medium.

a Describe how particles in a medium move when a longitudinal wave passes through it.   (1 mark)
b Explain how your answer to part a would change if a wave with a larger amplitude moved through the same medium.   (1 mark)
   (2 marks)

6 Describe how a simple microphone works. **(4 marks)**

7 The table shows the speed of sound in three different materials: A, B, and C.

Material	Speed in m/s
A	1250
B	300
C	5000

a Write down which material, A, B, or C, is probably a solid.   (1 mark)
b Write down which material, A, B, or C, is probably a gas.   (1 mark)
c Suggest a reason why the three speeds are different.   (1 mark)
   (3 marks)

8

a Write down which of the frequencies below is ultrasound: (1 mark)
   2000 Hz   25 kHz   300 Hz
   1000 kHz   100 000 Hz
b Suggest how dolphins use ultrasound to detect fish.   (2 marks)
c Explain why dolphins can communicate using sound over much larger distances than a human can.
   (2 marks)
   (5 marks)

9 The speed of sound in water is 1500 m/s. The depth of a sea is 4500 m. A ship sends down an ultrasound signal. Calculate how long it takes to detect the echo.

Hint: first, work out the *total distance* that the sound travels.

Then divide this by the speed of sound in water to get the time taken.

(4 marks)

3 Light

In this chapter you will learn about light – where it comes from, and the journey it takes from a source to a detector, like an eye or a camera. You will find out how it can be reflected and change direction, and how fast it travels. You will also find out about the colours of light and filters, and how they can be used to change the way objects look. Understanding light means we can build telescopes that use light to see far into the Solar System and the Universe. This can give us clues about where the Universe came from. We can also take photos of what we see.

Reactivate your knowledge

1. Name one transparent object, one translucent object, and one opaque object.

2. Describe a situation where you can see your own shadow.

3. Describe how you see a cat on a street in the daytime.

You already know

Some objects emit light.

Light can travel through some objects. They are transparent. Objects that light cannot travel through are opaque. They form shadows.

Light travels in straight lines.

 How to calculate distance.

 How to work scientifically to: Identify independent, dependent, and control variables.

Journey through P1

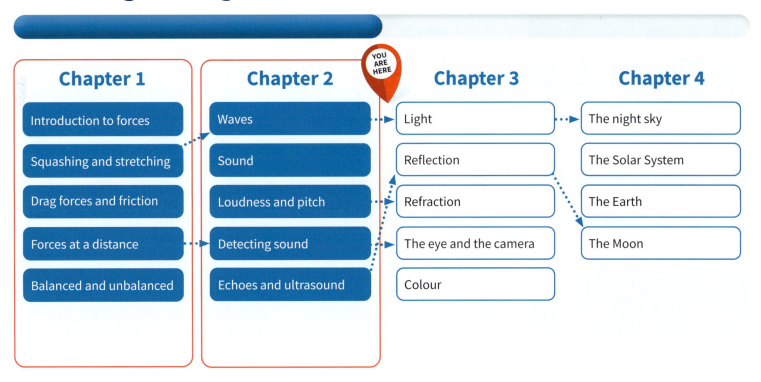

3.1 Light

Learning objectives
After this topic, you will be able to:
- describe the journey light takes
- describe how the speed of light is used to define distance.

Reactivate your knowledge
1. Name 3 objects that give out light.
2. Name 3 objects that you can see through.
3. Name 3 objects that you cannot see through.

As you go deeper and deeper into an ocean it gets darker and darker until you can hardly see a thing. Some fish that live there make their own light. Why is it so dark?

Key words
source, emit, reflect, absorb, ray, eye, luminous, non-luminous, transmit, transparent, translucent, opaque, light-time

What happens to light as it travels?

What happens when someone looks at a book? A **source** of light, like a light bulb, **emits** light. This light **reflects** off the book and into their eye. They see the book when the light is **absorbed** in their **eye**.

We draw lines called **rays** to model what beams of light do. You can see this in Figure 1.

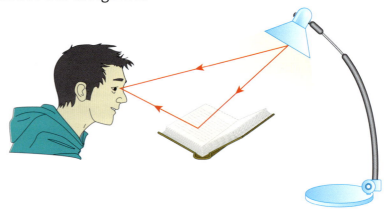

▲ **Figure 1** Objects are visible because light reflects off them.

▲ **Figure 2** Water absorbs light, so it is dark at the bottom of the ocean.

Objects that give out light are **luminous**. Most objects that you look at are **non-luminous**. They do not emit light. They are visible because they reflect light into your eyes. Light spreads out, just like sound.

When someone looks through a window, light travels through the glass and into their eye. The glass **transmits** the light. When light travels through glass, Perspex, or shallow water most of the light goes through. These materials are **transparent** and you can see through them. Transparent materials still absorb a small amount of light. In very deep water most of the light is absorbed. You can see this in Figure 2.

▲ **Figure 3** Frosted glass is translucent.

Reactivate your knowledge answers
1. E.g, sun, flame, light bulbs 2. E.g glass, water, air 3. E.g. brick, books, wood

P1 Chapter 3: Light

A Write down the difference between 'emit' and 'transmit'.

Materials like tissue paper or frosted glass, shown in Figure 3, are **translucent**. Light can travel through them, but it is scattered, so you cannot see through them clearly.

Materials that do not transmit light are **opaque**. Opaque materials produce shadows. You can predict the size and shape of shadows because light travels in straight lines.

B Write down the difference between a translucent and a transparent material.

What can light travel through?

Light can travel through gases, like the air. It can travel through some liquids, like water, and some solids, like glass. It can even travel through completely empty space, which is called a vacuum. It travels as a wave, but does not need a medium to travel in.

How fast does light travel?

It takes light about eight minutes to reach the Earth from the Sun, a distance of 150 million km (Figure 4). The speed of light is about 300 000 km/s. Sound travels about a million times slower than light. Astronomers use '**light-time**' to measure distances in space.

- A light-minute is the distance that light travels in one minute.
- A light-year is how far light travels in a year.

Light-time is a measure of distance, not time.

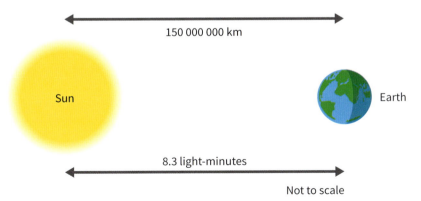

▲ **Figure 4** There are two ways of showing the distance to the Sun.

C Define 'light-second'.

Sort those words

Use the words below to make up three sentences involving a light bulb and a flower in a vase of water. The words can be used more than once but try to use them only once if you can.

**emit   transmit
reflect   absorb   luminous
non-luminous   transparent
opaque**

Link

You can learn more about the properties of waves in P1 2.1 *Waves,* and more about light time in P1 4.1 *The night sky.*

Summary Questions

1 Copy and complete the following sentences.

The Sun is **luminous/nonluminous** because it **emits/transmits** light. The light **reflects/transmits** off an object that is **luminous/non-luminous** into the eye. Most objects do not transmit light; they are **translucent/opaque**. A 'light-year' is the **distance/time** light travels in a year. (6 marks)

2 Explain why it is so dark at the bottom of the ocean even though water is transparent. (2 marks)

3 Use key words from these pages to describe the journey that light takes from the Sun to the eye when someone looks at fish in a pond. (4 marks)

169

3.2 Reflection

Learning objectives

After this topic, you will be able to:
- describe what can happen when light is reflected
- explain how images are formed in a plane mirror.

Reactivate your knowledge

1. Where do you see your 'reflection'?
2. Complete the sentence: 'Light travels in _____ lines'.
3. What do you call a reflection of sound?

▲ **Figure 1** You might be able to see your reflection in a window.

In everyday life, many objects create reflections, like in Figure 1. Shop windows, saucepans, car doors… but why do some surfaces create reflections and not others?

Why might you see an image in the mirror?

When you look in the mirror, you might see someone who looks just like you behind the mirror. There is an **image** in the mirror.

The brain uses the fact that light travels in straight lines to work out where the light appears to be coming from. This is where you see the image. It is a **virtual** image because light has not travelled from it to the eye. You can see how this works in Figure 2.

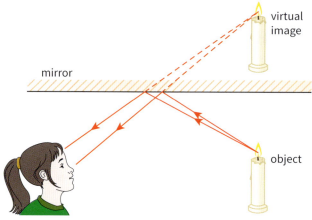

▲ **Figure 2** You can see an image in a mirror.

When something is reflected in a flat, or **plane**, mirror the image is:
- the same shape and size as the real object
- as far behind the mirror as the real object is in front of the mirror.

Left and right appear swapped, but the mirror is actually swapping back and front.

> **A** If you stand 1 m in front of a mirror, looking directly at it, how far are you from your image?

Key words
image, virtual, plane, normal, incident ray, reflected ray, angle of incidence, angle of reflection, law of reflection, specular reflection, diffuse reflection

Reactivate your knowledge answers
1 Example: mirror, saucepan, window 2 Straight 3 Echo

P1 Chapter 3: Light

What is the law of reflection?

You know that you need light to be reflected from an object for you to see it. Light reflects off a mirror in the same way that a wave reflects off a barrier, or a sound wave reflects off a building.

There is an imaginary line at 90° to the mirror called the **normal**.

You measure angles from the normal to the rays of light. The angle between the incident ray and the normal is the **angle of incidence**. The angle between the normal and the reflected ray is the **angle of reflection**. You can see how to do this in Figure 3.

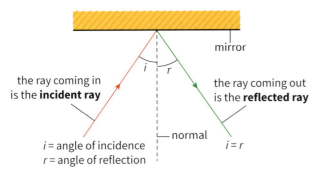

▲ **Figure 3** Light is reflected at equal angles.

When light is reflected from a mirror, the angle of incidence is equal to the angle of reflection. This is the **law of reflection**.

B If the angle of incidence is 30°, what is the angle of reflection?

How does light reflect off rough surfaces?

Every surface reflects at least some light. Figure 4 shows how light is reflected off two different surfaces. You can only see your image in surfaces that reflect light in a regular way.

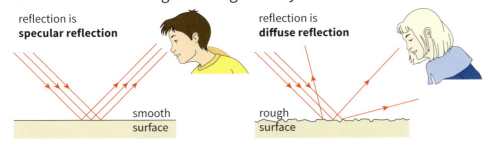

▲ **Figure 4** You can only see an image in a smooth surface.

To form an image, the rays from each part of the object have to reflect off a surface in the same way. If two rays that are parallel are reflected off a surface at different angles you won't see an image.

C State the type of reflection when light hits a shiny metal saucepan.

Bouncing light

A student wants to investigate the light that is reflected from different types of material using a light meter. Explain why they should repeat the experiment a few times. State and explain what type of graph they should use to plot the results.

Summary Questions

1 Copy and complete the following sentences.

When an object is reflected in a mirror a _____ image appears. The image is the same _____, _____, and _____ from the mirror as the real object. If the object moves to the left the image appears to move to the _____. The image is formed because light reflects off the mirror so that the angle of _____ is equal to the angle of _____. (7 marks)

2 Explain why no image is created by objects facing a white wall, even though most of the light hitting it is reflected. (2 marks)

3 Design a model to demonstrate how light can be diffusely scattered but still obeys the law of reflection. Use marbles and card instead of light and a mirror in your model. Explain how it works. (4 marks)

171

3.3 Refraction

Learning objectives
After this topic, you will be able to:
- describe and explain what happens when light changes direction
- describe how a convex lens affects light.

Reactivate your knowledge
1. What is a 'normal' on a ray diagram?
2. What is a 'virtual image'?
3. What is the law of reflection?

▲ **Figure 1** Pencils look bent when you put them in water.

You can bend a pencil without touching it. Put it in a glass and fill it with water. It looks bent, but it isn't. Why?

Why does a pencil in water look bent?

The pencil reflects light and the light travels from the pencil through the water. It then travels through the air into your eye. As the light leaves the water, the direction it is travelling in changes. This is called **refraction**.

Refraction happens whenever light travels from one **medium** (material) to another. The change in direction explains why the pencil appears to be bent, which you can see in Figure 1.

The brain thinks that the light has travelled in a straight line, and the end of the pencil looks to be in a different place to where it actually is. The pencil looks bent. Refraction also explains why a swimming pool looks shallower than it actually is, like in Figure 2.

Key words
refraction, medium, lens, convex, converging, focal length, focus, focal point

Watch that spelling!
In each list below, choose the correct spelling of the word. Make up a rule that will help you remember the spelling.
a. lense, lens, lenz
b. parallel, parralell, paralell

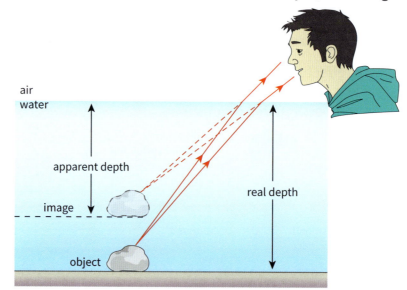

▲ **Figure 2** A rock at the bottom of a pool looks closer to the surface than it actually is.

A Explain why the image of the pencil in the water is virtual.

Reactivate your knowledge answers
1 A line at 90° to a surface where a ray hits, you measure the angles between the rays and this line. 2 An image formed when the brain uses light travelling in straight lines to work out where the light appears to have come from 3 The angle of incidence is equal to the angle of reflection

Why does light change direction?

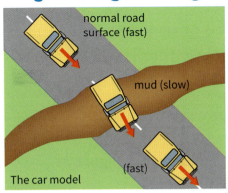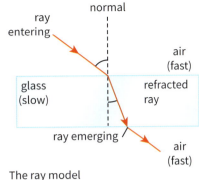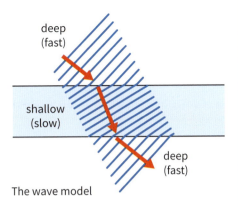

▲ **Figure 3** Like a truck that changes direction when it slows down, light and waves get refracted when they slow down.

Imagine a truck driving from a road onto mud as shown in Figure 3. When the first wheel of the truck hits the mud, it slows down. The other wheels keep going and this changes the truck's direction. This is similar to what happens when light travels from air into water or glass, or when water waves go from deep to shallow.

B Describe the difference between reflection and refraction.

When light enters a glass block it slows down. When it comes out it speeds up again. Its direction changes twice. Light bends towards the normal when it goes into glass and bends away from the normal when it comes out. The rays going into the block and the rays coming out are parallel.

What does a lens do?

There are two lenses in your body. The **lenses** in your eyes are **convex** or **converging** lenses. They focus the light and allow you to see. The light is refracted as it goes into the lens and as it comes back out. Figure 4 shows how a lens focuses light.

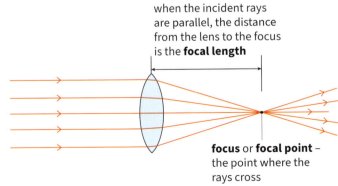

▲ **Figure 4** A piece of glass shaped like a lens focuses light.

C Describe what happens to the speed of the light when it comes out of the lens.

Summary Questions

1 Copy and complete the following sentences.

When someone looks at a rock at the bottom of a swimming pool it appears **above/below** where it actually is. This is because the light **reflects/refracts** when it travels from water into air. It bends **towards/away** from the normal as it goes into the air. This is because it **slows down/speeds up**. A **convex/plane** lens focuses light. (5 marks)

2 Write down and explain what would happen to:

a the speed and direction of light waves if they went straight into an area of shallow water rather than at an angle (2 marks)

b the speed and direction of light waves if they went straight into a glass block rather than at an angle. (2 marks)

3 Suggest and explain what happens to the focal length when you make the lens thinner. (2 marks)

173

3.4 The eye and the camera

Learning objectives
After this topic, you will be able to:
- describe how the eye works
- compare a simple camera with the eye.

Reactivate your knowledge
1. What is the light detector in the human body called?
2. What is refraction?
3. What does a lens do?

▲ **Figure 1** No-one has the same pattern in their iris as you.

Link
You can learn more about specialized cells in B1 1.3 *Specialised cells*.

Key words
lens, optic nerve, cornea, pupil, retina, iris, inverted, photoreceptor, camera, aperture, real (image), pixel, charge-coupled device (CCD)

The iris is the coloured part of your eye, shown in Figure 1. Everyone's iris is unique, like a fingerprint.

How do eyes work?

When someone looks at a tree, like in Figure 2, an image of the tree is formed on the retina of their eye.

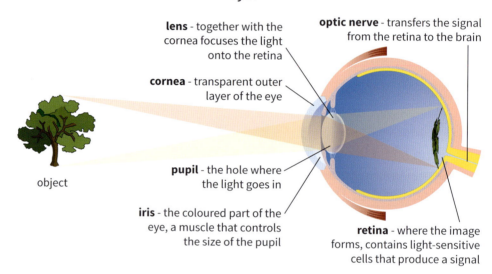

▲ **Figure 2** How an image is formed in the eye.

A Suggest why your pupil gets smaller in bright light.

The image is **inverted** (upside down), but your brain sorts it out so you see an image of the tree that is the right way up. The retina is a photosensitive material that contains cells that respond to light. These cells are called **photoreceptors**. When light hits a photoreceptor, chemical reactions produce an electrical impulse that travels up the optic nerve to your brain.

B Name the nerves connecting your eyes and ears to your brain.

Reactivate your knowledge answers
1 The eye 2 The bending of light when it goes from one medium to another 3 Focuses light

P1 Chapter 3: Light

How is the eye like a camera?

A **camera** produces an image, just like your eye. The hole at the front of the camera is the **aperture.** You can see how a camera works in Figure 3.

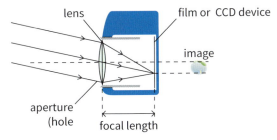

▲ **Figure 3** A lens in a camera focuses light.

▲ **Figure 4** Cameras used to use photographic film.

Cameras used to contain photographic film, which was photosensitive (Figure 4).

- When light hit the film a chemical reaction changed the chemicals in the film.
- When you processed the film, you saw the image.

At the back of a digital camera shown in Figure 5 there is a grid of photosensitive picture elements, or pixels. This is called a **charge-coupled device (CCD).** When light hits each **pixel** it produces a charge. The light produces an electrical, not chemical, effect. When you take a picture, this charge is moved off each of the pixels and stored. That is why there is a slight delay before you can take another picture.

▲ **Figure 5** A lens in a camera focuses light. Most phones now have cameras too.

C Suggest a value for the focal length of the camera lens in a smart phone in centimetres.

An image that is formed on a CCD, camera film, or your retina, is a **real** image. Your image in a mirror cannot be put onto a screen. Any image that you can make on a screen is a real image.

A pinhole camera, in Figure 6, models what happens in a camera.

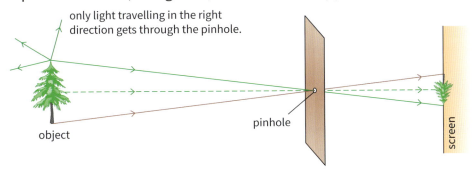

▲ **Figure 6** A pinhole camera works in a similar way to your eye.

Light enters the camera through the pinhole, just like it does through your pupil. You see a representation of the object on a screen.

Summary Questions

1 Copy and complete the following sentences.

When someone looks at an apple, light _____ off the apple into their eye. The light enters the eye through the _____. The _____ and the _____ focus the light onto the _____. A chemical reaction produces an _____ signal that is sent down the _____ to your brain.
(7 marks)

2 Describe how the camera in a smart phone is different to a pinhole camera. (2 marks)

3 Compare the eye, a phone camera, and a pinhole camera.
(4 marks)

175

3.5 Colour

Learning objectives

After this topic, you will be able to:
- describe how primary colours add to make secondary colours
- describe and explain the effects of prisms, filters, and coloured materials on light.

Reactivate your knowledge

1. What 4 things can happen when light hits a material?
2. How do we see things?
3. What are wavelength and frequency?

Key words

prism, spectrum, dispersion, continuous, primary colour, secondary colour, filter

Rainbows are beautiful patterns of light you might see after it rains. But where do the colours in a rainbow come from?

How do you split white light?

White light is made up of seven different bands of light, each of a different colour. You can use a **prism** to split white light into a **spectrum**. This is called **dispersion**. The spectrum of white light is **continuous**, meaning there are no gaps between the colours. Sir Isaac Newton first did this experiment (shown in Figure 1) in about 1666.

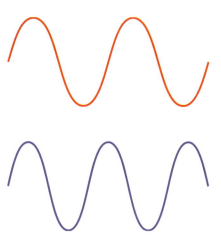

▲ Figure 2 Red light has a lower frequency than violet light.

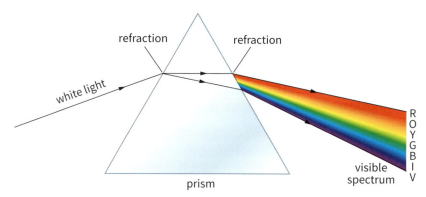

▲ Figure 1 A prism splits white light into a spectrum.

Dispersion happens because light with a high frequency, like violet, is refracted more than light with a lower frequency, as shown in Figure 2.

The white light spectrum is part of a larger spectrum called the electromagnetic spectrum. Waves of this spectrum include visible light, infrared radiation, and ultraviolet radiation.

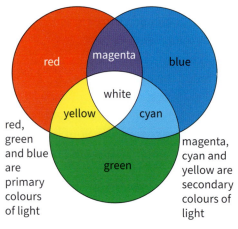

▲ Figure 3 This Venn diagram shows the primary and secondary colours of light.

A Suggest whether the frequency of red light is higher or lower than that of green light.

Reactivate your knowledge answers

1. It can be reflected, transmitted, refracted, absorbed 2. Light is emitted by or reflects off objects and enters our eyes 3. Wavelength is the distance between the peak of one wave to the peak of the next wave, frequency is the number of waves per second.

P1 Chapter 3: Light

What happens when you add light?

The eye detects three colours of light, called the **primary colours** of light.

When you mix two primary colours, you get **secondary colours** of light: cyan, yellow, and magenta. You get white light when you mix all three primary colours of light together as shown in Figure 3.

> **B** Suggest how you combine primary colours of light to make orange light.

What do filters do to light?

A red **filter**, like the one in Figure 4, subtracts colours from white light. It transmits red light and absorbs the rest. It does not change the colour of light.

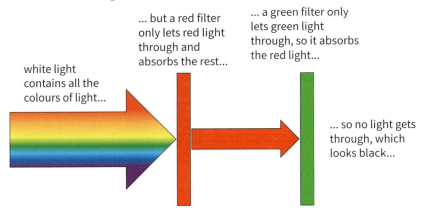

▲ **Figure 4** Filters transmit the colours that they are and absorb the rest.

> **C** State what a blue filter does to white light.

Why are objects different colours?

A blue car reflects blue light into the eye. When the white light from the Sun hits the car, the paint absorbs all the other colours except blue. Any coloured object reflects the colour that it is and absorbs the rest. Figure 5 shows how light reflects from red, white, and black objects.

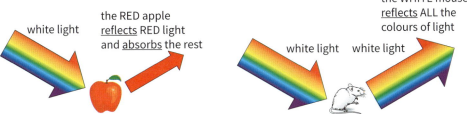

▲ **Figure 5** Red objects reflect red light but absorb all other colours. White objects reflect all colours of light, and black objects absorb all colours of light.

What table?

A student wants to record data in an experiment where she is shining all the primary and secondary colours of light onto pieces of coloured material. Draw a table to show how she could record her results.

Summary Questions

1 Copy and complete the following sentences.

When white light goes through a prism, red light is **reflected/refracted** the **most/least** and violet light is refracted the **most/least.** This is called **dispersion/refraction**. A green filter **absorbs/transmits** green light and **absorbs/transmits** the rest. A cyan object **absorbs/reflects** red light, **absorbs/reflects** blue light, and **absorbs/reflects** green light. A magenta object would look black in **blue/green** light. (10 marks)

2 Explain why a green shirt looks black in red light. (2 marks)

3 Explain why you cannot have a white filter or a black filter. (6 marks)

177

3 Chapter 3 Summary

In this chapter you have learnt that light is emitted by sources and can be transmitted, reflected, or refracted before being absorbed. You have seen how eyes detect light and produce a signal that is sent to the brain. You learnt how light is reflected at equal angles from plane mirrors and that the law of reflection can explain the formation of images. You have seen that by thinking of light as a wave that changes speed we can understand refraction. You have also learnt that white light is made up of different colours, which can be split by a prism to show the different colours. The eye can detect the primary colours of light. You saw that the way the colour of an object looks depends on the frequencies that it absorbs and reflects. Filters absorb different frequencies of light and can be used to change how something looks.

Metacognition and self-reflection task

Flashcards are a great way to summarise important facts. Being able to make your own cards will help you to remember the information in this chapter. It's also a really useful skill that you will use all the way through your science lessons. Make a flashcard for each spread, then test yourself to see how much you can remember from each card. As you go through the course you can mix flashcards from different topics or subjects.

Journey through P1

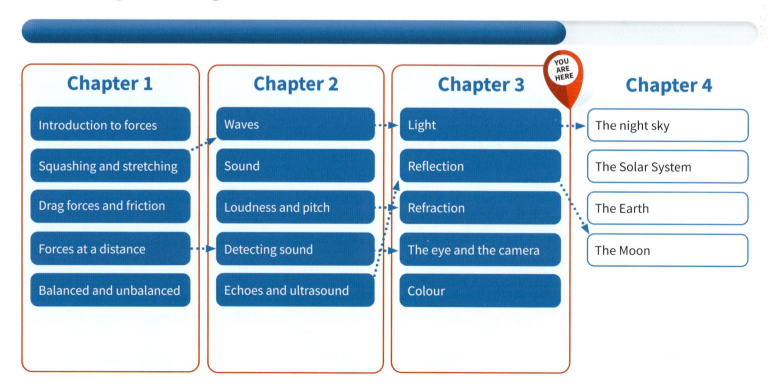

Chapter 3 Summary Questions

1 Match the words to the definitions:

Diffuse scattering — Ray hitting mirror
Specular reflection — Reflection from a rough surface
Incident ray — Reflection from a smooth surface
Reflected ray — Ray leaving mirror
(3 marks)

2 Choose a word from this list to complete the sentences about how the eye and camera are similar

aperture   CCD device   lens

a The retina of the eye is like the
_____ in a camera.
b The lens of the eye is like the
_____ in a camera.
c The pupil of the eye is like the
_____ in a camera.
(3 marks)

3 A hunter is trying to spear a fish.

a Explain why she aims at a place above where she sees the fish. (2 marks)
b Explain why diving birds dive straight down to catch fish. (2 marks)
(4 marks)

4 An actor is wearing a uniform that has a blue jacket and red trousers. Explain what the audience would see if he stood on stage in:

a white light (2 marks)
b green light (2 marks)
(4 marks)

5 A student has collected data about different types of plastic block. She measured the mass and the angle of refraction of a ray of light going into the block. Each block is the same size.

Here are her results.

Mass of block in g	Angle of refraction in °
250	27
220	32
275	24
300	21

a State **one** variable that the student must keep the same during this investigation. (1 mark)
b Name the dependent variable. (1 mark)
c Name the independent variable. (1 mark)
d Describe the relationship between the mass of the block and the angle of refraction. (1 mark)
(4 marks)

6 Copy and complete the diagram to show what happens when light travels through a lens. (4 marks)

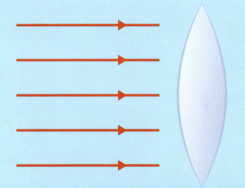

7 Light travels at 300 000 km/s in air. It slows down to 200 000 km/s in glass and to 226 000 km/s in water. A ray of light enters each medium with an angle of incidence of 40°. State and explain whether the angle of refraction would be bigger or smaller in water than in glass.
(3 marks)

8 The Sun is 8.3 light-minutes away, which is 150 000 000 km. The Moon is about 1.3 light-seconds away. Use these data and ratios to estimate the distance to the Moon in km. (4 marks)

4 Space

In this chapter you will learn about what we see in the night sky, and how far away things are. You will learn about the planets and the formation of the Solar System. You will find out why we have seasons, and why they are different in different places. You will learn about the phases of the Moon and why there are eclipses.

Reactivate your knowledge

1 Name the planets of the Solar System.

2 Name one object in the night sky that emits light, and one object that reflects light.

3 Describe three differences between the days in summer and in winter.

You already know

It is hotter in the summer than the winter, and it is daylight for longer.

Stars emit light. Other objects in space, such as planets and moons, reflect light.

There are objects outside the Earth's atmosphere, such as the moons and planets of our Solar System.

The Earth spins, which is why we have day and night. It is also why the Sun and the stars appear to move.

 How to multiply numbers and use units.

How to work scientifically to: Make a model of the Earth and Moon system and the planets of the Solar System.

Journey through P1

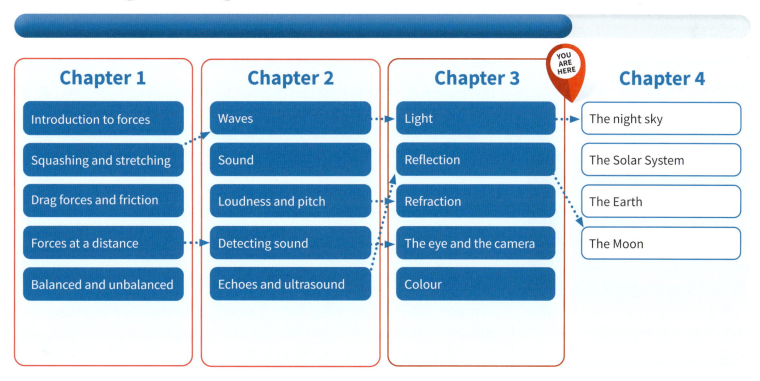

4.1 The night sky

Learning objectives

After this topic, you will be able to:
- describe the objects that you can see in the night sky
- describe the structure of the Universe.

Reactivate your knowledge

1. What is a light-year?
2. What is the star in our Solar System?
3. What is an orbit?

▲ **Figure 1** An astronaut on a spacewalk is repairing part of the ISS.

Key words

artificial satellite, natural satellite, Solar System, comet, meteor, meteorite, star, galaxy, Milky Way, Universe

When you look at the stars in the night sky you do not see them as they are today. The light from them has taken years to get here. You are looking back in time.

What is orbiting the Earth?

The nearest objects in the night sky that you can see without a telescope are **artificial satellites**. They orbit the Earth. In Figure 1 an astronaut is repairing the International Space Station (ISS). You can see the ISS with the naked eye (without using binoculars or a telescope). The light reflected from the ISS reaches us in a fraction of a second.

Light reflected from the Moon reaches us in just over a second. The Moon orbits the Earth. It is the Earth's only **natural satellite**. It is a celestial body because it is a natural object that exists outside of the Earth's atmosphere.

> **A** Write down which is closer to Earth: the Moon or the ISS.

What is wandering across the sky?

There are five planets that can be seen with the naked eye: Mercury, Venus, Mars, Jupiter, and Saturn. Like the Earth they orbit the Sun. Venus gets closest to the Earth, about two light-minutes away. Light from Saturn takes about 1.5 hours to reach Earth. The planets and the Sun form part of the **Solar System**.

> **B** Name three types of object in the night sky that you can see with the naked eye.

What are the streaks of light?

A **comet**, like the one in Figure 2, is an object in the night sky that appears to have a tail. The name 'comet' means 'hairy star'. They are made up of dust, rock, and ice. They disappear and then return because they orbit the Sun.

▲ **Figure 2** In 2020 Comet NEOWISE was visible from Earth.

Reactivate your knowledge answers

1. The distance light travels in a year 2. The Sun 3. The path (usually circular) that a moon takes around a planet, or a planet around the Sun.

Meteors are bits of dust or rock that burn up as they move through the Earth's atmosphere and produce streaks of light. Any meteor that makes it to the ground is called a **meteorite**.

> **C** State the differences between a comet and a meteor.

What is in the Universe?

Most of the dots of light that we see in the sky at night are **stars** in our own **galaxy**, the **Milky Way**, represented in Figure 3. A galaxy is a collection of billions of stars. A star is made of gases that produce enough energy to emit light. Our sun is just one of the many stars in the Milky Way.

Light takes about eight minutes to get to us from the Sun, our nearest star. Our next-nearest star is over four light-years away.

Some of the dots of light in the night sky are other galaxies. The Milky Way is just one of billions of galaxies that make up the **Universe**, each containing billions of stars.

Our nearest large galaxy is Andromeda, which you can see with the naked eye. The image of Andromeda shown in Figure 4 was made by a telescope. Light from Andromeda takes 2 million years to get to Earth. Both Andromeda and the Milky Way have smaller galaxies orbiting around them.

▲ **Figure 3** This shows the approximate position of our star, the Sun, in a simplified image of the Milky Way galaxy as it would be seen from the side and above.

▲ **Figure 4** The Andromeda galaxy is made of billions of stars, just like the Milky Way.

How do we know?

Astronomers have learnt about the objects that we see in the night sky from the observations they have made. You can make observations and collect data, but you cannot do experiments in astronomy. Find out how astronomers work out the distances to objects in the night sky.

Link

You will learn about how the Sun and other stars store energy in P2 2.2 *Energy adds up*.

Summary Questions

1 Copy and complete the following sentences.

There are thousands of satellites in orbit around the **Sun/Earth**. The Moon is a natural satellite of the **Sun/Earth**. Comets are huge snowballs that orbit the **Sun/Earth**. Planets orbit the **Sun/Earth**. The celestial body in orbit around the Earth is the **ISS/Moon**. (5 marks)

2 When you look up at the night sky you see dots of light that don't appear to move. Write down what the dots of light could be. (2 marks)

3 Compare the time it takes for light to reach us from the different objects that you can see in the night sky. (4 marks)

4.2 The Solar System

Learning objectives
After this topic, you will be able to:
- compare the planets of the Solar System
- describe how the Solar System formed.

Reactivate your knowledge
1. Name the planets of the Solar System.
2. How are planets different from stars in terms of light?
3. Which dwarf planet used to be called a planet?

▲ **Figure 1** An illustration of the planets of the Solar System.

Key words
asteroid, asteroid belt, ellipse, dwarf planet, terrestrial, gas giant, moon, astronomer

Remember that order!
Before Pluto was renamed a dwarf planet, people used to remember the order of the planets using this mnemonic:

My **V**ery **E**asy **M**ethod **J**ust **S**peeds **U**p **N**aming (**P**lanets).

A mnemonic uses first letters to make up a sentence. Make up your own mnemonic for the planets as they are now: M, V, E, M, J, S, U, N.

No-one has ever seen all of the Solar System at once because it is too big. Scientists have used observations to build a model of the Solar System. We produce images of the planets using data from telescopes and space probes (Figure 1).

What's in our Solar System?

Starting from the Sun and moving outwards, the Solar System contains four inner planets and four outer planets. Between the orbits of the inner and outer planets there is a region of space filled with **asteroids**, called an **asteroid belt**. A planet is a roughly spherical object orbiting a star. Its gravitational field is big enough to attract smaller objects so that it has cleared its orbit of debris.

All of the planets in our Solar System orbit the Sun. Each orbit is a slightly squashed circle called an **ellipse** (Figure 2).

> **A** Suggest why an astronaut cannot 'take a photo' of the Solar System.

What are the planets like?

The inner planets – Mercury, Venus, Earth, and Mars – are all **terrestrial** planets: they are made of rock. The temperature of each planet is very different, as shown in Table 1. Mercury does not have an atmosphere. Venus has an atmosphere of carbon dioxide that traps energy from the Sun.

The outer planets – Jupiter, Saturn, Uranus, and Neptune – are called **gas giants**; they are made mainly of gases such as hydrogen and helium. All of the gas giants are very cold and are much bigger than the inner planets.

Many of the planets have moons in orbit around them. Saturn has over 80 **moons** but Earth has only one.

> **B** List the planets in size order, starting with the smallest.

Reactivate your knowledge answers
1. Mercury, Venus, Earth, Mars, Jupiter, Saturn, Uranus, Neptune 2. Planets reflect light, stars emit light 3. Pluto

P1   Chapter 4: Space

Planet	Diameter in km	Distance from Sun in light minutes	Temperature in °C
Sun	1 391 000	-	-
Mercury	4879	3.2	−180 to 430
Venus	12 104	6.0	465
Earth	12 756	8.3	−89 to 58
Mars	6787	12.7	−82 to 0
Jupiter	142 800	43.3	−150
Saturn	120 660	79.0	−170
Uranus	51 118	159.0	−200
Neptune	49 528	250.0	−235

▲ **Table 1** Information about the planets.

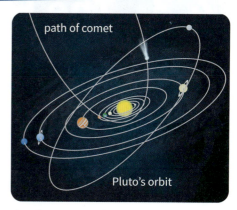

▲ **Figure 2** A diagram showing how the orbits of Pluto and a comet are different to the orbits of the planets.

What is on the edge of the Solar System?

Pluto used to be called a planet but in 2006 it was renamed a **dwarf planet**. Beyond Pluto's orbit is a region called the Kuiper Belt. The Kuiper Belt is a bit like the asteroid belt, but contains mainly icy objects.

Astronomers used to think that comets came from the Kuiper Belt. Now they think that comets come from outside our Solar System in a region called the Oort Cloud, beyond the Kuiper Belt. The orbits of Pluto and a comet are shown in Figure 2.

▲ **Figure 3** Our sister planet, Venus, is too hot to live on.

> **C** Suggest why Pluto was reclassified as a dwarf planet.

How did our Solar System form?

Scientists think that gravity pulled gas, rocks, and dust together to form our Sun about 5 billion years ago (Figure 4). They think planets formed from a disc of gas and dust surrounding the Sun.

The Kuiper Belt and the Oort Cloud are left over from the original cloud of dust, gas, and rocks that formed our Solar System. Astronomers are trying to observe clouds of gas and dust around other stars to see if they can detect planets forming.

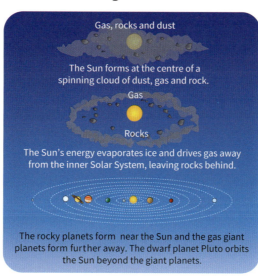

▲ **Figure 4** The formation of the Solar System

Summary Questions

1 Copy and complete the following sentences.

There are _____ inner and _____ outer planets in the Solar System. The band of dust and rocks between Jupiter and Mars is called the _____ _____ . Pluto is a _____ planet. _____ planets are rocky and _____ planets are gaseous. In general, the temperature of planets _____ as you move further from the Sun.   (8 marks)

2 Describe how both rocky and gaseous planets formed in the Solar System.   (2 marks)

3 Compare inner planets, outer planets, and asteroids.   (4 marks)

185

4.3 The Earth

Learning objectives

After this topic, you will be able to:
- explain the apparent motion of objects in the sky
- explain why hours of daylight and temperature change during the year
- describe seasonal changes in different places on Earth.

Reactivate your knowledge

1. Why does the Sun appear to move across the sky?
2. Which object does the Earth orbit?
3. What causes day and night?

▲ **Figure 1** This photograph of the night sky was taken over 10.5 hours.

Key words

axis, day, night, year, season, hemisphere, constellation

February 29th

It takes 21 600 seconds longer to orbit the Sun than just the 365 days you use for one year. Show that in 4 years these extra seconds add up to one day.

Is there day and night on other planets? Do they have seasons? How could you find out without going there?

Why do we have day and night?

Some people found it hard to believe that the Earth spins on its **axis**. However, if you take a photograph over a long time (Figure 1), the stars appear to move in circles. This shows that the Earth is spinning.

> **A** Suggest why people found it hard to believe that the Earth was spinning.

There is **day** and **night** on Earth because Earth spins on its axis. It takes 24 hours to complete one full spin. The Sun rises in the east each morning, reaches its highest point at noon, and then sets in the west in the evening. The Sun isn't moving– you are!

> **B** Give the direction in which the Sun rises if you are in the southern hemisphere.

Why do we have seasons?

Earth takes 365.2422 days to orbit the Sun. One **year** is 365 days. This means that there is an extra day in a leap year every four years.

As the **seasons** of the year change, so do the following: day length, the height of the Sun at noon, average daily temperature, the stars you see at night.

We can explain these observations using the fact that the Earth's axis is tilted, as shown in Figure 2. When the North Pole is tilted towards the Sun (Figure 4), it is summer in the northern half of the Earth (**hemisphere**). The angle of tilt is 23.4°.

Reactivate your knowledge answers
1 The Earth spins 2 The Sun 3 The Earth spins

P1 Chapter 4: Space

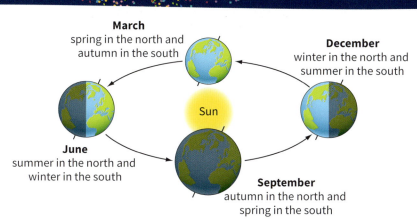

▲ **Figure 2** The tilt of the Earth's axis produces the seasons.

▲ **Figure 3** Diagram showing the effect of the Sun's rays hitting the Earth at different angles.

In the summer in *either* **hemisphere** (half of the Earth):

- the axis is tilted *towards* the Sun
- days are longer
- the Sun's rays spread over a smaller area, as in Figure 3a. It is warmer.

In the winter in *either* hemisphere:

- the axis is tilted *away* from the Sun
- days are shorter
- the Sun's rays spread over a larger area, as in Figure 3b.

In the summer at the North Pole the Sun does not set. This is called the 'Land of the Midnight Sun' (Figure 5).

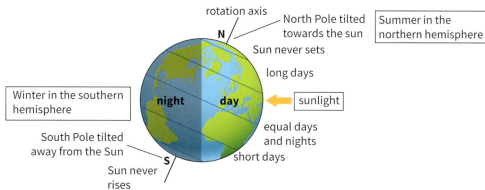

▲ **Figure 4** When the Earth spins, half the Earth is in the light and half is in the dark.

▲ **Figure 5** In the Arctic summer, the sun never sets.

In the winter at the North Pole, the Sun does not rise. At the equator there is very little difference between summer and winter.

The groups of stars, or **constellations**, that we see in the summer at night are different to the stars that we see in the winter. This is because the Earth is moving around the Sun.

Summary Questions

1 Copy and complete the following sentences.

You see the Sun rise in the **east/west** and set in the **east/west** because the Earth **spins/orbits**. A **month/year** lasts approximately 365 days. This is the time that it takes the Earth to **orbit the Sun/spin once**. The days are **longer/shorter** in the summer and the Sun is **higher/lower** in the sky at noon.
(7 marks)

2 Answer the following questions.

a Explain why it is hotter in the summer than it is in the winter. (2 marks)

b Explain why the seasons in the southern hemisphere occur at different months to those in the northern hemisphere. (1 mark)

3 Explain what you would experience in both hemispheres throughout the year if the axis of the Earth were *not* tilted.
(4 marks)

187

4.4 The Moon

Learning objectives
After this topic, you will be able to:
- describe the phases of the Moon
- explain why you see phases of the Moon
- explain why eclipses happen.

Reactivate your knowledge
1. What is a moon?
2. How do we see non-luminous objects?
3. How much of the Earth is lit up at any time?

Key words
phases of the Moon, umbra, total solar eclipse, penumbra, partial solar eclipse, lunar eclipse

Many years ago, people used to have different ideas about space. The ancient Chinese thought a solar eclipse was a demon eating the Sun.

Why does the Moon look different?

The Moon takes 27 days and 7 hours to orbit the Earth once. We see it because light reflects from it into our eyes.

A Suggest what shape the orbit of the Moon around the Earth is.

As the Moon moves around the Earth its shape appears to change. The changing shapes are called **phases of the Moon,** shown in Figure 1. The Moon only appears a different shape when viewed from the Earth. It might seem that the Earth should block the Sun's light during a full moon. It does not because the orbit of the Moon is slightly tilted.

▲ Figure 2 There is a side of the Moon that you never see from Earth

◀ Figure 1 The motion of the Moon around the Earth produces phases.

A lunar month is the period of time from one new moon to the next new moon.

B Write down how much of the Moon's surface is lit up by the Sun during a new moon.

The Moon spins on its axis. The time it takes to spin all the way around is the same time that it takes to orbit the Earth.

Farewell, Moon
The moon is 38 000 000 000 cm away and is moving away from the Earth at a rate of about 3.8 cm a year. Work out how much closer to the Earth it was when you were born.

Reactivate your knowledge answers
1 A celestial body that orbits a planet/natural satellite of a planet 2 Light reflects from them into our eyes 3 Half

P1 Chapter 4: Space

This means that the same side of the Moon always faces the Earth. The side we don't see is often called the 'dark side of the moon' (Figure 2).

> **C** Suggest why people did not see the far side of the Moon until 1959.

Why do we see eclipses?

Solar eclipses

When the Moon comes between the Sun and the Earth it makes a shadow on the Earth's surface (Figure 3). If you are standing in the **umbra**, the Moon completely blocks the light from the Sun and you see a **total solar eclipse.** If you are standing where only part of the Sun's light is blocked, the **penumbra**, you will see a **partial solar eclipse**. You should never look directly into the Sun or at a solar eclipse.

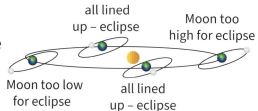

▲ **Figure 5** The tilted orbit of the Moon explains why solar and lunar eclipses do not happen monthly.

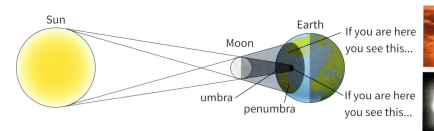

▲ **Figure 3** A solar eclipse happens when the Moon blocks the light from the Sun. A partial solar eclipse is shown on the top right and a total solar eclipse is shown underneath it.

Lunar eclipses

A **lunar eclipse** happens when the Earth comes between the Sun and the Moon (Figure 4). Light from the Sun is refracted by the Earth's atmosphere, which makes the Moon look red during a total lunar eclipse.

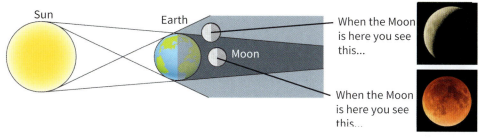

▲ **Figure 4** A lunar eclipse happens when the Earth comes between the Sun and the Moon. A partial lunar eclipse is shown on the top right and a total lunar eclipse is shown underneath it.

Why don't we see eclipses every month?

Figure 5 shows how the tilt of the Moon's orbit also explains why we do not see lunar and solar eclipses very often.

Summary Questions

1 Copy and complete the following sentences.

You see a _____ moon when the Sun lights up the whole of the side that you can see. When the side of the Moon that you can see is in shadow you see a _____ moon. A solar eclipse happens when the _____ comes between the Sun and the _____. A lunar eclipse happens when the _____ comes between the Sun and the _____. (6 marks)

2 Describe how you could use a torch, a beach ball, and a tennis ball to demonstrate the difference between a full moon and a lunar eclipse. (4 marks)

3 Explain why you would see an eclipse if you were on some of the planets in the Solar System but not others. (1 mark)

189

Chapter 4 Summary

In this chapter you have learnt that you can see the Moon, the International Space Station, and the nearest planets without a telescope. You saw that our star, the Sun, is one of billions in our galaxy, the Milky Way, and that there are billions of galaxies in the Universe. You learnt that we use light-seconds, light-minutes, and light-years as a measure of very large distances. Other galaxies are millions of light-years from us. You saw that the Solar System consists of four inner planets, an asteroid belt, and four outer planets that formed when gravity brought together dust and gas. You learnt that it is hotter in summer than winter due to the tilt of the Earth's axis, which affects the angle of the light and how much daylight we get. The spinning Earth explains where day and night come from, and the appearance of the Moon. You saw how the phases and eclipses depend on the location of the Moon compared to the Earth and Sun.

Metacognition and self-reflection task

Comparing and contrasting objects or systems is a great way of checking that you understand the relationships between them. Use a Venn diagram to compare the similarities and differences between objects in the night sky and objects that orbit the Sun.

When you have finished, look at each part of the diagram and ask if there is anything else you could add.

Journey through P1

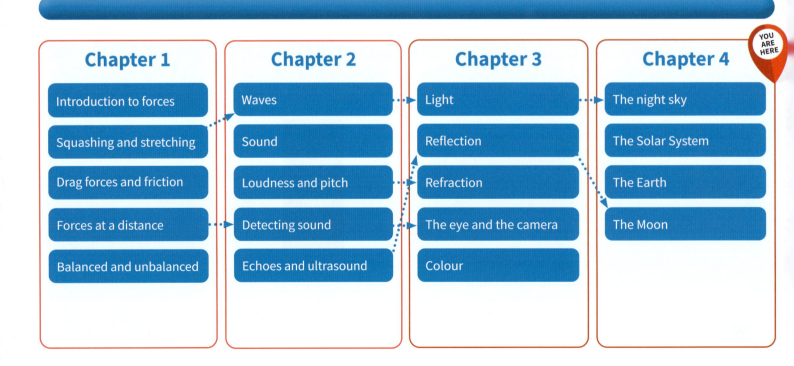

Chapter 4 Summary Questions

1 Here is a list of objects that you can see in the night sky. Sort the objects into those that are in orbit around the Sun and those that are in orbit around the Earth.

comet   planet   Moon   satellite
asteroid   International Space Station
(2 marks)

2 Complete the following sentences using these words.

half   all   full   solar   lunar

We see phases of the Moon because _____ of the Moon is lit up at all times. When we see the side that is lit by the Sun, we see a _____ Moon. When the Moon comes between the Earth and the Sun we can see a _____ eclipse. **(3 marks)**

3 The diagram shows the Earth in orbit around the Sun:

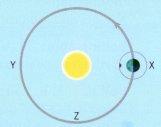

a Copy the diagram and label the Sun, the Earth, and the Moon. (3 marks)
b It is summer in the southern hemisphere when the Earth is at position X. State which season it is in the UK when the Earth is at position Y. (1 mark)
c Write down how many months it takes the Earth to move between X and Z. (1 mark)
(5 marks)

4 This diagram shows how the Sun moves across the sky during the day in summer:

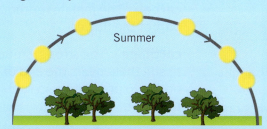

a Copy the diagram and add these labels:
east   west   sunrise   sunset   noon   (2 marks)
b On the diagram sketch the path of the Sun in winter. (2 marks)
c Explain why the path of the Sun in the sky is different in autumn and in winter. (2 marks)
(6 marks)

5 Describe how the Solar System formed. **(2 marks)**

6 Explain why we see lunar eclipses and solar eclipses. **(2 marks)**

7 Here are some objects in the Universe:

Sun   inner planet   outer planet
galaxy   our nearest star   The Moon

a State which object or objects are a distance of light-seconds away and which are light-years away. (2 marks)
b Describe a problem with communicating with people on a spacecraft travelling through the Solar System. (2 marks)
(4 marks)

8 The table below shows the angle of tilt of the axes of the planets in the Solar System.

Use the information in the table and your scientific knowledge to compare the seasons on Mercury and Venus with those on Earth. **(4 marks)**

Planet	Angle of tilt (in °)
Mercury	0
Venus	177
Earth	23.5
Mars	25
Jupiter	3
Saturn	27
Uranus	98
Neptune	30

Glossary

absorb Taken into a material.

accurate data Data that is close to the true value of what you are measuring.

acid An acid is a solution with a pH value less than 7.

adaptations (cell) The structure and features of a cell that make it suited to carrying out a particular job.

adolescence The period of time when a child changes into an adult.

air resistance The force on an object moving through the air that causes it to slow down (also known as drag).

alkali An alkali is a soluble base.

alveolus A structure inside the lungs where gas exchange takes place with the blood.

amoeba A unicellular organism.

amplify To increase the amplitude of a sound so that it sounds louder.

amplitude The distance from the middle to the top or bottom of a wave.

analyse The process of looking at data and writing about what you have found out.

angle of incidence The angle between the incident ray and the normal line.

angle of reflection The angle between the reflected ray and the normal line.

anomaly A result that is very different from the other repeats of that measurement.

antagonistic muscles A pair of muscles that work together to control movement at a joint – as one muscle contracts, the other relaxes.

anther The part of a flower that produces pollen.

aperture The hole at the front of a camera.

artificial satellite A manmade spacecraft.

asteroid belt A region of space filled with asteroids.

asteroid Lumps of rock orbiting the Sun left over from when the Solar System formed.

asthma A condition where triggers, such as dust, cause inflammation and narrowing of the airways, making it difficult to breathe.

astronomer A scientist who studies space.

atom The smallest part of an element that can exist.

audible range The range of frequencies that you can hear.

auditory canal The passage in the ear from the outer ear to the ear drum.

auditory nerve An electrical signal travels along the auditory nerve to the brain.

axis The imaginary line that the Earth spins around.

balanced (forces) Forces acting on an object that are the same size but act in opposite directions.

balanced formula equation In a balanced formula equation, chemical formulae represent the reactants and products. The equation shows how atoms are rearranged, and gives the relative amounts of reactants and products.

bar chart A way of presenting data when one variable is discrete or categoric and the other is continuous.

base A base is a substance that neutralises an acid.

binary fission When a unicellular organism splits itself into two identical cells.

biomechanics The study of muscle and joint movement.

boiling point The temperature at which a substance boils.

boiling The change of state from liquid to gas that occurs when bubbles of the substance in its gas state form throughout the liquid.

bone marrow A soft tissue found inside bones that makes red and white blood cells.

bone A tissue that forms a hard structure, used to protect organs and for movement.

camera A device that produces an image.

carpel The female reproductive part of the flower.

cartilage The strong, smooth tissue that covers the end of bones to prevent them rubbing together.

catalyst A catalyst speeds up reactions without being used up.

categorical A variable that has values that are words.

cell membrane The cell component that controls which substances can move into and out of the cell.

cell wall The plant cell component that surrounds the cell, providing support.

cell The smallest functional unit in an organism – the building block of life.

cervix The ring of muscle at the entrance to the uterus. It keeps the baby in place while the woman is pregnant.

change of state The process by which a substance changes from one state to another.

charge-coupled device (CCD) A grid of pixels at the back of a digital camera that absorbs light and produces an image.

chemical formula A formula that shows the relative number of atoms of each element in a compound.

chemical reaction A change in which atoms are rearranged to create new substances.

chemical symbol A one- or two-letter code for an element that is used by scientists in all countries.

chloroplast The plant cell component where photosynthesis takes place.

cilia Tiny hairs on the surface of cells.

circulatory system A system of organs that help transport substances around the body in the blood.

cochlea Snail-shaped tube in the inner ear with the sensory cells that detect sound.

combustion reaction A chemical reaction in which a substance reacts quickly with oxygen and gives out light and heat.

comet Dust particles frozen in ice that orbit the Sun.

compound A substance made up of atoms of two or more elements, strongly joined together.

compress To squash into a smaller space.

compression The part of a longitudinal wave where the air particles are close together.

concentrated A solution is concentrated if it has a large number of solute particles per unit volume (litre or cubic metre).

concentration A measure of the number of particles of a substance in a given volume.

conclusion What you write down to say what you have found out during an investigation.

condense The change of state from gas to liquid.

condensing The change of state from gas to liquid.

condom A barrier method of contraception, which prevents semen being released into the vagina.

confidence How sure you are of your conclusion based on the data.

conservation of mass In a chemical reaction, the total mass of reactants is equal to the total mass of products. This is conservation of mass. Mass is conserved in chemical reactions and in physical changes.

conserved In a chemical reaction, the total mass of reactants is equal to the total mass of products. This is conservation of mass. Mass is conserved in chemical reactions and in physical changes.

constellation A collection of stars that make a pattern in the sky.

contact force A force that acts when an object is in contact with a surface, air, or water.

continuous A variable that has values that can be any number.

contraception A method of preventing pregnancy.

contraceptive pill A chemical method of contraception.

control measure Something you put in place to reduce the risk of a hazard causing harm.

control variable A variable that you have to keep the same in an investigation.

converging Bringing rays of light together.

convex A lens that produces converging rays of light.

cornea The transparent layer at the front of the eye.

corrosive A substance is corrosive if it can burn your skin or eyes.

crest The top of a wave.

cytoplasm A 'jelly-like' substance found in cells, where all the chemical reactions take place.

data Words or numbers that you obtain when you make observations or measurements.

day The time it takes a planet to make one full spin on its axis.

Glossary

decibel A commonly used unit of sound intensity or loudness (dB).

decomposition A chemical reaction in which a compound breaks down to form simpler compounds and/or elements.

deform To change shape.

density The mass per unit volume – how heavy something is for its size.

dependent variable A variable that changes when you change the independent variable.

diaphragm (breathing) The sheet of muscle used in breathing.

diaphragm The part of the microphone that vibrates when a sound wave hits it.

diffuse reflection Reflection from a rough surface.

diffusion The movement of liquid or gas particles from a place of high concentration to a place of low concentration.

digestive system A system of organs that break down food into smaller molecules and then absorbs them.

dilute A solution is dilute if it has a small number of solute particles per unit volume (litre or cubic metre).

discrete A variable that can only have whole-number values.

dispersion The splitting up of a ray of light of mixed wavelengths by refraction into its components.

drag The force acting on an object moving through air or water that causes it to slow down.

driving force The force that is pushing or pulling something.

dwarf planet A small lump of rock in orbit around the sun.

ear The organ of the body that detects sound.

eardrum A membrane that transmits sound vibrations from the outer ear to the middle ear.

echo A reflection of a sound wave by an object.

egg cell A cell containing female genetic material.

ejaculation When semen is released from the penis.

elastic limit The point beyond which a spring will not return to its original length when the force is removed.

electrostatic force The force acting between two charged objects.

element A substance that cannot be broken down into other substances.

ellipse A squashed circle or oval shape.

embryo A ball of cells that forms when the fertilised egg divides.

emit To give out.

endothermic change An endothermic change transfers energy from the surroundings.

energy Energy is needed to make things happen.

equilibrium Balanced.

euglena Unicellular organism that performs photosynthesis.

evaluation To discuss the quality of data collected during an investigation and suggest improvements to the method.

evaporation The change of state from liquid to gas that occurs when particles leave the surface of the liquid only. It can happen at any temperature.

exhale Breathing out, to remove carbon dioxide.

exothermic change An exothermic change transfers energy to the surroundings.

extension The amount by which an object gets longer when a force is applied.

eye Organ of sight, which focuses and detects light.

female (adjective) of the sex that can bear offspring or produce eggs.

female (noun) a person, animal, or plant of the sex that can bear offspring or produce eggs.

fertilisation The process where the nucleus of a sperm cell joins with the nucleus of an egg cell.

filament The part of a flower that holds up the anther.

filter A piece of material that allows some radiation (colours) through but absorbs the rest.

flagellum A tail-like structure that allows euglenas to move.

fluid sac Contains fluid. This acts as a shock absorber, protecting the foetus from bumps.

focal point The point at which the rays refracted by a convex lens cross over.

focus Another name for the focal point.

foetus The name given to an unborn baby from eight weeks of development.

force A push or pull that can change the shape or movement of objects.

fossil fuel A fuel made from the remains of animals and plants that died millions of years ago. Fossil fuels include coal, oil, and natural gas.

freezing The change of state from liquid to solid.

frequency The number of complete waves or vibrations produced in one second (measured in hertz).

friction The force that resists movement because of contact between surfaces.

fruit The part of a plant that contains seeds.

fuel A material that burns to transfer useful energy.

galaxy A number of stars and the solar systems around them grouped together.

gametes Reproductive cells. The male gamete is a sperm cell and the female gamete is an egg cell.

gas exchange system A system of organs that absorb oxygen into the blood and remove carbon dioxide from the blood.

gas exchange The transfer of gases between an organism and its environment.

gas giant An outer planet in the Solar System made mainly from gas.

gas In the gas state, a substance can flow and can also be compressed.

germination The period of time when a seed starts to grow.

gestation The time from fertilisation until birth.

gravitational field strength The force of gravity that acts on each kilogram of mass.

gravity A non-contact force that acts between two masses.

hazard symbol A sign that warns people of things that could cause harm.

hemisphere Half of the Earth – either from the equator to North Pole or from the equator to the South Pole.

hertz The unit of frequency (Hz).

Hooke's law A law that says that if you double the force on an object the extension will double.

image The point from which rays of light entering the eye appear to have originated.

implantation The process where an embryo attaches to the lining of the uterus.

incident ray The ray coming from a source of light.

incident wave The wave coming from a source of light.

independent variable A variable you change that changes the dependent variable.

indicator A substance that changes colour to show whether a solution is acidic or alkaline.

infrasound Sound below a frequency of 20 Hz.

inhale Breathing in, to take in oxygen.

inner ear The semi-circular canals that help you to balance, and your cochlea.

interaction pair When two objects interact there is a force on each one that is the same size but in opposing directions.

interval A gap between measurements.

inverted Upside down.

investigation An experiment or set of experiments designed to produce data to answer a scientific question or test a theory.

iris The coloured part of your eye.

kilogram (kg) A unit of mass, symbol kg.

kilohertz 1 kilohertz (kHz) = 1000 hertz (Hz).

law of reflection The angle of incidence is equal to the angle of reflection.

leaf cell The plant cells that contain chloroplasts, where photosynthesis takes place.

lens A device made of shaped glass that focuses light rays from objects to form an image.

ligament Joins two bones together.

light-time Distance measured in terms of how far light travels in a given time.

line graph A way of presenting results when there are two numerical variables.

line of best fit A smooth line on a graph that travels through or very close to as many of the points plotted as possible.

Glossary

linear (graphs) A straight-line graph.

liquid In the liquid state, a substance can flow but cannot be compressed.

litmus An indicator. Blue litmus paper goes red on adding acid. Red litmus paper goes blue on adding alkali.

longitudinal A wave where the vibrations are in the same direction as the direction the wave moves.

loudness How loud you perceive a sound of a certain intensity to be.

lubrication A substance that reduces friction between surfaces when they rub together.

luminous Gives out light.

lunar eclipse An eclipse that happens when the Earth comes between the Sun and the Moon.

lung volume The volume of air your lungs can hold.

lungs The organ in which gas exchange takes place.

male (adjective) belonging to the sex that reproduces by fertilising egg cells produced by the female.

male (noun) a person, animal, or plant belonging to the sex that reproduces by fertilising egg cells produced by a female.

magnetic force The force between two magnets, or a magnet and a magnetic material.

mass The amount of matter (stuff) a thing is made up of.

material The different types of stuff that things are made from.

mean An average of a set of data, found by adding together all the values in the set and dividing by the number of values in the set.

medium The material that affects light or sound by slowing it down or transferring the wave.

melting point The temperature at which a substance melts.

melting The change of state from solid to liquid.

menstrual cycle The monthly cycle during which the uterus lining thickens, and then breaks down and leaves the body if an egg is not fertilised.

meteor A piece of rock or dust that makes a streak of light in the night sky.

meteorite A stony or metallic object that has fallen to Earth from outer space.

method The steps you must follow to carry out an investigation.

microphone A device for converting sound into an electrical signal.

microscope An optical instrument used to magnify objects, so small details can be seen clearly.

middle ear The ossicles (small bones) that transfer vibrations from the outer ear to the inner ear.

Milky Way The galaxy containing our Sun and Solar System.

mitochondria The cell component where respiration takes place.

mixture A material whose properties are not the same all the way through.

molecule A group of two or more atoms, strongly joined together.

Moon A rocky body orbiting Earth; it is Earth's only natural satellite.

multicellular organism An organism made up of many cells.

muscular skeletal system A system of organs and tissues that allow animals to move.

natural satellite A moon in orbit around a planet.

nerve cell An animal cell that transmits electrical impulses around the body.

neutral A solution that is neither alkaline nor acidic. Its pH is 7.

neutralisation In a neutralisation reaction, an acid cancels out a base or a base cancels out an acid.

newton (N) The unit of force, symbol N.

newtonmeter A piece of equipment used to measure weight in newtons.

night The period on one section of the Earth or other planet when it is facing away from the Sun.

non-contact force A magnetic, electrostatic, or gravitational force that acts between objects not in contact.

non-luminous Objects that produce no light.

non-renewable Some fuels are non-renewable. They form over millions of years, and will one day run out.

normal An imaginary line at right angles to a surface where a light ray strikes it.

nucleus The cell component that controls the cell and contains genetic material.

observation Carefully looking at an object or process.

opaque Objects that absorb, scatter, or reflect light and do not allow any light to pass through.

optic nerve A paired sensory nerve that runs from each eye to the brain.

organ system A group of organs working together to perform a function.

organ A group of tissues working together to perform a function.

organism A living thing.

oscillation Something that moves backwards and forwards.

oscilloscope A device that enables you to see electrical signals, like those made by a microphone.

ossicles The small bones of the middle ear (hammer, anvil, and stirrup) that transfer vibrations from the eardrum to the oval window.

outer ear The pinna, auditory canal, and eardrum.

oval window The membrane that connects the ossicles to the cochlea.

ovary (human) Contains egg cells.

ovary (plant) The part of a flower that contains ovules.

oviduct Tube that carries an egg to the uterus.

ovulation The release of an egg from an ovary.

ovule The female gamete of a plant.

oxidation reaction A chemical reaction in which substances react with oxygen to form oxides.

partial solar eclipse A solar eclipse where only part of the Sun is covered by the Moon.

particle model A way to describe the movement and arrangement of particles in a substance.

particle The tiny things that materials are made from.

pattern When the results follow a predictable direction.

peak The top of a wave.

penis The structure that caries sperm and semen out of the body.

penumbra The shadow on Earth where the Sun is only partially blocked by the Moon.

period Loss of uterus lining through the vagina.

Periodic Table A table of all the elements, in which elements with similar properties are grouped together.

petal The brightly coloured part of a flower that attracts insects.

pH scale The pH scale shows whether a substance is acidic, alkaline, or neutral. An acid has a pH below 7. An alkaline solution has a pH above 7. A solution of pH 7 is neutral.

phases of the Moon Shape of the Moon as we see it from the Earth.

photoreceptors Specialised cells that are sensitive to light.

physical change A change that is reversible, in which new substances are not made. Examples of physical changes include changes of state, and dissolving.

pinna The outside part of the ear that we can see.

pitch A property of sound determined by its frequency.

pixel A picture element found at the back of a digital camera.

placenta The organ where substances pass between the mother's and the foetus's blood. It acts as a barrier, stopping infections and harmful substances reaching the foetus.

plane A mirror with a flat, reflective surface.

pollen The male gamete of a plant.

pollination The transfer of pollen from the anther to the stigma.

primary colour The colours red, blue, and green.

prism A triangular-shaped piece of glass used to produce a spectrum of light.

product A substance that is made in a chemical reaction.

property A quality of a substance or material that describes its appearance, or how it behaves.

puberty The physical changes that take place during adolescence.

Glossary

pull   A type of force.

pupil   The hole in the front of your eye where light goes in.

push   A type of force.

rarefaction   The part of a longitudinal wave where the air particles are spread out.

ratio   A ratio is a way of comparing values.

ray   Lines used to model beams of light.

reactant   A starting substance in a chemical reaction.

reaction   The support force provided by a solid surface like a floor.

real (image)   An image that you can put on a screen; the image formed in your eyes.

receiver   The device that absorbs the sound waves.

red blood cell   An animal cell that transports oxygen around the body.

reflect   Bounce off.

reflected ray   The ray that is reflected from a surface.

reflected wave   The wave that is reflected from a surface.

reflection   The change in direction of a ray or wave after it hits a surface and bounces off.

refraction   The change in direction of a ray or wave as a result of its change in speed.

relative number   The number of atoms of one type compared with the number of atoms of another type in an element or compound.

reproductive system   A system of organs that work together to make new organisms.

resistive force   Any force that acts to slow down a moving object.

respiration   A chemical reaction where food and oxygen are converted into energy, water, and carbon dioxide.

retina   The layer of light sensitive cells at the back of the eye.

reversible   A chemical reaction or physical change that can be reversed (changed back).

ribcage   The bones that protect the lungs.

root hair cell   A plant cell that takes in water and minerals from the soil.

salt   A salt is a compound in which the hydrogen atoms of an acid are replaced by atoms of a metal element.

scrotum   The bag of skin that holds the testes.

season   Changes in the temperature during the year as the Earth moves around its orbit.

secondary colour   Colours that can be obtained by mixing two primary colours.

seed dispersal   The movement of seeds away from the parent plant.

seed   The structure that develops into a new plant.

semen   Fluid containing sperm.

semi-circular canal   Part of the inner ear that contains fluid to help with balance.

sepal   The special leaves found under the flower, which protect unopened buds.

sex hormones   Chemical messengers that travel in the blood and cause the changes that take place during puberty and reproduction.

sexual intercourse   The process where the penis releases semen into the vagina.

skeleton   All the bones in an organism.

Solar System   The Sun and the planets and other bodies in orbit around it.

solid   In the solid state, a substance cannot be compressed and it cannot flow.

sonar   Using ultrasound and reflections to detect objects underwater.

source   Things that emit (give out) light or sound.

specialised cell   A cell whose shape and structure enable it to perform a particular function.

spectrum   A band of colours produced when light is spread out by a prism.

specular reflection   Reflection from a smooth surface.

speed of light   The distance light travels in one second (300 million m/s).

speed of sound   The distance sound travels in one second (330 m/s).

sperm cell A cell containing male genetic material.

sperm duct Tube that carries sperm from the testes to the penis.

stamen The male reproductive part of the flower.

star A body in space that gives out its own light.

states of matter The three forms in which a substance can exist – solid, liquid, and gas.

stigma The part of a flower that is sticky to catch grains of pollen.

streamlined The three forms in which a substance can exist – solid, liquid, and gas.

stretch An object can be stretched if you exert a force on it.

style The part of a flower that holds up the stigma.

sublimation The change of state from solid to gas.

substance A material that is not a mixture. It has the same properties all the way through.

superpose When waves join together so that they add up or cancel out.

tendon Joins a muscle to a bone.

tension A stretching force.

terrestrial Made of rock.

testis (testes) The testes produce sperm and the male sex hormones.

tissue A group of similar cells working together to perform a function.

total solar eclipse An eclipse where all of the Sun is covered by the Moon.

trachea A large tube running down the throat and connecting the mouth and nose to the lungs.

translucent Objects that transmit light but diffusing (scattering) the light as it passes through.

transmit When light or other radiation passes through an object.

transmitter A device that gives out light or sound.

transparent Objects that transmit light and you can see through them.

transverse The vibrations are at right angles to the direction the wave moves.

trough The bottom of a wave.

ultrasound Sound at a frequency greater than 20 000 Hz, beyond the range of human hearing.

umbilical cord Connects the foetus to the placenta.

umbra The shadow on Earth where the Sun is completely blocked by the Moon.

unbalanced (forces) Opposing forces on an object that are unequal.

undulation A smooth up and down movement.

unicellular Consisting of just one cell.

universal indicator An indicator that changes colour to show the pH of a solution. It is a mixture of dyes.

Universe Everything that exists.

urethra Tube that carries urine or sperm out of the body.

uterus Where a baby develops until its birth.

vacuole The plant cell component that contains cell sap and helps to keep the cell firm.

vacuum A space in which there is no matter.

vagina Receives sperm during sexual intercourse. This is where the male's penis enters the female's body.

vibration Backwards and forwards motion of the parts of a liquid or solid.

virtual An image that cannot be focused onto a screen.

volume The amount of space an object takes up.

water resistance The force on an object moving through water that causes it to slow down (also known as drag).

wavelength The distance from the peak on one wave to the peak on the next wave.

weight The force of the Earth on an object due to its mass.

year The length of time it takes for a planet to orbit the Sun.

Index

A
absorption 168
acid rain 131
acids 126, 132
    acids and bases 133
    acids and metals 133
    concentrated or dilute? 126–127
    indicators and pH 128, 129
    neutralisation 130, 131
    using acids and alkalis safely 126
adaptations 30
adolescence 56, 57
air resistance 140, 145
alkalis 126–130
    using acids and alkalis safely 126
alveoli (alveolus) 42, 43
amoebas 34
amplitude 154
analysing data 18
    identifying patterns and trends 18
    lines of best fit 18–19
    writing a conclusion 19
angle of incidence 171
angle of reflection 171
animal cells 28
    specialised cells 30, 31
anomalies 15
    identifying anomalies 21
antagonistic muscles 51
anther 66
apertures 175
artificial satellites 182
asteroids 184
    asteroid belt 184
asthma 45
astronomers 185
atoms 98, 99
    chemical reactions 111
    relative number 103
audible range 161
auditory canal (outer ear) 160
auditory nerve 160
axis (axes) 186

B
babies 62
    how does a baby develop? 63
    what happens during birth? 63
    where does a baby grow? 62–63
balanced forces 148
balanced formula equations 119
bar charts 16–17
bases 130, 131
    acids and bases 133
binary fission 34
biomechanics 48
birth 63
blood cells, red 30
blood cells, making 47
boiling 86
    boiling point 86
    measuring boiling points 86–87
    using boiling points 87
bones 46
    bone marrow 47
    joints 48, 49
breathing 42–43
    how do you breathe? 44
    inhalation and exhalation 44–45
    measuring lung volume 45
    why do we breathe in and out? 43

C
cameras 175
carbon dioxide 102
carbon monoxide 102
carpel 66
cartilage 49
catalysts 109
categorical data 16
cells 26
    cell membranes 28
    cell walls 29
    diffusion 32–33
    movement of substances 32
    multicellular organisms 40
    specialised cells 30, 31
    unicellular organisms 34, 35
    what's inside a plant cell? 29
    what's inside an animal cell? 28
cervix 59
changes of state 84–89
    endothermic and exothermic 120–121
    physical changes 109
charge-coupled devices (CCDs) 175
chemical formulae 102, 103
chemical reactions 108
    balanced formula equations 119
    decomposition reactions 114, 115
    how do you know it's a chemical reaction? 108–109
    how fast are chemical reactions? 109
    not all changes are chemical reactions 109
    oxidation reactions 112, 113
    rearranging atoms 111
    representing reactions 110
    why are chemical reactions useful? 109
    word equations 111
chemical symbols 97
chloroplasts 29
cilia 60
circulatory system 41
cochlea (inner ear) 160
colours 176
    filters 177
    how do you split white light? 176
    primary and secondary colours 176, 177
    why are objects different colours? 177
combustion reactions 112–113
comets 182
compounds 100, 101
    naming compounds 102–103
    why are carbon–oxygen compounds different? 102
compressions 142, 155
concentration 32, 90, 126–127
conclusions 19
condensation (condensing) 43, 89
condoms 65
conservation of mass 84, 118
    calculating masses 118–119
constellations 187
contact forces 140
continuous data 16
continuous spectrum 176
contraception 65
contraceptive pill 65
control measures 11
control variables 9
converging lenses 173
convex lenses 173
cornea (eye) 174
crests 154
cytoplasm 28

D
data 8
    accurate data 13
    analysing data 18, 19
    evaluating data 20, 21
    presenting scientific data 16, 17
    recording data 14, 15
    spread of data 21
    three types of scientific data 16
day 186
decibels (dB) 159
decomposition reactions 114
    comparing reactions 115
    thermal decomposition reactions 115
deforming 142

density 82
　　how does state affect density? 83
　　how does the particle model explain density? 82
dependent variables 9
diaphragm 44
diffuse reflection 171
diffusion 32–33
　　diffusion in plant cells 33
diffusion of particles 90
　　factors affecting speed of diffusion 91
digestive system 41
dilution 126–127
direction 149, 173
discrete data 16
discrete variables 115
dispersion 176
drag forces 145
driving force 148
dwarf planets 185

E
ears 160
　　eardrum 160
　　inner ear 160
　　middle ear 160
　　outer ear 160
Earth 149, 186
　　what is orbiting Earth? 182
　　why do we have day and night? 186
　　why do we have seasons? 186–187
echoes 162
　　measuring distances 162–163
eclipses 189
　　why don't we see eclipses every month? 189
egg cells 31, 60, 61
ejaculation 61
elastic limit 143
electrostatic force 146
elements 96, 97, 98
　　water 100–101
ellipses 184
embryo 61
emissions 168
endothermic change 120–121

energy 154
equilibrium 148
equipment 13, 21
errors 21
euglenas 35
evaluations 20
　　checking for errors 21
　　identifying anomalies 21
　　identifying strengths and weaknesses in data 20–21
　　improving investigations 21
　　spread of data 21
evaporation (evaporating) 88
　　how is evaporating useful? 88–89
exhalation 43, 45
exothermic change 121
extension 143
eyes 168, 173, 174
　　how do you see? 174
　　how is the eye like a camera? 175

F
fertilisation 60, 61
　　plants 68
fields 146
filament 66
filters 177
flagellum 35
flowers 66
fluid sac 62
focus 173
　　focal length 173
　　focal point 173
foetus 62, 63
forces 140
　　balanced forces 148
　　drag forces 145
　　fields 146
　　forces acting at a distance 146, 147
　　how can the floor push you up? 142–143
　　how do forces affect solid objects? 142
　　interaction pairs 141
　　measuring forces 141
　　stretching 143
　　stretching a spring 143
　　unbalanced forces 148–149

freezing 84
frequency 154
　　what frequencies can animals hear? 161
　　what frequencies can you hear? 161
friction 140, 144
fruit 68
fuels 112
　　fossil fuel alternatives 113
　　fossil fuels 113
　　what happens when fuels burn? 112–113

G
galaxies 183
gametes 60
gas exchange 42, 43
　　gas exchange system 41
gas giants 184
gases 80, 81
germination 69
　　how does a plant grow? 69
gestation 62
Globally Harmonized System (GHS) 10
gravitational field strength 147
gravity 140

H
hazards 10
　　hazard symbols 10
hearing 160
　　ear structure 160
　　frequencies 161
　　how can you damage your hearing? 161
hemispheres 187
hertz (Hz) 159
Hooke's Law 143

I
images 170, 175
　　inverted images 174
implantation 61
incident rays 171
incident waves 155
independent variables 9
indicators 128, 129
　　which plants make good indicators? 128

infrasound 161
inhalation 43, 44–45
interaction pairs 141
interval 13
investigations 8
　　choosing the right equipment 13, 21
　　improving investigations 21
　　measurements 13
　　planning a scientific investigation 12
iris (eye) 174

J
joints 48
　　types of joints 48
　　what does a joint look like? 49

K
kilograms (kg) 147
kilohertz (kHz) 159

L
leaf cells 31
lenses 173, 174
ligaments 49
light 168
　　colours 176, 177
　　how does light reflect off rough surfaces? 171
　　how fast does light travel? 169
　　light-time 169
　　reflection 170, 171
　　refraction 172, 173
　　speed of light 157
　　what can light travel through? 169
　　what happens to light as it travels? 168–169
　　why does light change direction? 173
line graphs 16, 17
linear graphs 143
lines of best fit 18–19
liquids 80, 81
litmus paper 128
longitudinal waves 155
loudness 158
　　measuring loudness 159
lubrication 144
luminous objects 168

Index

lunar eclipses 189
lungs 42
    measuring lung volume 45

M
magnetic force 146
magnification 27
mass 82, 147
    difference between weight and mass 147
materials 78, 156, 169, 172
mean 15
measurements 13
    interval 13
    range of results 13, 21
    repeat measurements 15
medium (material) 156, 172
melting 84
    melting point 84–85
menstrual cycle 64
    stages of the menstrual cycle 64–65
metals and acids 133
meteorites 183
meteors 183
methods 12
    repeatable methods 21
microphones 158, 161
microscopes 26
    magnification 27
    parts of a microscope 27
Milky Way 183
mirrors 170, 171
mitochondria 28
mixtures 78
molecules 100
Moon 149, 182
    phases of the Moon 188–189
    why do we see eclipses? 189
moons 184
movement 48–51
multicellular organisms 40
muscles 48, 52
    how do muscles work? 50
    how do pairs of muscles work together? 51

measuring muscle strength 49
muscular skeleton system 46

N
natural satellites 182
nerve cells 30
neutral solutions 129
neutralisation reactions 130
    acidic lakes 131
    pH changes in neutralisation 130
    soil for crops 131
    which substances neutralise acids? 130
newtonmeters 141
newtons (N) 49, 141
night 186
night sky 182
    what are the streaks of light? 182–183
    what is in the Universe? 183
    what is orbiting Earth? 182
    what is wandering across the sky? 182
non-contact forces 140
non-luminous objects 168
non-renewable fuels 113
normal 171
normal force 143
nucleus 28

O
observations 8, 26
opaque materials 169
optic nerve 174
organ systems 41
organisms 26
    multicellular organisms 40
    unicellular organisms 34, 35
organs 40–41
oscillations 154
oscilloscopes 158
ossicles (middle ear) 160
oval window(middle ear) 160
ovaries 57, 59
ovary (flowers) 66

oviducts 59
ovulation 64
ovule 66
oxidation reactions 112, 113
oxygen 102

P
partial solar eclipses 189
particles 78
    diffusion 90, 91
    how can particles explain properties? 81
    particle model 79, 82
patterns 18
peaks 154
penis 57, 58–59
penumbra 189
Periodic Table 96–97
periods 64
petals 66
pH scale 129
    pH changes in neutralisation 130
photoreceptors 174
physical changes 109
pie charts 16, 17
pinna (outer ear) 160
pitch 159
pixels 175
placenta 62, 63
planes 170
planets 182
    what are the planets like? 184–185
plans 12, 13
plant cells 29
    diffusion 33
    specialised cells 31
    why do plants wilt? 33
pollen 66, 67
pollination 66–67
    insect-pollinated plants 67
    wind-pollinated plants 67
predictions 9
    predicting states 87
primary colours 176, 177
prisms 176
products 110
properties 79, 80, 81
puberty 56

females 57
males 57
pull forces 140
pupil (eye) 174
push forces 140

R
random errors 21
range of results 13, 21
rarefactions 155
ratios 116
    calculating values with ratios 117
    simplifying ratios 116–17
rays 168, 171
reactants 110
reaction force 143
real images 175
receivers 163
recording data 14
    calculating a mean 15
    checking for anomalous results 15
    recording repeat measurements 15
    results tables 14
reflected waves 155
reflection 155, 168, 170
    how does light reflect off rough surfaces? 171
    law of reflection 171
    reflected rays 171
    why might you see an image in the mirror? 170
refraction 172
    what does a lens do? 173
    why does a pencil in water look bent? 172
    why does light change direction? 173
relative number 103
repeat readings 15, 21
repeatable methods 21
reproductive system 41
    female reproductive system 59
    male reproductive system 58–59
resistive forces 148
results tables 14
retina (eye) 174

reversibility 84
ribcage 42
risks 11
    control measures 11
    risk assessment 11
root hair cells 31

S
safety 10
    hazard symbols 10
    hazards 10
    risks 11
    using acids and alkalis safely 126
salt 101
    how can you make salt crystals? 133
    making salts 132, 133
    what are salts? 132
    which reactions make salts? 132–133
satellites 182
scientific questions 8
    control variables 9
    developing ideas into questions 8
    making a prediction 9
    suggesting ideas 8
    what is a variable? 9
scrotum 58
seasons 186–187
secondary colours 176, 177
seed dispersal 70
    animal dispersal 70–71
    water dispersal 71
    wind dispersal 70
seeds 68
    what do seeds need for growth ? 69
    what's inside a seed ? 69
semen 58
semi-circular canals (inner ear) 160
sepals 66
sex hormones 57
sexual intercourse 59
    what happens during sexual intercourse? 60–61
skeleton 46
    why do we have a skeleton? 47
soil pH 131
solar eclipses 189

Solar System 182, 184
    how did our Solar System form? 185
    what are the planets like? 184–185
    what is on the edge of the Solar System? 185
    what's in our Solar System? 184
solids 80, 81
sonar 163
sound waves 156
    detecting sound 160, 161
    echoes 162–163
    loudness 158–159
    pitch 159
    seeing sound 158
    speed of light 157
    speed of sound 156–157
    ultrasound 163
    what does sound travel through? 156
sources of light 168
spectrum (spectra) 176
specular reflection 171
speed 81, 149
    speed of light 157
    speed of sound 156–157
sperm cells 31
sperm cells 60, 61
sperm ducts 58
spread of data 21
springs 143
squashing 142
stamen 66
stars 183
states of matter 80, 83
    changes of state 84–89, 109
    diffusion of particles 91
    gas state 81
    liquid state 81
    predicting states 87
    solid state 81
stigma 66
streamlining 145
stretching 142, 143
style 66
sublimation (subliming) 89
substances 78, 79, 80
    identifying substances 87
    states of matter 80, 81
Sun 182
superposed waves 155

symbols 10
    Globally Harmonized System (GHS) 10
systematic errors 21

T
temperature 91
tendons 50
tension 143
terrestrial planets 184
testes 57, 58
thermal decomposition reactions 115
tissues 40
total solar eclipses 189
trachea 42
translucence 169
transmission 168
transmitters 163
transparency 168–169
transverse waves 154
trends 18
troughs 154
true value 13

U
ultrasound 161, 163
    measuring distance 163
umbilical cord 62, 63
umbra 189
unbalanced forces 148
    causing changes in direction 149
    causing changes in speed 149
undulations 154
unicellular organisms 34, 35
universal indicator 129
Universe 183
urethra 58, 59
uterus 59

V
vacuoles 29, 33
vacuum 156
vagina 59
values 117
    true value 13
variables 9, 115
vibrations 154, 156
virtual images 170
volume 82

W
water 100–101
    water resistance 145
wavelength 154
waves 154
    features of a wave 154
    two types of wave 154–155
    what happens when waves hit a barrier? 155
    what happens when waves superpose? 155
weight 147
    difference between weight and mass 147
    weight in space? 147
wilting 33
word equations 111

Y
years 186

Periodic Table

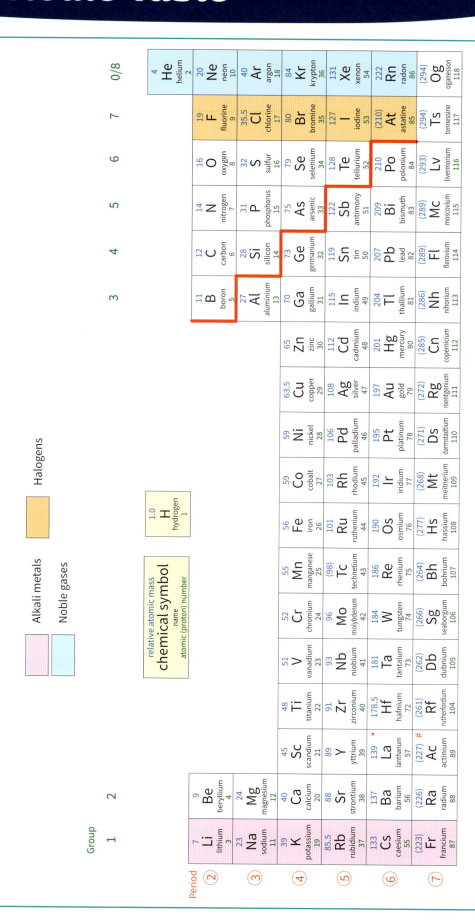

Great Clarendon Street, Oxford, OX2 6DP, United Kingdom

Oxford University Press is a department of the University of Oxford. It furthers the University's objective of excellence in research, scholarship, and education by publishing worldwide. Oxford is a registered trade mark of Oxford University Press in the UK and in certain other countries.

© Oxford University Press 2022

The moral rights of the authors have been asserted

First published in 2022

All rights reserved. No part of this publication may be reproduced, stored in a retrieval system, or transmitted, in any form or by any means, without the prior permission in writing of Oxford University Press, or as expressly permitted by law, by licence or under terms agreed with the appropriate reprographics rights organization. Enquiries concerning reproduction outside the scope of the above should be sent to the Rights Department, Oxford University Press, at the address above.

You must not circulate this work in any other form and you must impose this same condition on any acquirer

British Library Cataloguing in Publication Data
Data available

978-138-202106-7

978-138-202094-7 (ebook)

10 9 8 7 6 5 4 3 2 1

Paper used in the production of this book is a natural, recyclable product made from wood grown in sustainable forests.

The manufacturing process conforms to the environmental regulations of the country of origin.

Printed in the United Kingdom by Bell & Bain Ltd, Glasgow.

Acknowledgements

The authors would like to thank the following:

Philippa Gardom Hulme

Enormous thanks to Barney, Catherine, and Sarah Gardom for their superb support and sparkling suggestions. Thank you, too, to Helen Reynolds and Jo Locke; I love working with you both. Finally, huge thanks to my parents, Mary and Edward Hulme, for patiently correcting my holiday diaries all those years ago, and getting me into writing in the first place.

Jo Locke

Many thanks to my girls Emily and Hermione for all their support, encouragement, and delicious cakes, and to Dave for providing endless cups of tea and helpful ideas. It has also been an honour to write again with the original Activate team of Philippa Gardom Hulme and Helen Reynolds; I couldn't have done it without you.

Helen Reynolds

I would like to thank Michele, Roh, Lesa, and Bill for their support and innumerable cups of tea and walks. Many thanks also to Oleksiy and all those at the dance studio for their tremendous support and encouragement throughout the writing process. Finally, it has been an absolute pleasure working with Philippa Gardom Hulme and Jo Locke again. Thank you so much for your support, insight, and inspiration.

Thank you to Amanda Clegg and Karen Collins for their expert review of and contribution to the Working Scientifically chapter, and to Lauren Stephenson for the authoring of the Metacognition spreads.

The publisher and authors would like to thank the following for permission to use photographs and other copyright material:

Cover: Michal Bednarski. Photos: **p6**: A Bennion/Shutterstock; **p8**: Jan Martin Will / Shutterstock; **p10**: MyImages - Micha/Shutterstock; **p11**: Migren art/ Shutterstock; **p12**: wavebreakmedia / Shutterstock; **p20**: Alexandr Zadiraka / Shutterstock; **p22**: Science Photo Library; **p24**: FlashMovie/Shutterstock; **p26(t)**: World History Archive / Alamy Stock Photo; **p26(b)**: DR GOPAL MURTI / SCIENCE PHOTO LIBRARY; **p28**: DR GOPAL MURTI / SCIENCE PHOTO LIBRARY; **p29**: J.C. REVY, ISM / SCIENCE PHOTO LIBRARY; **p38**: Magic mine/Shutterstock; **p42**: Guzel Studio / Shutterstock; **p46**: Jarva Jar / Shutterstock; **p48**: itsmejust / Shutterstock; **p54**: DR G. MOSCOSO/SCIENCE PHOTO LIBRARY; **p56**: Vinicius Tupinamba / Shutterstock; **p57**: Pixel-Shot / Shutterstock; **p60**: EYE OF SCIENCE / SCIENCE PHOTO LIBRARY; **p65(t)**: energyy/iStockphoto; **p65(b)**: vertolena / Shutterstock; **p66**: Nnehring/Getty Images; **p67(t)**: Haiduchyk Aliaksei / Shutterstock; **p67(b)**: Philip Bird LRPS CPAGB / Shutterstock; **p70**: Malira / Shutterstock; **p71(t)**: ProstheticHead / Shutterstock; **p71(b)**: Kovaleva_Ka / Shutterstock; **p74**: iamlukyeee/Shutterstock; **p76**: IBM RESEARCH/SCIENCE PHOTO LIBRARY; **p78**: nik wheeler / Alamy Stock Photo; **p79**: t_kimura/ iStockphoto; **p80**: Africa Studio / Shutterstock; **p83**: Starkov Roman / Shutterstock; **p84**: candy3 / Shutterstock; **p85**: CHARLES D. WINTERS / SCIENCE PHOTO LIBRARY; **p88**: MZStock/Shutterstock; **p89(t)**: Werayuth Tes / Shutterstock; **p89(b)**: R_Tee/Shutterstock; **p90**: ANDREW MCCLENAGHAN / SCIENCE PHOTO LIBRARY; **p94**: Bjoern Wylezich/Shutterstock; **p96(l)**: Damian Palus / Shutterstock; **p96(m)**: SCIENCE PHOTO LIBRARY; **p96(r)**: Carolina K. Smith MD / Shutterstock; **p98(l)**: bonchan / Shutterstock; **p98(r)**: LAURENCE MARKS, NORTHWESTERN UNIVERSITY / SCIENCE PHOTO LIBRARY; **p99**: t_kimura/iStockphoto; **p100**: Novikov Alex / Shutterstock; **p101**: Creativa Images / Shutterstock; **p106**: SCIENCE PHOTO LIBRARY; **p108(t)**: Heikki Wichmann / Shutterstock; **p108(b)**: ASHUYADAV31 / Shutterstock; **p110(t)**: Doctor Jools / Shutterstock; **p110(l)**: MARTYN F. CHILLMAID / SCIENCE PHOTO LIBRARY; **p110(r)**: MARTYN F. CHILLMAID / SCIENCE PHOTO LIBRARY; **p112**: Cylonphoto / Shutterstock; **p113**: Paceman / Shutterstock; **p114**: Roman Kosolapov / Shutterstock; **p115**: SCIENCE PHOTO LIBRARY; **p116(t)**: Jagodka / Shutterstock; **p116(bl)**: Dmetsov Alexey / Shutterstock; **p116(br)**: Tim UR / Shutterstock; **p117**: CWIS / Shutterstock; **p118(t)**: wolv / Getty Images; **p118(b)**: ANDREW LAMBERT PHOTOGRAPHY / SCIENCE PHOTO LIBRARY; **p120**: Andrey_Popov / Shutterstock; **p121**: Nicvandum / Shutterstock; **p124**: GIPHOTOSTOCK IMAGES/ SCIENCE PHOTO LIBRARY; **p126**: mevans / Getty Images; **p128**: ANDREW LAMBERT PHOTOGRAPHY / SCIENCE PHOTO LIBRARY; **p131(t)**: SasinTipchai / Shutterstock; **p131(b)**: Universal Images Group / Getty Images; **p132(t)**: posteriori / Shutterstock; **p132(b)**: seb001 / Shutterstock; **p132(m)**: Jirik V / Shutterstock; **p136**: sommanas kotcharak/Shutterstock; **p138**: AndreyZH/ Shutterstock; **p140**: Stocktrek Images, Inc. / Alamy Stock Photo; **p141**: Michael H/Getty Images; **p142**: brave rabbit/Shutterstock; **p143**: Melinda Nagy/ Shutterstock; **p145**: ChrisVanLennepPhoto/Shutterstock; **p146(t)**: New Africa / Shutterstock; **p146(b)**: 262276 / Shutterstock; **p152**: Andrew Berezovsky/ Shutterstock; **p154**: ANDREW LAMBERT PHOTOGRAPHY/SCIENCE PHOTO LIBRARY; **p155**: sciencephotos / Alamy Stock Photo; **p156(t)**: STEVE ALLEN / SCIENCE PHOTO LIBRARY; **p156(b)**: Willyam Bradberry / Shutterstock; **p157**: Abaca Press / Alamy Stock Photo; **p158(t)**: ANDREW LAMBERT PHOTOGRAPHY / SCIENCE PHOTO LIBRARY; **p158(b)**: LightField Studios / Shutterstock; **p159**: Image Source Collection / Shutterstock; **p160**: STEVE GSCHMEISSNER / SCIENCE PHOTO LIBRARY; **p162**: Henrik Sorensen / DigitalVision / Getty Images; **p163**: THIERRY BERROD, MONA LISA PRODUCTION/ SCIENCE PHOTO LIBRARY; **p166**: Riccardo Solci/Shutterstock; **p168(t)**: Rich Carey / Shutterstock; **p168(b)**: SiwaBudda / Shutterstock; **p170**: F8 studio / Shutterstock; **p172**: Pat_Hastings / Shutterstock; **p174**: Tatiana Makotra / Shutterstock; **p175(t)**: Urte Baranauskaite / Shutterstock; **p175(b)**: Hrendon / Shutterstock; **p180**: Darryl Fonseka/Shutterstock; **p182(t)**: Artsiom P / Shutterstock; **p182(b)**: Jim Cumming / Shutterstock; **p183**: Todor Mishinev / Shutterstock; **p184**: MarcelClemens / Shutterstock; **p186**: DAVID PARKER / SCIENCE PHOTO LIBRARY; **p187**: DR JUERG ALEAN / SCIENCE PHOTO LIBRARY; **p188**: Stocktrek Images, Inc./Alamy Stock Photo; **p189(a)**: Warachai Krengwirat/Shutterstock; **p189(b)**: Elymas/ Shutterstock; **p189(c)**: Nedelea Cristian/Shutterstock; **p189(d)**: Chris Harwood/ Shutterstock.

Artwork by Q2A Media, Michal Bednarski, Erwin Haya, Aptara, Jeffrey Bowles, Wearset Ltd., Peter Bull Art Studio, and Oxford University Press.

Although we have made every effort to trace and contact all copyright holders before publication this has not been possible in all cases. If notified, the publisher will rectify any errors or omissions at the earliest opportunity.

Links to third party websites are provided by Oxford in good faith and for information only. Oxford disclaims any responsibility for the materials contained in any third party website referenced in this work.